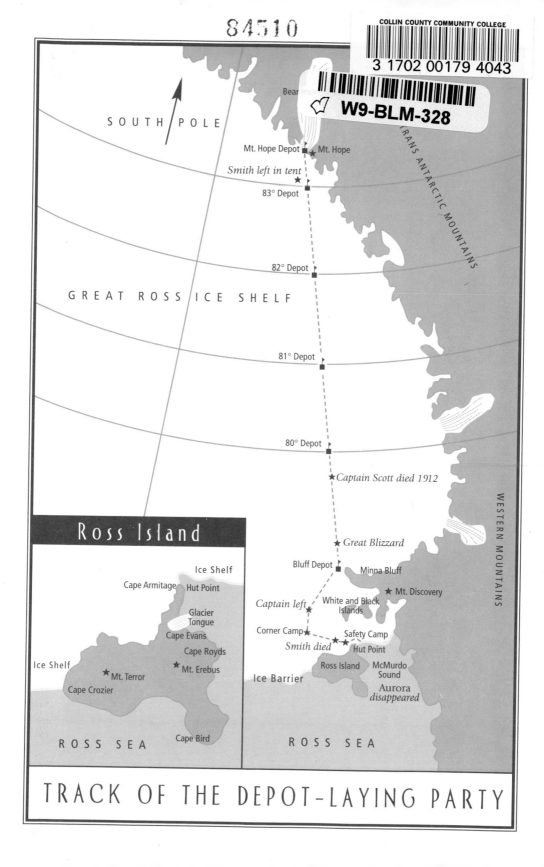

SOUTH POLE

Bear...

TRANS ANTARCTIC MOUNTAINS

Mt. Hope Depot ■ ★ Mt. Hope

Smith left in tent ★

83° Depot ■

82° Depot ▶
■

GREAT ROSS ICE SHELF

81° Depot ■

80° Depot ▶
■

★ *Captain Scott died 1912*

WESTERN MOUNTAINS

★ *Great Blizzard*

Bluff Depot ■ ▶ Minna Bluff

★ Mt. Discovery

Captain left ★ White and Black Islands

Corner Camp ★ Safety Camp

Smith died ★★ Hut Point

Ross Island McMurdo Sound

Ice Barrier *Aurora disappeared*

ROSS SEA

Ross Island

Ice Shelf

Cape Armitage Hut Point

Glacier Tongue

Cape Evans

Cape Royds

Ice Shelf

★ Mt. Terror ★ Mt. Erebus

Cape Crozier

ROSS SEA Cape Bird

TRACK OF THE DEPOT-LAYING PARTY

SHACKLETON'S FORGOTTEN MEN

THE UNTOLD TRAGEDY OF
THE ENDURANCE EPIC

SHACKLETON'S FORGOTTEN MEN

THE UNTOLD TRAGEDY OF THE ENDURANCE EPIC

BY LENNARD BICKEL

Foreword by Rt. Hon. Lord Shackleton, KC, PC, OBE

Series Editor, Clint Willis

adrenaline classics ™

Thunder's Mouth Press and Balliett & Fitzgerald Inc.
New York

An Adrenaline Classics Book™

Published by
Thunder's Mouth Press
841 Broadway, 4th Floor
New York, NY 10003

and

Balliett & Fitzgerald Inc.
66 West Broadway, Suite 602
New York, NY 10007

Distributed by Publishers Group West

Book design: Sue Canavan

frontispiece photo: Front row: R. W. Richards, I.O. Gaze, A.K. Jack, back row: A. Stevens, E Joyce, H.E. Wild, J.L. Cope; © Australian Antarctic Division

Manufactured in the United States of America

ISBN: 1-56025-256-1

Library of Congress Cataloging-in-Publication Data

Bickel, Lennard.
    Shackleton's forgotten men: the untold tragedy of the endurance epic/Lennard Bickel.—1st ed.
        p. cm
    ISBN 1-56025-256-1
        1. Aurora Relief Expedition (1916-1917) 2. Antarctica—Discovery and exploration. 3. Mackintosh, A.L.A. (Aeneas Lionel Acton), 1879-1916—Journeys. 4. Shackleton, Ernest Henry, Sir, 1874-1922. I. Title. II. Series.

G850 1916 B43 2000
919.804—dc21   99-045483

contents

Foreword

by Rt. Hon. Lord Shackleton, KC, PC, OBE

Lennard Bickel has done a great service in writing this book, not only for the benefit of polar historians, but even more so to honor the memory of men who carried out some of the most heroic and devoted journeys ever made in the Antarctic.

Those journeys were made, under appalling conditions, to set up depots to supply an expedition led by my father (Sir Ernest Shackleton), who planned to cross the Antarctic continent from the Weddell Sea to the Ross Sea. The achievements of the Ross Sea party were overshadowed by the saga of the *Endurance*, which was crushed in the Weddell Sea pack ice. The extraordinary story of my father's 800-mile open boat journey to get help has until now obscured the events so graphically described in this book.

Shackleton himself wrote about the Ross Sea party, "In making this journey the greatest qualities of endurance, self-sacrifice and patience were called for, and the call was not in vain . . . no more remarkable story of human endeavour has been revealed than the tale of that long march."

After the Ross Sea party under Captain Aeneas Mackintosh had landed, their ship the *Aurora* was torn from her moorings, leaving the expedition literally marooned without any of the essential supplies and equipment for their southern journeys. Using Scott's old bases at Cape Evans and Hut Point, they scrounged enough supplies to prepare for their arduous depot-laying journeys, imperfect and inadequate though the equipment was.

Three men in particular emerge as heroes: Captain Aeneas Mackintosh, a young Australian physicist, Dick Richards, and Ernest Joyce.

Lennard Bickel's account of the interplay of personalities, of the growing strength and leadership of Joyce, presents a remarkable chronicle of courage and loyalty, not for their own glory, but out of their devotion to the "Boss", Shackleton, whom they were determined not to let down. The tragic death of the young English clergyman, A. P. Spencer-Smith, probably from scurvy, is a moving story, as well as the loss of Captain Mackintosh and a companion as they tried to cross the sea ice in a blizzard against the advice of Joyce. The rescue of the survivors came after two long years.

Four great names have stood out in the annals of the heroic age of exploration of the Antarctic mainland—Roald Amundsen, Douglas Mawson, Captain Scott, and Ernest Shackleton—but there are now other names to add to the roll of honor, and those names are found in this moving story.

Lennard Bickel's previous books—on Mawson's epic journey of lone survival, and on the life of Frank Hurley, the remarkable explorer-photographer, who was with my father in the Weddell Sea drama—are well succeeded by this new work.

Author's Note and Acknowledgments

In 1915, a small party of men made one of the greatest journeys in Polar history. Abandoned by their ship, dependent on scavenged supplies, the men hauled sledges almost 2000 miles across the harsh interior of Antarctica. Their mission was to lay food depots for Ernest Shackleton's expedition, which hoped to make the first crossing of the continent.

Shackleton never came. But these forgotten men's long march to the Beardmore Glacier and back ended the Heroic Age of Antarctic Exploration. Its completion—with attendant tragedy—was a triumph of the human spirit. Yet more than 60 years passed before the astonishing story of their achievement could be told.

In part, the men's story has been overshadowed by the tale of Shackleton's own struggle on the other side of the continent—from the crushing of his ship *Endurance* to the open boat voyage to South Georgia. That epic—along with the still-fresh news of Robert Scott's last Antarctic journey—was followed by the grimmest years of World

War One. Together, those events helped obscure the feat of the Antarctic castaways, who served Shackleton as well as any man on the *Endurance*.

Other factors also played a part in suppressing the story. In 1928 the historian Dr Hugh Robert Mill wrote that ". . . the full tale had better remain unpublished for some time to come." He knew that haphazard organization had resulted in suffering and loss of life. Moreover, the only complete diary to return to civilization was the redoubtable Ernest Joyce's, an account somewhat lacking in modesty. Dick Richards kept only brief notes during the height of the group's peril, a time when the other party members left little or nothing. Captain Mackintosh disappeared beneath the ice of McMurdo Sound and Ernie Wild drowned in a warmer sea, neither man leaving a personal record of that grim time.

Over the years, people of special note in this field—Shackleton himself, his biographer Marjorie Fisher, Professor Frank Debenham and others—have drawn attention to the need for a full telling of this remarkable story. But the gaps in the record made that difficult. Fortunately, two events threw new light on the journey.

First, Harry King, the distinguished Librarian at the Scott Polar Institute at Cambridge University, discovered in 1976 that the last survivor of the saga, Richard Walter "Dick" Richards, GC, was living in southern Australia. King suggested that the National Library of Australia ask Richards to record his recollections for Antarctic annals. The Library invited me to conduct this interview, and Richards, then in his 84th year—still hale and hearty and his memory sharp—generously submitted to long hours of recorded interviews. He told a thrilling, heroic story; yet gaps remained.

In particular, there was no record of events in one of the party's two tents—a tent in which two men were slowly dying, while depending on another for their basic needs. In 1981, however, the diary of one of those men, the long-suffering clergyman A. P. Spencer-Smith, came to auction in London. The National Library of Australia bought the long-lost diary, written as his ailing body was dragged hundreds of miles across that terrible landscape, and at once resold it to the Scott Polar Institute (for the same sum).

The journal was the death-bed testimony of a very brave Englishman. I saw it before it went to England; the moving entries in the last testament of a victim of the worst case of sledging scurvy in history helped convince me to tell the tale of these men. Further study and research around the world proved this forgotten enterprise to be a major epic of human resolution against awesome odds. I am proud to recount it here.

I owe many debts to people and institutions who helped me with this book. Dick Richards made a priceless contribution to the history of exploration of this planet and my debt, and the debt of future historians, to him is plain. I am deeply grateful to Lord Shackleton for advice, guidance, kind encouragement, and for opening rich avenues. Harry King coiled the mainspring for the work.

I received valuable advice and contributions from the following: Dr. Gordon de Q. Robin, Director of the Scott Polar Institute; Dr. John Hemming, Director of the Royal Geographic Society; Duncan Carse, who scanned the Shackleton papers; Dr. Fred Jacka and Mrs Edna Sawyer, Director and Archivist of the Mawson Institute in Adelaide, Australia; officers of the National Library of Australia, Canberra, and the Mitchell Library, Sydney; Bob Reece of the Australian Antarctic Division, and the former Director, Dr. Philip Law; the ANARE Club of Australia.

I am especially grateful for the patient support of my dear wife, Pauline.

Lennard Bickel
Canberra
August, 1999

Shoveling ice from the deck of *Aurora*, 1911.

The Setting

From the very day it was discovered, in 1841, Antarctica's Great Ross Ice Shelf evoked awe and wonder among those who gazed upon it. Those first few men who came against its frozen ramparts in the mid-19th century stood on the decks of two small wooden sailing ships, necks craned, staring upward in stunned disbelief. Barring their southern passage was the greatest wall of ice human eyes had seen, towering high above the ships' topmasts, immobile—a frozen tidal wave. From the plateau beyond their view, polar gales blew streams and clouds of snow high above their heads out into the cold, heaving sea. Fronting that sea, the glittering cliffs ran in both directions—east and west—stretching far beyond the horizon.

Immediately the men named this cold, high wall that blocked their path the Great Barrier. Here, they reasoned, was the birthplace of those mighty flat-topped icebergs, the islands of ice many miles in length that they had met in their passage through the crowded fields of pack ice and floes.

Both ships and men were puny against this astonishing immensity—and these were men now well accustomed to new and impressive scenes, to the excitement of discovery. Many of them had spent years traversing the Arctic on many voyages with their commander, the handsome Captain James Clark Ross of the Royal Navy. Only a few weeks earlier, they had sailed out of Australia's southernmost port of settlement, Hobart, and slipped down the River Derwent.

Within three weeks of leaving Australia, Captain Ross had pushed his two little ships farther south than men had ever been before. Less than 70 years earlier, the intrepid James Cook in his ship *Resolution* had been the first explorer to cross the Antarctic Circle. Below 71° South, however, Cook had met with sheer impenetrable ice, which he thought might stretch clear to the South Pole, more than 1,200 miles away—or "to some land to which it has been fixed since Creation." Barred from moving southward by the ice, Cook went on to become the first man to circumnavigate the Antarctic continent. His record for furthest south stood for almost half a century, until the whaler captain James Weddell, on the opposite side of the continent in the south Atlantic, steered a vessel to a latitude of 74° South in that frigid sea that now carries his name; then he too came up against masses of ice that blocked his southerly progress.

Now, two decades later, Captain Ross drove the oak hulls of his ships through jostling floes and growlers (hard-sided slabs as big as cottages), squeezing between cavalcades of great, castellated icebergs—islands of ice a dozen or more miles across, monsters that would come close to wrecking these two ships the following year. Nothing like these had been seen in the Arctic (Sir James Hooker, aboard Ross's *HMS Erebus*, saw them as "grim sentinels of the Antarctic").

Through these floating colonnades, then, Ross took *Erebus* and *Terror* to beyond Weddell's southernmost point, to below 75° South, and there he sailed into a great sullen solitude of open water. Captain Ross exulted, "We are the first men to burst into this silent sea!"

Yet the "silent sea" that bears his name held both more surprises and disappointment for James Clark Ross. In his cabin was the prized

British flag he had unfurled on reaching the North Magnetic Pole. Now he held high hopes that this sea would carry him to the South Magnetic Pole—and there, a singular triumph—the honor of having unfurled the same Union Jack at each end of the globe.

The disappointment became clear at the southern boundary of the "silent sea." The surprise was in the form of a massive mountain, visible some 70 miles to the north, a hulking peak that, as they drew closer, brought further astonishment. They had come on the Antarctic's monolith—the southern continent's only live volcano. Dr. Robert McCormick, surgeon on Ross's command vessel, noted how the fumes from the lofty crater, some 12,600 feet above the sea, were smudging the sky to the horizon, "ejecting smoke and flame from the summit of its stupendous peak of thick-ribbed eternal ice and snow."

Soon they could see that the fuming mountain had a companion, some 2,000 feet lower; a quiet companion, an extinct volcano. They named the two peaks after their ships. Ross gave the active volcano the name of Mount Erebus, and dubbed the dead volcano Mount Terror. These peaks were later to serve as portals to journeys then unimagined, becoming symbols of hope and safety to desperate and dying men.

Mount Erebus and Mount Terror, Ross and his men found, were part of an island—Ross Island on today's charts—abutted by the gigantic wall of the ice shelf that spread to the east, running beyond the horizon, enticing them to explore its length, a mass of ice such as men had never before seen. Day after day they sailed along the face of the shelf, taking soundings as they went. They established to their surprise that this frozen immensity was hundreds of feet thick. The ice was stupendously deep, and yet it was floating on the waters of the sea.

In all they sailed for 300 miles along the icy cliffs. The monotony of the slow wind-borne passage was dispelled by the panorama of changing scenes. The walls of the Barrier were adorned with clusters of long, thin icicles shining blue, green, and mauve in the changing daylight; with endless arrangements of patterns in grottoes and caves, and huge echoing caverns, deeply carved by the dashing waves, reflecting light of luminous blues and yellows from the ice and the diatoms. The awe that fuming Erebus had inspired in these first men was forgotten in this massive wonderland. A poetic blacksmith aboard the command ship was moved to write:

> Aweful and sublime
> Magnificent and rare;
> No other earthly object
> With the Barrier can compare.

In that long sail against the face of the ice, however, only a brief glimpse of the interior was obtained, when the shelf dipped low in one spot to allow a brief look at what waited beyond. Magnificent? Sublime? Rare? It was all those things. And yet the poet-blacksmith could never have sensed the true nature of the ice shelf from the ship's deck. Its hostility to life, its climatic savagery, its immensity were then beyond imagination. Poetic insight could not envision the Great Barrier's true character. The Barrier was merely the facade of an enormous floating attachment to a high polar plateau of awesome cold; an appendage pinned against impressive arrays of alpine peaks and fed by the world's largest assembly of glaciers, rivers of ice creeping down from the altitudes of the world's only uninhabited continent. No mind's eye could begin to conjure up the fearful conditions that would beset travelers over the treacherous surface of the 250,000 square miles of ice, a frozen plain almost the size of Western Europe; conditions that would inflict suffering and death on those early explorers who struggled to cross that frigid threshold in their attempts to reach the South Geographic Pole.

Sixty years later, among the first few men to gain a clear sighting of the actual surface of the Great Ross Ice Shelf were two explorers who would also be among the first travelers to die and be buried in that white wilderness. They were Captain Robert Falcon Scott of the Royal Navy, and his close friend Dr. Edward Wilson.

On his initial foray into the Antarctic in 1901, Scott anchored off

Ross Island in *Discovery*, a vessel built of oak and elm especially for this expedition. Although the expedition was sponsored by the London-based Royal Society and Royal Geographical Society, it was essentially another naval enterprise in that all but nine members of its complement of 48 were subject to discipline under the Navy Act.

At Cape Crozier on Wednesday, January 22, 1902, Scott and Wilson went ashore with other officers in a longboat and climbed the shoulder of Mount Terror. To their left the ice cliffs cast a ribbon of black shadow on the water which, twisting and curving, ran clear to the hidden eastern horizon. But these men stared southward, the low Antarctic sun in their faces, the point where the snowy wastes met the sky lost in glittering reflection. They could see that well beyond the ramparts the ice shelf rolled on, as Scott put it, "indefinitely". In his notes he wrote, "So far as the eye can see there must be a plain stretching directly to the south."

The first view of that vast plain of ice rolling southward out of sight had an enormous impact on Scott's thinking. It buoyed his hopes that it might take him clear to the South Pole, with straight and level traveling all the way. He did not at first express this objective openly, but the hints crept into his secret diary writings. The plain could go on indefinitely, but to reach the Pole would entail a Homeric journey of some 1,600 miles there and back. It would demand enormous endurance and perseverance. Three strong men, with the aid of dog teams, would have to tow sledges carrying all their needs and protection. Who then would his two companions be? Certainly they would include his close friend Dr. Wilson. The third man? In the end, Scott chose a Royal Navy reserve officer, Lieutenant Ernest Shackleton.

By that time, it was far too late in the southern season to open preparations for this first sortie across the great ice shelf. They would now have to endure an Antarctic winter, and so Scott allowed *Discovery* to be set fast in the sea ice off the tip of a tongue of land pointing towards the Pole, south of Mount Erebus. In case the ship was crushed or lost to them from some other cause, Scott had his men erect an emergency hut on that point. Big enough to house the whole party of

40 men, the hut was nonetheless little more than a wooden shell of planking tough enough to withstand the battering blizzards and gales of winter. It was also used for storing equipment and supplies, and by parties in transit. Later it was to be a blessed sanctuary to a few debilitated wretches struggling back from one of the most harrowing sledge journeys of all time. That spot became known in Antarctic annals as Hut Point; it is still in use by the United States and New Zealand as a site for their bases of exploration.

Full of optimism, unsuspecting of the unimaginable suffering the ice shelf would impose, Scott, his two companions, and their dog team of 19 animals set off south from Hut Point on the first Sunday in November that same year, 1902. Their journey opened an age of heroic attempts to explore the southern ice.

Other men had nibbled at the edge of the continental mainland, and one party—the *Southern Cross* expedition under Carstens Borchgrevink—had wintered at Cape Adare six years before. But Scott, Shackleton, and Wilson were the first men to press deep into the interior of Antarctica. What they found, learned and suffered had a direct bearing on all of the events on the ice shelf in the ensuing 15 years.

They were placed in a setting no human had explored, facing conditions they had never experienced and could not imagine. Still, they were pioneers, sturdy explorers with an ample fund of courage and a driving desire to be first at the South Pole. So they marched with high hopes.

Hauling in his sledge harness, Scott still entertained the thought that this flat plain of ice would carry him directly to the South Pole—the glittering prize waiting to be won. Shackleton, strongest and biggest of the three, had his own dream of immortality, while the observant Dr. Wilson was quietly assured. Scott wrote of their optimism, "Confident in ourselves, confident in our equipment, confident in our dog team, we cannot but feel elated with the prospect that is before us."

The savage climate soon met their elation head-on. Within days they were tent-bound, lying in their sleeping bags, as a shrieking blizzard tore at their flapping tent and smothered the tethered dogs—all lacking in conditioning—beneath the driving snow. Scott had severely limited the amount of food and fuel they would carry (rations of 25 ounces a day for three men, for three months, and a diet for the dogs of dried fish stock) to reduce the strain of pulling. This seemed wise at the beginning of the journey, when the blizzards left deep snow that stuck to their boots like porridge and dragged at the sledge runners. This meant the men were forced to "relay"—heaving half of their load for a mile and then returning for the other half—three miles of hauling for an advance of one. It was backbreaking, discouraging toil, with the dogs soon weakening and becoming difficult to handle. The trio also made mistakes. They moved dogs from one team to another, for example, without taking into account the pack instinct in the huskies; as a result, there were fights among the animals, with the intruders on a team almost ripped to pieces.

Scott's confidence was already waning when the party had been out only a month. The South Pole was still 800 miles away, and the party was covering just three or four miles a day, with their strength ebbing and the dogs faltering. Living on bare rations of monotonous food, food lacking in vitamins now known to be essential for health, bending in endless labor with their faces against the wickedly cold winds, they struggled south from the 80th meridian to 82° South. Hunger, frostbite, and snow blindness from the solar glare that reflected off the ice began to strengthen their doubts. And always, whether the men were in or out of their sleeping bags, the relentless climate sapped their strength and their resolution.

Days of battering and bitter winds sometimes gave way to weird periods of silence and stillness, when the malevolent light played tricks in the still air, showing them double suns, bright-colored halos, green skies. Then the men caught their first glimpse of the southern mountains, the heaving ranges that killed Scott's hope of a flat walk to the Pole. Theirs were the first human eyes to view the new land sawing into space. They watched as the peaks, dark and brooding, changed suddenly to clearly etched heights against an open sky, then vanished in the white haze as sudden blizzards swept down from the high polar plateau behind.

Scott was now the sea captain afloat on a plain of ice, his two sledges the craft he commanded, the mountains ahead the landfall he planned. In the little pyramid tent, with the canvas banging against the poles, he wrote on December 10, 1902: "The coast cannot be more than 10 or 12 miles, but will we ever reach it? And in what state shall we be to go on?"

On that frozen plain the light deceived him, as it would deceive many who came after. Two weeks of struggle followed, yet on Christmas Day the peaks seemed no closer. Defeat now stared them in the face. Life for all three men had taken on a dreamlike quality; they were unsure of distance, of time, of their own capacity. That day Shackleton found some comfort for them all, producing a small plum pudding he had stowed away in the toe of a sock, complete with a crumpled sprig of holly.

With the Christmas camp behind them, the men faced more days of menace. The dogs dropped and died, one by one. Shackleton was ill, sometimes spitting up blood. Wilson diagnosed scurvy, and Shackleton was shaken, disturbed by his failure. None of the party realized that Shackleton's bigger body suffered greater heat loss and needed more nourishment than the other two; so they played their nightly game with heated pemmican, the famous "hoosh": two men turning their backs and the cook, filling a mug, asking, "Whose?" Shackleton's gums were black now and swollen, his legs were affected and he was lethargic and weak. Now Wilson found similar symptoms in Scott and himself. Scott noted, "We have almost shot our bolt."

The last day of the year was the last day of their outward journey. They had come some 460 miles on foot, and still had not reached the trans-Antarctic range. Yet, with Shackleton's illness, with most of the dogs dead and butchered to keep the others alive, Scott persisted. He wanted to reach the foothills, to be clear of this endless ice shelf. He wanted a few rocks to take back for the geologists to study.

"It has been a nightmare," he wrote, "that has got more terrible toward the end."

He did not reach the mountains—not on that journey. The ice shelf defeated his last efforts to reach the foothills. He found their way barred by yawning chasms that seemed impassable in the men's weakened state, and there was no time to seek a way around them.

All thought of getting to the Pole was banished now. They were just beyond the 82nd parallel. Scott philosophized, "If this compares poorly with our hopes and expectations when leaving the ship it is a more favourable result than when those hopes were first blighted by the failure of the dog teams." It was a sad conclusion, which would have tragic implications for Scott's future exploration. He blamed the dogs—not the way they were used or the fact that they had not been hardened for the conditions they had to endure.

The three men turned for home, and with the wind driving the snow into their backs, rigged sails to compensate for the loss of dog power; the last two of the 19 animals were dead, and Scott sorrowed: "I scarcely like to write of it . . . the finale to a sad tale." The men were bearded, their heads shrouded, but still the wind and the snow glare struck at their skin. Their rest was disturbed by dreams of food, Wilson waking to a shaking tent and the howling blizzard wind, with the vision still in his mind of fine suppers, of "sirloins of beef, cauldrons of steaming vegetables," of shouting to waiters to bring extra plates of food, food, food!

Shackleton began to stagger; he was unable to play his part in making or breaking camp. At times he rode on a sledge with Scott and Wilson hauling. Towards the end of January the party saw through the ice fog the bulky shape of Mount Erebus, rising above the protuberance they called Minna Bluff. For the first time men welcomed the sight of that volcano as the precursor of warmth, comfort and safety. Wilson wrote as they reached a critical depot of food and fuel, "Our main object now is to get Shackleton back to the ship before we get caught in another blizzard."

But the ice shelf had not finished with them. The movement of the ice, fed from the polar plateau, caused strain along the areas where it was held against solid rock; wide crevices, reaching down to abyss, opened in the path of the three men. Some of these gaps filled with driven snow that masked them, making them potentially deadly to three exhausted men stumbling toward sanctuary. In one day Wilson fell eight times; he was badly bruised. Scott was almost lame, and Shackleton was virtually a passenger. Finally, the party crossed the sea ice to where the *Discovery* was still held fast off Hut Point. The first long sledge journey in the Antarctic was ended.

The expedition had taken the three men 480 miles into the unknown, with a total distance of 960 miles covered in 93 days under appalling conditions. They had won fame, but had not attained the goal of the South Pole; they had shown, moreover, that the accolade for being first at the South Pole would be far harder to win than expected. Scott, tirelessly writing his diary, noted that "we have striven and endured with all our might." True. Given what they had encountered, with the preparations made and the provisions they had carried, they were fortunate to be alive. Theirs had been an epic journey in the history of exploration of the planet, and had laid a foundation of knowledge and experience for the feats that were to follow.

Comrades in adversity during the stress and peril of the first ice shelf expedition, Scott and Shackleton, once back in the safety of the ship, were never again to know that same companionship. Scott ordered Shackleton home on the relief ship *Morning*, ostensibly on the grounds of his poor health. A picture of Shackleton stayed with those who remained on the ice: a big, broad-shouldered man on the afterdeck of the retreating ship, weeping tears of anger at his dismissal.

Shackleton was a natural leader, a man of action and keen imagination and also a forthright man, whose outgoing nature was reported to have caused tension between him and the rigid naval commander of the *Discovery* expedition. Now Shackleton's return to England worked in his favor. For traveling "farther south than any men before," he was at once a celebrity, even though the attempt to reach the Pole had failed. As would happen with other failures to come, the journey was hailed as a triumph of courage.

Scott returned to England after a further southern summer and a notable 600-mile sledge journey up a glacier onto the plateau of Victoria Land to find that Shackleton had become the first man to announce to the world his intention of reaching the South Pole. By early 1907 Shackleton had raised enough money to buy and equip a 200-ton schooner, *Nimrod*. He had handpicked a party headed by Frank Wild (who had also been with Scott), a man destined to rank high among Antarctic explorers. Furious at the notion that Shackleton was going back to the ice shelf, Scott forced a promise from his former subordinate: Shackleton would not use Scott's old hut at Hut Point. Scott could not claim sovereignty over the shelf, he acknowledged, but the hut was his. Hut Point was farther south than any subsequent base and gave added security for sledging parties, removing some of the risk of traveling over sea ice that could break away. So Shackleton sailed, having sworn that he would not land in the McMurdo area that Scott had pioneered.

In Sydney, Shackleton won further financial support and recruited several outstanding men, including the remarkable professor of geology T. W. Edgworth David and a strapping young geologist, Dr. Douglas Mawson. Searching along the ice barrier, however, *Nimrod* could find no safe anchorage. With regret and misgiving regarding his promise to Scott, Shackleton was forced to land on Ross Island in McMurdo Sound. He built his base shelter, not at Hut Point but some 20 miles farther north on Cape Royds, the point named for one of Scott's officers.

This site was at the foot of the towering, smoking Mount Erebus, the volcano named for an ill-fated ship that itself was named for the mythical god of "darkness personified." So strongly did the volcano dominate the Shackleton camp that Edgworth David and Mawson were fired with ambition to scale Dr. McCormick's "stupendous peak of thick-ribbed eternal ice and snow," and to peer into the flaming fumeroles of the crater and collect samples—all, of course, in the interest of the science of geology. Shackleton agreed, and along with a doctor from Sydney, Alistair McKay (later to die in the Arctic), and a supporting party, the men fought their way through blizzards, up the icy slopes to the summit, where they discovered a second crater.

Later in 1907 these same men completed the longest unsupported man-haul of sledges in Antarctic exploration, following a similar trail to the one Scott took on his 600-mile trip, up the glacier onto the Victoria Land plateau. Fighting snow blindness, frostbite and crevasses, the party reached the area of the South Magnetic Pole—the target Ross had sought back in 1841. All told, Edgworth David (then 52 years old), Mawson and McKay walked 1,260 miles over sea ice, angled glaciers, mountain slopes and deep polar plateau snowdrifts.

The outstanding performance of this first Shackleton expedition came on the Ross Ice Shelf. Shackleton and three companions (one of them Frank Wild) attempted the 1,600-mile journey to the South Pole itself, and came within 100 miles of their target. For the first time they took ponies to the ice plain, Manchurians selected to withstand the cold of the implacable shelf that Shackleton now knew so well. Shackleton reasoned that the ponies, replacing dogs, not only provided speed and power but also added to the stock of human food when their usefulness as beasts of burden was ended.

Shackleton left for his great trek on November 3, 1908, a day later on the calendar than the date that began his expedition with Scott. He had passed Scott's farthest south position by November 26. The men on this trip also discovered that mountains crossed their path, but found a way to the polar plateau up the great Beardmore Glacier. Their last pony dead, the party made the first human footprints in the snows beyond the Queen Maud Mountains. By then, they were toiling on reduced rations in cold, oxygen-thin air at an altitude of 9,000 feet.

Shackleton faced this dilemma: He could go on and achieve the prize of the South Pole, but he knew if he did this he and his party would likely not make it back. On January 6, 1909—the men were then 112 miles from the Pole—a terrible blizzard struck their tent. For two days, half-dead from cold and nearly starving, the small group waited for the blow to finish. Then they struggled on to what Shackleton claimed was the latitude of 88°23' South—97 miles from the Pole. They planted the flag, knowing they had crossed the limit of safety, and turned back north with the wind now behind them.

The party reached the top of the glacier within two weeks and found their last food depot. The descent of Beardmore Glacier brought them to exhaustion. A meal of pony meat repaid them with severe dysentery. The struggle back across the ice shelf was a nightmare of survival, a gritty fight against terrible conditions, with their strength failing and the southern summer running out.

The smoking peak of Mount Erebus welcomed them late in February. When the men finally reached Hut Point and then Cape Royds, they found that the ship had lost its moorings because of icy conditions—but happily only briefly. With every man aboard, not a life lost, Shackleton turned the *Nimrod* north, the most successful of the southern expeditions behind him. True, he had not reached the Pole, but his party had been farther south than any other men; his Australian team had scaled Mount Erebus and had reached the South Magnetic Pole. It was hailed as a triumph, and he was happy to see Scott greet him and congratulate him on his return. But each man knew that the job was not done. For all Antarctica's perils they would go back again; both of these fine leaders were destined to rest forever in those cold latitudes—Ernest Shackleton in the desolate South Georgia Islands, and Captain Scott in the ice of the Great Ross Shelf.

The epic of Captain Scott's ill-starred second voyage to the bottom of the world is legendary. Norwegian Roald Amundsen, beaten to the North Geographic Pole by American Robert Peary, turned his ship toward the South Pole. When the telegram announcing his intention reached Scott, then aboard *Terra Nova* in Melbourne, Australia, the seeds of tragedy were sown: a race was on.

The tragic but heroic details are well-known: Scott used ponies—as did Shackleton—and motor sledges and dogs, and finally reached that "awesome place." By then, however, Amundsen was well on his way back to his base at the Bay of Whales, his motive power being his teams of superb dogs, thoroughly trained and conditioned for travel across that terrible, frozen plain. The dogs were cared for, fed properly, housed at times in bell tents, and given days of rest between the hard days of travel. On Tuesday, December 12, 1911, Amundsen, heading his team of sledges, drivers and dogs, had held up his hand at three in the afternoon and called a halt. The sledge meters told him the distance his party had traveled. He wrote, "The goal was reached, the journey ended . . . we proceeded to the most solemn act—the planting of our flag. Five weather-beaten, frost-bitten hands . . . grasped the pole, raised the waving flag in the air, and planted it as the first at the South Geographical Pole."

Meanwhile, Scott was still struggling on the lower Beardmore Glacier, complaining of "bogged" sledges and recording an advance for the day of only four miles. Another five weeks of body-sapping toil lay ahead before he and his four companions faced that flag and the "appalling possibility." On January 16, 1912, his diary bore these words: "The worst has happened . . . the Norwegians have forestalled us . . . all the day dreams must go . . . now for the run home. I wonder if we can do it."

Dejected, defeated, rundown by cold, work, and lack of food, they faced a man-haul of more than 800 miles, the major part across the great shelf from the foot of the Beardmore Glacier, the huge river of ice marked at its base by a peak called Mount Hope.

Each one of the party of five was to die on that shelf. Petty officer Evans, the biggest, strongest man of the group, perished first, near the foot of the Beardmore. The others died weeks later: "Titus" Oates walking out to his death on the shelf on frostbitten legs; Scott's old friend Wilson, Lieutenant "Birdie" Bowers, and Scott himself lying blizzard-bound, waiting for the end in their little gale-wracked tent. Their frozen bodies rested beneath the canvas, their sad tale recorded in the diaries, until November 12, 1912, eleven months after Roald Amundsen reached the Pole. That day a search party saw the hump of snow made by the tent in the desolate white waste. The last three men had died a mere 11 miles from One Ton Depot, a cache of food and fuel that Scott had originally planned to site some 20 miles farther south.

When news of Amundsen's success and Scott's death reached the world, Ernest Shackleton's driving ambition to be first at the South Pole was vanquished. Within months, however, he had conceived another daring and perilous adventure. He would undertake the "last great journey." "With Amundsen's success," he declared with typical promotional flair, "only one great object of Antarctic journeying remains—the crossing of the South Polar Continent, from sea to sea."

His plan of operation was to take one ship down into the Weddell Sea, below the South Atlantic, and find a landing place on the unknown coast there. He and five experienced companions would then walk onto the polar plateau—carrying all they needed on sledges—to reach the tent Amundsen had left at the South Pole. They would march on to the great chain of mountains he had first seen with Scott from the immense ice shelf, find the huge river of ice he had named the Beardmore Glacier, and climb down to the foot of Mount Hope, the peak that marked the glacier's entry into the Ross Ice Shelf.

At that spot they would pick up food and fuel from a series of depots that were to be laid by another party of six men, working south from a base on McMurdo Sound. These men, based at Hut Point, would cover the same journey Shackleton had made with Scott and Wilson in 1902. Like those earlier travelers, these men would have to haul the supplies needed to sustain themselves to the foot of the polar plateau and back. But they also had to carry the supplies that would be left for the six men of Shackleton's party. "The programme involved some heavy sledging," Ernest Shackleton was to write later, "but I had not antici-pated the work would be extremely difficult."

The daring of his plan caught the public's imagination. The Royal Geographical Society members had just been told that "the continen-tal mass of Antarctica was as little known as the interior of the moon," and Shackleton's timely announcement salved Britain's national pride. He was deluged by thousands of letters from men who wanted a chance to march with him across the bottom of the earth. Ernest Shackleton knew better than anyone living the fearful toll of man-hauling sledges across the south polar plateau—a toll that had come near to taking his own life. He was fully aware this expedition was a challenge fit only for a very select few. At best it would require a trek of five or six months under appalling conditions in thin, freezing polar air, lugging heavy sledges for a distance of 1,800 miles across the most hostile terrain on the planet. There was no romance in this venture; the only prize was achievement, and the likely penalty of failure was death in the white wastelands.

Meanwhile, Shackleton was busy raising money for the trip. He told potential backers that there would be scientific dividends; other sledge parties would make exploratory journeys; the magnetism of the area would be studied, the weather patterns logged, ice formations recorded. It would be ascertained whether the great chain of mountains they had seen from the ice shelf extended clear across the continent to link with the Andes of South America, whether the south polar plateau dipped towards the Weddell Sea or whether there was another great chain of peaks. The most powerful pull on the public purse, however, was his demand that this "last great journey" to open up unknown lands, "should be made under the British flag, since the whole of the area southward to the Pole is British Territory." He added that his proposal should appeal urgently to "all those interested in the White Warfare of the South."

Shackleton's phrase, made on the eve of the Great War, played well to the hawkish spirit of the times.

Two ships had been bought for this expedition. One was a 350-ton schooner from Norway, *Polaris*, which Shackleton prophetically renamed *Endurance*. The other vessel was in Australia, a former Newfoundland sealer. This second vessel had won distinction in the Arctic in the relief of the Greely expedition, and had gained greater fame aiding Douglas Mawson's discoveries of the western Antarctic coastland. This was the ship that Shackleton asked the noted ballerina

Anna Pavlova to christen: *Aurora*. Shackleton had bought the vessel from Mawson; it would transport to McMurdo Sound the men who would lay the depots across the Great Ross Ice Shelf, which Shackleton's party would then use to survive in the second half of their journey across the continent.

Leaving Plymouth, *Endurance* braved a wartime crossing of the Atlantic to reach Buenos Aires. There she took on the redoubtable explorer-photographer, Frank Hurley; he was a Mawson veteran, whom Shackleton had called from a remote corner of northern Australia to act as official photographer. From Buenos Aires *Endurance* sailed south for the capital of the islands of South Georgia, the whaling port of Grytviken, which announced its location with a stench of rotting carcasses before it was sighted. This wind-battered port, described by Shackleton as "the southernmost British outpost," is some 800 miles north of the Antarctic Circle.

Shackleton sailed south on December 4, 1914, to seek his historic landing on an unknown coast, ignoring Norwegian whaling captains who warned of the perils of ice in the Weddell Sea. There he would begin his "last great journey," for which he had already selected several men: Frank Wild, who had been with Scott and had also been in charge of Mawson's far western party; Frank Worsley, captain of *Endurance*; Frank Hurley, a tried and tested sledger; and Tom Crean, a naval petty officer. Crean had been with Scott's final expedition, and had served in the last supporting party; he had wept with disappointment when he was sent back with Lieutenant Evans little more than 100 miles from the Pole.

Endurance was beset by the massive ice fields, and the fight for survival that followed is without parallel in polar history. The story of these men, and what they endured and achieved in order to survive, has been told numerous times. Their ship destroyed, Shackleton and 27 men crossed shifting ice and rough seas on sledges and small boats to a series of camps. Finally, Shackleton led five men 800 miles in a small boat to South Georgia Island; from there, he eventually was able to organize a rescue for the remaining men.

For that feat, Shackleton has been hailed as a modern Argus. His unflinching courage, his constant watchfulness over his men, his indomitable will—all hallmarks of leadership of the highest order— were praised by brave men who traveled with him. They paid tribute to him as a leader who never lost a man under his direct command, and as a man who sacrificed his own health and strength for the sake of others. One of Shackleton's men, the intrepid Australian photographer Frank Hurley, gave the most personal of accolades for Shackleton and his fellow explorers in his book *Argonauts of the South*.

But what of the other Antarctic party, with its orders to lay supplies for Shackleton? While the men of *Endurance* struggled merely to survive, their counterparts who disembarked from the *Aurora* on the other side of the continent went on to make the most horrendous sledge march in polar history—in a cause of the highest nobility and the utmost futility. Committed to lay food-fuel depots for Shackleton and his party—one depot every 60 miles all the way down to the south polar plateau—this group also lost its ship, a disaster equal to the loss of *Endurance*. With no more than the clothes they were wearing, dependent on the discarded supplies from past expeditions, using improvised equipment and shelter, these heroes achieved a march of almost 2,000 miles across the polar plains. These starving, half-frozen wretches spent 10 months in the field of ice, laying down food and fuel weighing thousands of pounds—supplies they badly needed themselves—for the men of Shackleton's planned transcontinental party: for six men who would never come.

The effort killed three of their party. Yet their loss, and the group's feat of brave futility, was overshadowed by the saga of the *Endurance*. Their self-sacrifice became a footnote in history and was quickly forgotten, even though Shackleton himself summed up their long agony by saying that "no more remarkable story of human endeavour has been revealed than the tale of that long march."

There was more to the heroic march to the Beardmore Glacier than even Shackleton knew. The few documents—notes, letters and diaries— brought back by the survivors were soon mislaid. The precious food hauled by starving men is still where they left it, on the Ross Ice Shelf, buried with the carcasses of a dozen faithful dogs beneath the snows and blizzard winds of more than 80 Antarctic winters. Those depots, for which men and dogs died, are invisible to modern travelers in their heated aircraft cabins or tractored vehicles. Yet they are there—memorials to the human spirit that shone briefly on the vast stage of ice during that longest sledge journey—a journey that brought down the curtain on Antarctica's heroic age.

Aurora

Chapter 1

Passage to the Southland

Young Dick Richards's adventure in the white wastes of Antarctica began on the sparkling summer waters of Sydney Harbor. Wearing a neat suit, his moustache carefully trimmed, Richards surveyed the harbor's colorful scene from the deck of a ferry chugging its way to Cockatoo Island, where the ship known as *Aurora* was berthed at the naval dockyard undergoing a refit. Ocean-going ships sat at their moorings, while small craft cut through the waves, leaving white wakes against the blue. The shoreline held manifold coves and bays, pretty little inlets hidden behind bluffs clothed with eucalyptus, soft grey-green in the morning light.

The young man found reassurance in the beauty of Port Jackson and in the fresh sea breeze flushing between the Heads, the harbor's bulky sentinels to the great waterways beyond. Between those hulks of rock, ships came and went to all the corners of the world—but no corner more remote and so strange as that land to which Richards had offered himself, in a sense of adventure common to young Australians in late 1914.

There was that other adventure, of course, the one called the Great War. That one had tugged at him, too: The bloodbath had hardly started in Flanders, and war, in the spirit of the times, was still associated with glorious cavalry charges, gallant enemies, and the ideals of King and Country. Also, it was generally accepted that the Russian steamroller would soon flatten Germany. Many young Diggers on their way overseas worried that it would all be over before they saw any action. But war had not appealed strongly enough to young Richards.

He had doubts about this Antarctic venture as well; in fact, he sometimes wondered what had made him apply for a place in the expedition. On the long, hot train ride of more than 600 miles from Ballarat, Victoria, to Sydney, he had sought an answer but hadn't found one. He had seen the advertisement in a Melbourne newspaper: young physicist, fit and ready for adventure, invited to join Imperial Trans-Antarctic Expedition. Well, he was young and fit all right, and he'd studied physics and science in his training as a technical teacher at Melbourne University. The undertaking sounded very grand, and so he had applied. The shining memory of Captain Scott and his noble companions was still fresh, and the challenge of this journey was ineluctably alluring compared with the thought of passing endless hot summer days in the Technical School at Ballarat.

Still, Richards had been surprised when the telegram came asking him to come for an interview. Now, as he stood on the ferry, he wondered what they'd think of him. Suppose they thought him too young? He was only 21, new to his teaching post, fresh out of college, and here he was offering himself as a physicist. He didn't think of himself as immature—on the contrary, he was strong and enterprising and self-assured—but the expedition's planners might think him too inexperienced to join a group of men exploring unknown parts of the world.

However, that would all come out in the interview, and here it was approaching. The grey buildings and slender cranes of the dockyard began to loom larger against the peacock sky. He thought again about the telegram—how it could change his life, and why he had responded. It had been signed by somebody named Mackintosh, and it called him to report aboard a vessel named *Aurora*. Richards knew about *Aurora*; only that very same year it had brought the famous Douglas Mawson back from his great epic of survival. Perhaps the name of the ship added to this venture's appeal.

Dick Richards had carried that telegram in his pocket on the train journey, and he fingered it now as the ferry closed with the timbered wharf. The ropes were thrown and the craft was tied against bollards immediately astern a small, drab vessel topped by a thin, blackened smokestack, with tired rigging drooping from a foremast. Richards would never forget the moment: stepping down the gangplank, he asked the ferryman where he could find *Aurora*. His work-soiled thumb jerking at the other craft, the man grunted, "Right there, sport!"

Even to Richards's inexperienced eye, the ship had the stained look of an old coal-burner, a lumbering veteran prone to roll and buck in a small swell. It looked tiny in these surroundings, and totally inadequate for ocean travel. He stepped back momentarily on the jetty and stared. His first thought was that it would be a risk to take this ship beyond those Heads into the Tasman Sea. Imagine her butting into the ferocious gales of the Southern Ocean! Then he remembered she had been south twice on the Mawson expedition.

Finally he went aboard—only to have his doubts of her seaworthiness strengthened. He made his way aft of the blackened funnel to a narrow, steep companionway below the little poop deck, stooping and bending to get into the wardroom; so he did not see the solid eight-foot-thick block of wood, armoured with steel plates, that was the ship's prow for riding the ice pack; he did not see the tiers of oak and greenheart timber that lent the vessel great strength in the buffeting of stormy seas and shifting ice floes. He saw only that the wardroom was barely eight feet wide and just twice as long, with bunks built into the walls to accommodate some 20 persons. In that confined space, he also saw for the first time the bulky figure of the man who had sent the telegram—the captain of *Aurora* and commander of the Ross Sea operation in the Imperial Trans-Antarctic Expedition, Captain Aeneas Mackintosh. To Richards's surprise, the man had only one eye.

In time, Richards would learn how Mackintosh had served before the mast and with Sir Ernest Shackleton in the merchant marine; how he had been an officer on a P&O ship, and had served as second mate on the *Nimrod* with Shackleton's 1908 venture, losing his right eye when a cargo hook broke loose from a sling unloading cargo at the Cape Royds landing. The *Nimrod*'s surgeon, Dr. Marshall, had excised the smashed eye, and Shackleton had sent Mackintosh back to New Zealand for the winter; but the tough seaman had returned in the spring to take part in sledging to lay depots.

Douglas Mawson's old commander of *Aurora*, the seasoned John King Davis, had praised the injured man's grit. Davis saw Mackintosh as "eager, adventurous, with a spirit nothing could quell". Richards learned this later; he also heard that in consoling the injured man Shackleton had been heard to say, "Never mind, Mack. If there is ever anything I can do for you—anything at all—you have only to ask." When John King Davis turned down the offer to command *Aurora* and the Ross Sea party, Shackleton had appointed the man who had lost his right eye in his service—a resolute man who had shown his ability to survive in difficult circumstances.

In the little wardroom on *Aurora*, however, Richards saw only a weatherbeaten seaman, a veteran sledger and a man given to some impetuosity. Mackintosh sat with his ginger brows drawn down into a frown, his one good eye staring at the young applicant. The captain seemed anxious to get the business of the interview over with quickly. There were questions to answer: Yes, he was R. W. Richards, born at Bendigo on 11 November 1893. Yes, he had trained to become a science and technical teacher and now held a post at the Ballarat Technical School. Yes, he knew enough to navigate and take readings, and yes, he was aware that life in the southern climes would not be all "beer and skittles."

Mackintosh told Richards the bare details of the expedition: Sir Ernest was the overall Boss; Mackintosh himself was in charge of this end, including ship, men, and shore operations for the Ross Sea party. Their orders were to proceed to McMurdo Sound, the base of earlier expeditions; from there, Mackintosh and his men would travel across the Ross Ice Shelf to lay depots of food and fuel. Those supplies would see Shackleton and his sledgers through the second half of their journey across the continent. Along the way, the Ross Sea party would also make studies of the environment, of wild life and weather patterns and other features, work for which a physicist might prove useful.

Did that mean that the expedition's physicist would not be involved in the journey across the Ross Ice Shelf? Mackintosh knew Richards was the youngest applicant, and though he looked strong and resolute, it had been Sir Ernest's plan that only experienced men would lay the supplies. The captain shook his head and said he doubted that the young physicist would be asked to travel very far on the ice; he added that the King had given the whole show his blessing, that it was a privilege to have the chance to serve not only His Majesty and the Empire but also Shackleton—"the Boss" to his men and admirers. The captain spoke in haste, and made his decision just as quickly: "Well, laddie, will you join us?"

He would. Richard soon had his instructions: Collect his belongings from home, then make his way across Bass Strait and down to Hobart to join *Aurora* at a date in mid-December, of which he would be advised. Before Christmas, Mackintosh told him, they would be well out to sea and heading for the southern lands.

Not until he was back on the train and rolling south again to Melbourne did Richards realize that the question of pay had not been mentioned. It didn't seem to matter then, nor did it later.

Setbacks and delays in Sydney dashed Mackintosh's hopes of getting an early start; not until December 15 did the blunt nose of *Aurora* turn down the harbor for Sydney Heads, with the sirens of ships and klaxons of small craft sounding the parting. She made the slow passage of 600 sea miles to Hobart, then threaded her way past several troopships and arrived alongside the wharf on the morning of December 22.

There Richards found *Aurora* in an even worse condition than when he'd first seen her. His first days aboard ship were marked by physical discomfort, confusion, and disorder amid frantic endeavors to load stores. Mackintosh was determined to be at sea before Christmas. All the hours of daylight were a flurry of haste and hurry, with every hand aboard taking part in the breakneck loading of the vessel's stores. Tons of coal were dumped on the open deck, along with stacks of petrol cans for the motor sledge; these cans were laid directly above the galley along with endless cases of tinned foods and stacks of equipment, and the livestock they would leave off at Macquarie Island for the party that had been maintained there since Douglas Mawson erected a radio station on the island in 1911. They also had their own sheep on the open deck, to be slaughtered when *Aurora* reached the ice.

Richards was convinced the ship was grossly overloaded, and that only her registration with the Royal Yacht Squadron saved her from the normal marine inspections. There was one comfort: They had no time, and there were no hands to spare, to light the galley fires while the race to load the ship was in progress. This meant that all hands had to eat their meals in dubious shoreside cafes—but there was also less risk that the fuel stored above the galley would explode.

Further delay: The carriage of the Governor of Tasmania, Sir William Macartney, arrived with due pomp on December 23; His Excellency and his lady were shown aboard, and Lady Macartney, a sister of the late Captain Scott, presented the ship with a framed portrait of her famous brother—a gift to remind the men of the perils they would face in the south.

On Christmas Eve, the toil of carrying stores aboard went on from daylight until late afternoon. Then the vessel slipped her lines and moved to Taroona Bay, to anchor there for the night near the old quarantine station amid the setting of green paddocks, orchards, crop fields, and wooded slopes. Soon after dawn on Christmas Day, they brought the dogs on board from quarantine. It was a difficult undertaking: The snapping, snarling animals weighed 100 pounds or more apiece, and they were showing their wolf strains, baring fangs to the men who tried to move them. It took hours of work to convey the dogs by boat to the ship, hoist them on deck, and usher them into the waiting kennels.

* * *

Two men, Richards noticed, were prominent in the difficult work of moving the dogs. One was a bearded man with a piratical appearance—Ernest Joyce, already a legendary figure in his circle and the most experienced man in the Ross Sea party. Joyce had been a petty officer on Scott's first expedition to the ice shelf in 1902. Shackleton liked to tell of how he was sitting in his office in Lower Regent Street in 1907, planning his first attempt to reach the South Pole, when he looked out of the window to see Joyce on a passing open-top omnibus. Instantly he sent an aide racing after the veteran. They had sledged together on the first Scott expedition, and Shackleton at once pressed Joyce to join his *Nimrod* venture, where the man distinguished himself—although Shackleton disappointed him by leaving him off the team that tried for the Pole. Two years later, Douglas Mawson had enlisted Joyce to select dogs for the discovery and exploration of King George V Land and the territory east of Commonwealth Bay.

This time around, Joyce had been working for the Sydney Harbor Trust when Shackleton enlisted him—by letter and cable—to join the Ross Sea party. His areas of responsibility were to play the lead role in laying the depots, to be "in charge of all equipment, stores, sledges, clothing, dogs etc.," and to compile a zoological collection. This rather broad assignment sowed the seeds for eventual conflict with the impetuous Captain Mackintosh; but that would come later.

The other man handling the huskies seemed calm and capable. This was Ernest Wild, younger brother to Frank Wild. Frank had been to the Antarctic with Scott, had marched to within 100 miles of the Pole with Shackleton, had led Mawson's western party, and had even been on *Endurance*, facing a fight for survival as Shackleton's second-in-command. The Wild brothers came from a large Yorkshire family of eight sons and two daughters; they had been born near Marston, the birthplace of the renowned Captain James Cook, with whom they claimed kinship. Mrs. Wild had been christened Mary Cook, and though Captain Cook's children left no issue and Cook was a common name, the Wilds felt themselves related to the great explorer. Indeed, while he was serving with

Scott, Frank Wild openly declared that his "illustrious great-great-grandfather had been the first man to sail among the mountainous bergs and meet the terrors of the Antarctic."

Ernest Wild had come out from England on the steamship *Ionic,* along with the dogs and the majority of the *Aurora* expedition members, including the ship's officers and several scientists and specialists. Among these was the man whom his companions would call Padre: the Reverend Arnold Patrick Spencer-Smith. A 31-year-old Cambridge graduate, he had been ordained at All Saints' Episcopalian Church in Edinburgh. Shortly afterward, he joined the Imperial Trans-Antarctic Expedition in the dual role of chaplain and photographer. He would be the first clergyman to die in the southern continent; Hugh Robert Mill later praised him as "one of the finest spirits who ever joined in exploration." The full tale of his agony and long suffering on the march south remained hidden for more than 60 years, until his last diary came into the possession of the Scott Polar Institute in Cambridge in 1981.

Spencer-Smith found a cousin among the ship's staff. This was Irvine Gaze, an Australian resident; he was among the men enlisted by Mackintosh in Sydney, along with Dick Richards and Lionel Hooke (later, as Sir Lionel, he would head the giant electrical firm of AWA for many years). Hooke's task was to operate the primitive radio equipment on *Aurora,* which Mawson had left lodged in a corner of the steward's pantry.

On Christmas morning, with the noisy huskies finally ensconced in their deck kennels, Mackintosh hoisted the anchors. *Aurora*'s coal-fed 98-horsepower engine thrust its steel-clad nose out of the Derwent estuary into the rare quiet of Storm Bay. The rocky line of the Port Arthur peninsula, site of an old British convict settlement, was on their quarter, and the southern summer sun was directly over their heads. The ship's complement gathered on the poop deck to offer prayers for the safety and success of their mission, the gentle voice of Spencer-Smith intoning the words over the quiet water. Behind them, the last vestige of civilization and comfort faded into the haze.

They would often remember this day in the times that lay ahead. It was a smooth beginning to the voyage south, and before them was the pleasant prospect of a halfway call to land stores and livestock at Macquarie Island in the New Year. The new comrades celebrated Christmas night with plentiful food and drink; along with the quiet sea, this made it easier to face the discomforts of life aboard *Aurora*, with her limited space and facilities.

The merriment over, the goodfellowship still ringing in their ears, they went to their "sleeping quarters"—a phrase, Dick Richards was to recall, that had little relation to reality. His bunk, along with those of five others—all of them big men—was located right above the upsweep of the ship's after-counter, in an area that extended across the ship's stern on either side of the rudder, with three bunks on each side. These accommodations were slotlike regions only two feet high, which the men had to crawl into by way of a row of wooden slats nailed into the upsweeping deck. Nature's calls at night were marked by cursing and growling as one of the men from the inner positions struggled to emerge from his confinement over the other sleeping bodies.

In fact, as the voyage went on and the seas grew rough, it was the man using the lavatory who was often to be pitied most. There were two such facilities topside in the waist of the vessel, and they emptied directly into the sea, a mere few feet above the normal water line. *Aurora* was heavily laden, and when the ship rolled on a wave the sea would burst up the opening with the fury of a coastal bore hole, catching the unfortunate occupant of the wooden seat unawares.

Other trials and tribulations appeared as the ship pushed farther south, and the sea grew colder. No ablutions or washing of clothes could occur in the confined space below deck. These functions had to be performed topside, with water obtained by heaving a bucket attached to a rope over the ship's side. Fresh water was at a premium, as it had been for the men of Mawson's first expedition. The various tasks assigned to all aboard made for a constant struggle to keep clean.

There were only three able seamen on the ship, and these men took the wheel in four-hour watches. Expedition members shared deckhand duties and other jobs—tasks such as setting and taking in the canvas when *Aurora* was under sail, saving coal, look-out, performing depth soundings and weather recording, and the worst job of all: the disposal of ashes from the engine room, a back-breaking, knuckle-skinning ordeal. On every watch, two men had to haul huge buckets of damped ashes, each weighing about 224 pounds, up a vent, foot by foot, making progress only as the ship came to an even keel. Then they had to carry the buckets across a lurching deck and dump the furnace residue into the sea, without losing the steel bucket. Richards soon evaded this horror by volunteering for a less odious job: trimming coal from between decks to the bunkers, and doing oiling and greasing tasks in the engine room.

Inevitably, the barometer fell soon after *Aurora* put out to sea. The slowly wallowing ship took on a new liveliness; rolling and pitching in the rising swell, she quickly displayed the inadequacy of the poorly funded refit in Sydney. She began showing leaks in the upper planking. The less experienced men gave way to seasickness, but the captain had every man stand to his duty, ill or not, in the belief that the best cure for *mal de mer* was work.

They came to their first relief on the last day of the year, dropping anchor in a stiff breeze off Macquarie Island, where the wind whipped creamy surf against the forbidding crags. A longboat took supplies and livestock ashore for the resident mission, while the provident Joyce went about the grisly business of finding fresh meat for the howling huskies—killing enough seals to last the animals until the ship reached the ice. There were seals aplenty on Macquarie Island, some of them huge animals weighing above a ton.

Joyce also garnered a supply of penguins for the human larder. Some of the men blanched at this, but Joyce wagged his head at their ignorance, telling them they'd soon find that penguin breast compared favorably with wild duck, and that seal livers, hearts, and kidneys were delicacies for the table. "And seal meat," he pronounced, "will be welcomed by you all before much longer. Not for its taste, but what it will do for your health."

The unloading of stores and livestock completed, the men wrote letters to folk back home and left them for the island mission to post
months later, when they were relieved. *Aurora* turned south, and the
breeze filled the fully set sails, sending her butting into the Southern
Ocean under a sky of scudding cumulus clouds. The men were in good
spirits and the ship's routine was running smoothly when the first
storm struck. Green seas sluiced over the ship's heavy nose and flooded
down the scuppers; waves raced in abeam, carrying over the waist of
the ship. Soaking wet, the men went about their various duties. At
night, darkness added to the peril: Black banks of clouds shut out the
light from the sky, and all hands had to feel their way across the clut-
tered open spaces of the laden decks, with the dogs moaning and howling and the sheep bleating. Men and beasts alike grew more wet and
miserable as the air grew colder and the gale blew stronger.

On January 4 the storm blew itself out, and as the weather cleared
the men sighted their first iceberg. They were beyond 62 degrees latitude South when the chief officer, John Stenhouse, yelled from the
bridge that he could see land off the port beam. The sighting mysti-
fied Mackintosh, for the chart showed no land there. He altered
course to investigate this discovery, and soon the crew could see that
the "land" was actually an immense berg, several miles long with three
icy pinnacles rising to nearly 300 feet—part of the Great Barrier that
had broken away. The island of ice threw dark shadows on the sea,
giving the impression of land.

The next day the sky cleared for a time, and in chill sunshine Joyce
released the dogs from the kennels for some exercise, finding them
frisky and healthy on their diet of fresh seal meat. The break was short-
lived, however; next morning brought the first snow. The fall became
heavy, with big flakes settling on the decks and giving *Aurora* a new,
clean aspect. It was the coldest weather they had met so far, and before
long they were well into the pack ice and could hear the sinister hiss—
what sailors called the "song of the pack"—caused by the ice floes rubbing against each other in the muted swell. In character with the
region (they were now below 64° South), there was sudden and bois-

terous change. Driving sleet replaced the softly falling snow, and a biting wind whistled through the rigging. The sails were furled, and the
ship bumped her way along through the heavy hunks of ice.

The cold, wet weather further increased the misery of the dogs and
the few sheep on the open deck. Joyce persuaded the cook to allow
preparation of a stew of hot seal meat minced into a mash to relieve
their condition. For the sheep it was their last meal; on the following
day, January 6, they were killed, it being judged then that the air was
cold enough to preserve their carcasses in good condition.

Each day now brought some new item of interest or excitement.
From the port bow on January 7 the men caught their first sight of
Antarctica's mainland: the towering hazy mass of Mount Sabine rising
12,000 feet above Cape Adare, the bleak gravel strip where men first
wintered in the Antarctic. The peak was first sentinel in the transcontinental range that Shackleton had surmised to be linked with the American Andes, broken only by the dip beneath the waters south of Cape
Horn. The men aboard *Aurora* sighted Sabine from some 70 miles away.
Now they could claim to be within the Ross Sea, whose clear waters
were the summer home for hundreds of whales—seen now everywhere,
emerging, blowing, and then submerging again, shiny barnacles showing clearly on their backs. Some of the bigger mammals were fearless,
coming very close to the little wooden vessel.

Aurora's destination was now only 400 miles away. Clear skies and
slanting sunshine graced the next several days of running. The
Admiralty Range lay to the western part of the majestic alpine
panorama—going south, they knew, for at least 1,000 miles, with
peaks reaching 15,000 feet or more into the green-blue southern sky.
For its first 500 miles, this great mountain chain forms the western
boundary of the Ross Sea and then continues as the western flank of
the great ice shelf, its peaks subsiding thereafter into the 12,000-foot-
high polar plateau.

Aurora found the place in its gentler mood; pastel-tinted clouds
adorned the sky between the crests, and loose pack ice dappled the sea
as the ship threaded its way toward McMurdo Sound and Ross Island.

The practical Ernest Joyce, out exercising his dogs in twos and threes as he enjoyed the scenic wonder, was moved to write in his diary: "The snow, with the sun shining upon it, glistens in all its glory, while the scene inspires one to face with courage the solitude and vastness of the Polar Regions."

Dick Richards, when not perched in the crow's nest staring at the western range, spent much of his time leaning over the after-rail gazing at killer whales "disporting like giant lizards in the clear water"; or watching a mammoth blue whale, the largest mammal in the world, rise ponderously like a new blue island being born and then sound again with a great swirl of water. "The scene in the pack ice at times is entrancing," he noted. "Imagine a calm sunny day with water tones from the deepest of shades to green and light blue, and scattered about, here and there, dazzlingly white pack ice some few feet above the water, relieved by dark shadows cast by the sun . . . Whales in the water lanes, and penguins both in and out of the water, swimming with most elegant grace and then leaping some feet into the air to alight on the ice. Skuas and petrels overhead, and somnolent seals on the ice, it made a picture one never forgets."

Idyllic, entrancing, glorious—and entirely deceptive. For a brief moment, the light of the sun masked for them the region's utter hostility to life. At the end of the following decade, in 1929, the American explorer Admiral Richard Byrd conned a triplane above the ice shelf and over those mountains, becoming the first man to fly over the South Pole; he too found a scene of calm, mysterious beauty. He was later to write: "At the bottom of this planet is an enchanted continent in the sky, pale like a sleeping princess. Sinister and beautiful, she lies in frozen slumber." But Richard Byrd was destined to see another side to the face of that sleeping princess, as were the men aboard *Aurora*. And like them, he was to come close to death in the blizzards and the killing cold of those open spaces. (Undeterred, in 1946 the aging Admiral headed the largest expedition ever mounted in the Antarctic. Still engrossed by the mysterious beauty of the great white south he took thirteen ships and 4,000 men on Operation Highjump, to make a detailed photographic survey of the magnificent mountains and much of the continent's coastline from aircraft.)

For the 28 men on *Aurora*, no such Byrd's-eye view was possible. They had only sails and their small coal-fed engine to propel them along the coast of Victoria Land and past Coulman Island—a long whitened mound with brown streaks of exposed rock. There they caught their first sight of the peak of Mount Erebus, the steam from its snowy tip still invisible from *Aurora*'s deck, 120 miles away to the north.

With a day to spare before the first landfall, at Ross Island, every man bent his back down the narrow companionway to bring stores, equipment, and a small prefabricated hut up onto the top deck. Mackintosh held a conference with Joyce and his chief officer, Stenhouse, to review Shackleton's plan to land a few men under the command of the group's biologist, Dr. John Cope, who was also medico to the expedition. This small party was supposed to study the breeding habits of emperor penguins at the rookery known to exist each winter at Cape Crozier, the northeastern point of the triangular island, where the land is joined to the steep ice cliffs of the Barrier.

In another memorable journey in midwinter 1911, which came near to taking their lives, Dr. Edward Wilson, Lieutenant Bowers, and the historian Apsley Cherry-Garrard had sledged the 40 miles across the island to Cape Crozier to look for the eggs of these large penguins, which breed in the heart of the Antarctic winter. Cherry-Garrard could find no words to describe the horror of this journey. It was, he wrote, "the weirdest bird-nesting expedition there ever was."

The 36-day sledge trek from the western point of the island, opposite Cape Evans, where Scott had his winter quarters, was made in temperatures below a hundred degrees of frost and was fraught with raging blizzards, which at one stage tore their tent from over their heads. They came back, Scott recorded, "more weather-worn than anyone I have ever seen . . . faces scarred and wrinkled, eyes dull, and hands whitened and creased with the constant exposure." The trio carried back with them three penguin eggs, which naturalists in England later treated as no more than an oddity.

Now, in Shackleton's concession to biological circles—a concession made when he was raising funds—he had committed three men to a tiny hut for the winter, to study the enigmatic penguins. The project fortunately caused no human suffering, though it did result in an accident that could have spelled disaster for the whole expedition.

On Saturday evening, January 9, 1915, Mackintosh eased the ship close to the junction of the Barrier and the steep frozen face of Cape Crozier. A boat was lowered, and Joyce and an excited chief officer went ashore to scale the cliffs in order to reconnoiter a site on which to erect the hut that would house the study group. The two men—the chief officer clearly thrilled to be setting foot on the land of Antarctica—laboriously cut their way to the top of the cliff, hacking out steps in the ice with their axes.

The captain, meanwhile, kept *Aurora* slowly moving in the open water between the floes. He soon fell a victim to a deception that has tricked many travelers in this region—an illusory merging of landscape into white mist that has taken many lives. The pale shroud billowed down from the Barrier, blotting out all sense of distance and definition for the men on watch. *Aurora* was moving headlong into the face of the ice front when the lookout finally yelled his warning.

On the bridge, Mackintosh yanked his telegraph to "astern." Before the engineer could react and set the propeller into reverse, however, the ship's jibboom smashed into the cliff face, the shock of the collision bringing down the topmast and many tons of ice rocks onto the forward decks, which scared both the men and the chained dogs into uproar.

While the debris was being cleared away, the longboat went to collect Joyce and Stenhouse, who came back to report disappointment at not finding a single suitable site for the little hut, or even an area where the stores and the hut could be landed. To ease the tension these events had brought, an issue of rum was made that night to all hands. Then, threading its way between the many icebergs, the little wooden vessel started on the last stage of the sea journey—to an anchorage in McMurdo Sound.

In the early hours of Sunday, some 20 miles from the old Scott base at Cape Evans, *Aurora* came up alongside the sea ice and was laid fast with grappling anchors. When full light lit the scene, Joyce took some of his dogs for a run on the ice sheet—which was several feet thick—and then organized a teaching session in flat skiing for the inexperienced members of the party. While men and dogs "disported themselves like penguins on the ice," he went off and shot some two dozen skua gulls to provide fresh meat for the men.

That afternoon, with the ship motionless and quiet for the first time in weeks, Joyce and Richards stood together and surveyed the scene about them. High summer in the Antarctic! To the west, the southern sunshine glinted from glaciers webbing the mountains, the peaks showing sharp against a pale sky, from the magnificent conical Mount Discovery to the towering Mount Lister, a 13,000-foot peak. (Lister was guardian to the Skelton Glacier, which Sir Edmund Hillary was to ascend on his way overland to the South Pole, the first man to make that journey since Scott's death). They drank in the wonderful play of light and shadow, the sky now and again suffused with shades of pale pink or green, sometimes even purple, slashed with deep-toned "earth shadows." Warmer air, inverted over the cold strata, created fascinating appearances of light, just as it created mirages across the frozen wastes.

To the side of where *Aurora* lay anchored to the face of the sea ice in McMurdo Sound loomed the triangular Ross Island, its southern extremity clutched within the Great Barrier. The side of the island they faced ran roughly north to south against the backdrop of mighty Erebus, the mass of Mount Terror, and another extinct volcano, which had been named Mount Terra Nova. This inhospitable coastline stretched 48 miles from the northernmost tip of Cape Bird to the end of a peninsula of land finishing with Cape Armitage and Pram Point, both bedded into the Barrier ice. Opposite, but separated by steep ice-clad hills, was Hut Point, located nearly 50 miles south of Cape Bird, 23 miles from the Cape Royds promontory where Shackleton pitched his hut in 1908, and 13 miles across the sea ice from Cape Evans, the Scott base in 1910. The whole coast was precipitous with icebound rocky cliffs and impassable glaciers—one of which, Glacier Tongue, blocked the direct route from Cape Evans to Hut Point. Its mass stuck out into the sea ice for more than five miles, with a face a mile wide and hundreds of feet high.

Joyce could call upon rich memories of McMurdo Sound. It had been named for one of the officers on *Terror*, the ship of James Clark Ross. McMurdo Sound was a frigid gulf, 30 miles wide and 20 deep, which from its frozen surface between Ross Island and the western range gave easier access to the Barrier ice via snow slopes rising some 40 feet to the shelf. Ernest Joyce had crossed that sea ice many times. He knew that it could not always be trusted, except in midwinter, to bear the weight of men and laden sledges. Away to his right the sun gleamed on the Ferrar Glacier; it was there, when he was with Scott in 1902, that the surface of that river of ice had frozen so hard it had ripped the metal runners of the sledges they were pulling, as they cut a path up onto the polar plateau for the first time. Over on Ross Island itself was Observation Hill, which Scott's team had scaled to peer south for sight of the missing polar party—and where *Discovery* lay snared for two years, caught in the same sea ice they were now tied against.

To the south, out on the great, cold shelf, the Black and White Islands thrust through the thick ice, imposing a 20-mile diversion to the east for southerning parties. Beyond them, still farther south, the long hard tongue of Minna Bluff ran westward from the main range. This was the Bluff where Joyce had laid a critical food depot for the return of the Shackleton party that had got to within 97 miles of the South Pole.

Shackleton had denied Joyce a place on that party, but Joyce's depot had saved Sir Ernest's life, and the Boss knew it. Hugh Robert Mill recorded the strange circumstances of that event: how Shackleton and his companions, fighting back from so close to the Pole, had been miles off their course, starving and weak, when by "an almost incredible coincidence the signal flag Joyce had mounted on the depot was raised into sight by a mirage, just in time to save the returning party." It was one of the few times when the Antarctic refraction of light, caused by the meeting of colder and warmer layers of air and millions of tiny crystals of floating ice, came to the rescue of men.

The miracle of the miraged depot created a lasting bond between Joyce and the Boss. The 1908 trek had been a hard slog with the season well advanced, down to the Bluff and around those islands that bar a direct north-south approach from Hut Point. Joyce took a tyro sledger on that excursion—the second officer on *Nimrod*, a strong young man named Aeneas Mackintosh. Now here was Mackintosh, back again as captain of *Aurora* through his own bond with Shackleton.

Mackintosh had the ship, but he and Joyce had not yet entirely agreed upon who would command the sledging operations. Mackintosh, in his fierce devotion to Shackleton, demanded the right to make all decisions—after consultation. He had his direct orders, he told the veteran sledger, explicit from the Boss: "to make a base at some convenient spot in McMurdo Sound, land stores and equipment, and lay depots on the Great Ice Barrier down to the Beardmore Glacier to support the party coming across the continent from the Weddell Sea coast."

But Joyce also had specific instructions from Shackleton, in writing. They stated that he was to "take charge of all sledging equipment and would lay the food-fuel depots along that same course as in previous expeditions." In a letter of appointment the Boss had concluded: "Well, Joyce, old chap . . . if there is one man I can trust to lay the depots it is your good self—that was proved at a critical time in 1908 when I returned from the long trek south."

The overlap of responsibilities was enough to set the two strong-willed men at odds with each other: the Captain, hasty of judgment and, in Joyce's eyes, inexperienced, versus the toughened veteran, didactic and opinionated, and proud of his past role in polar exploration. There was a common ground between them that was formed by the power of Shackleton's charisma and by their admiration for his leadership. That link was strained, however, when Mackintosh decided to form four sledging parties for the early depot-laying.

Joyce was already upset, therefore, when he opened the packages of sledging gear that had been shipped from the expedition's London office direct for loading at Hobart. Now he became downright angry: Less than half the required clothing—weatherproof overgarments, protective underwear, and their sledging boots, the fur finneskoes—had been sent. There was barely enough gear on hand to send ten men onto the ice. "One day," Joyce vowed, "I will interview the person responsible for this disgraceful omission!"

Within a single day the sun was lost to their world. Heavy snow began falling and the air grew much colder. Then came a driving wind, which opened a battle with pack ice. The ice in the Sound had been some six feet thick, but some undercurrent of warmer water caused melting, and soon lanes were opening, allowing the ship to move farther south down the island peninsula. Movement was not without risk, however. At times *Aurora* butted into solid ice, the bow riding up on its steel plating and the weight cracking new leads in the frozen mass. This sent huge sharp-sided blocks sweeping down the beam, putting the single propeller in danger. While most men chose to be below, out of the wind, Dick Richards was suspended over the stem, hanging onto a rope just above the screw, where he used a long pole to fend off the pieces that might have bent the blades and caused disbalance to their only means of propulsion.

On Thursday, having made 15 miles toward Cape Evans, they were given respite and a chance to replenish the ship's supply of fresh water. They tied against a huge iceberg, and the men attacked its sides with pickaxes. The lumps were chain-handled down to the steam tanks in the hold, where they were melted. This took place offshore from Cape Royds—named for Charles Rawson Royds, first officer on the *Discovery*, on Scott's first expedition—and Joyce scaled the side of the iceberg to peer landwards. He came back to tell Richards and the others that he had seen Shackleton's base hut on Cape Royds.

Behind the Cape, the bulk of Erebus rose. Its "peak of thick-ribbed eternal snow and ice" (as Ross had described it), was all but obliterated from view by a descending blizzard cloud that would soon sweep across the Sound and all about the ship. Joyce had seen this occur many times during earlier adventures. On Cape Royds he'd often relied on Erebus as a natural barometer, a forecaster of weather that might imperil Shackleton and his companions after their attempt on the Pole. Now his thoughts dwelt again on Shackleton, and the man's unconquerable spirit.

* * *

On the same day that *Aurora* pushed through the pack toward the Scott base on Cape Evans, Ernest Shackleton was also fighting sea ice—but his was on the other side of the continent, indeed, the other side of the world. *Aurora* was below 78° by this point and ready to anchor, but *Endurance*, in the Weddell Sea, had not reached much beyond 76° South. Shackleton was still searching for his landing site, and about to make the error that would cost him his chance of attempting to cross the continent.

It was late at night, under sail in clear weather, that the commander of *Endurance*, Captain Frank Worsley, wafted the ship abeam the floating tongue of a huge glacier. This massive ice flow rose some 400 feet above the surface of the sea. It ran outward for many miles, forming a sheltered area that Shackleton named Glacier Bay. He saw at once that it would make an excellent landing site, shielded from gales rampaging from the south. But he rejected the prospect, arguing, "Every mile we gain to the south means a mile less sledging when we come to start our great journey." Open water leads beckoned beyond the mass of floating ice—and so they went on, only to run into yet another great glacier with a tongue more than 40 miles wide, with new land beyond rising to 3,000 feet.

The ship ran into heavy pack ice as a blizzard came bursting down from that land, which Shackleton had named for his generous Scottish backer James Caird. They eased *Endurance* into shelter behind a stranded berg—the last time she would answer the helm. The position was fixed as 76°34′ South, and 31°30′ West.

During the howling night, the pack closed around both ship and berg. On January 20, a fateful Wednesday, Shackleton recognized their plight: "A survey of the position showed *Endurance* firmly beset. As far as the eye can reach from the masthead, ice is packed heavily and firmly all round the ship—in every direction."

She would never escape that frozen grip. In a short time, the tremendous forces of the Weddell Sea ice pack would destroy her completely. And Shackleton would recall the lines by St. John Lucas that he had carried in his memory for so long, and which he had quoted often:

> We were the fools who could not rest
> In the dull earth we left behind
> And burned with passion for the South
> And drank strange frenzy from its wind.

Men and dogs land from *Aurora* near Hut Point, 1915

The First Sledge Journey

T
hree miles of treacherous bay ice still lay between *Aurora* and Scott's last base on Cape Evans. Captain Aeneas Mackintosh gazed across the white expanse at Scott's hut, standing on the summer-bared shore at the foot of the steaming volcano. Mackintosh could not resist the wish to be the first man to cross the hut's threshold since that day in 1913 when Scott's mission had departed after finding the bodies of its leader and his last two companions in their tent on the ice shelf.

Yet Mackintosh dared not go alone across that ice. Moreover, he felt that another veteran aboard should share the moment. Joyce, with his experience in these regions, would be able to help decide whether the deserted Scott hut was their best choice for a base. Mackintosh and Joyce skied across the remaining distance together until they reached a strip of gravel. They stared at the wooden planking of the famous hut, standing so silently beneath the towering white headstone of Mount Erebus. Scott's trip had been called the most lavishly equipped expedition ever sent south. There was evidence of this in the piles of scattered cases littering the slopes, many of which still held their original contents. There was evidence too of the mission's hurried and despondent departure: Sledges and sledging equipment had been left to rot in the elements, and old tents, boots and tarpaulin covers lay in bundles on the snow.

Mackintosh and Joyce had no trouble pushing their way into the building. They found it clean and free of snow and ice, indicating that it was still weatherproof. When they discovered that the acetylene gas lights that Scott had installed for winter comfort still worked, Mackintosh was convinced: The Cape Evans hut would be their shore base, and they would find some good anchorage nearby for *Aurora* to sit out the winter.

Joyce debated this decision. The natural starting point for southern journeys, he noted, was Hut Point; across the ice from Hut Point was access to the Barrier. Hut Point in turn was a good 15 miles across the bay ice from Cape Evans, and that ice, warned Joyce (prophetically), could not be trusted until the depths of midwinter. "If this is base," Joyce said, "then sledging parties will face a journey across that ice that at best will take more than five hours solid dragging. And you know how the weather can change here; a good blow—a blizzard off the Barrier—and suddenly the ice is gone."

Joyce also warned that the ship could be trapped here, just as *Discovery* had been in 1902. The relief ship *Morning* was blocked some 20 miles away by solid sea ice the following year, and when she came back with *Terra Nova* in January 1904 the same thing happened. Finally, Joyce reminded Mackintosh that they'd had a similar experience with *Nimrod* in 1909.

But Mackintosh decided the risks would have to be taken. He would order his chief officer to land 10 tons of coal and 100 cases of oil to fit out the Cape Evans hut for a winter occupation, and would ask Stenhouse to look for a secure place to winter the ship while he, Mackintosh, was away laying the first depots. Just the same, he said to Joyce, he would like to know what state the old *Discovery* Hut was in down at the end of the peninsula. "I'll have to ask Stenhouse to land some stores there, too, if it is at all livable."

Despite Joyce's forebodings, they were lucky that year of 1915. The ice began to break up unusually early, and by January 18 the expedition was within nine miles of Hut Point with the ice cracking under *Aurora's* bow. Joyce agreed to lead a party of six to inspect the *Discovery* Hut. Besides Joyce, the party would consist of Stenhouse, the first officer; Irvine Gaze (Spencer-Smith's cousin); dour Ernest Wild; Victor Hayward, who helped Joyce with the dogs; and Fred Stevens, the expedition's chief scientist.

They worked most of the day hauling stores from the holds to the upper decks, getting ready for the work of allocating sledging rations. It was a rare calm day, with the mountains standing sharply etched against the horizon. The fumes from Erebus were piling straight up into the sky, undisturbed by wind. This convinced Joyce the men had good weather for traveling on the bay ice. So they ate a hearty meal and then climbed down the side of the ship and set their skis to the south.

The six soon discovered it would not be smooth sliding; there were signs the ice could go out very soon due to severe undercutting by the currents. There were cracks all the way to Hut Point, some of them made more perilous by a covering of snow. In several places the men fell into traps where the ice pack gave way, or small floes tilted under the pressure of the skis. Stenhouse and Irvine Gaze fell through and got soaked with cold sea water, and Joyce himself went into the water later. The caution these mishaps imposed caused them delay, and they did not reach Hut Point until after five the next morning, their clothes frozen stiff and all of the men chilled to the marrow.

Discovery Hut was a disappointment. The new hands found the conditions appalling. They had to force their way into the hut, which was half-filled with accumulated ice and hard-packed drift and littered with old refuse, discarded clothes, broken cartons and boxes. Four years after it had last been used, the place still reeked with the stench of burned seal blubber. In one corner was the source of the smell: the primitive blubber stove that the ill-fated Captain "Titus" Oates had used to melt snow for drinking water and to cook bran mash for the ponies Scott took to the ice shelf. A few fat-soaked bricks lay on the sodden floorboards, supporting a plate of steel blackened from use. With the skill of the hardened campaigner, Joyce found a small pile of slabs of seal fat, and soon had the blubber sizzling and flaring under the steel sheet. The other five men crowded round, defying smoke and smell to absorb some of the light and warmth, while Joyce cooked a pot of pemmican—the famous "hoosh"—and gave them their induction to a sledging diet.

In the early hours of that morning Joyce assumed his tutorial role as the hot mash and the fat fire gradually thawed the men's bodies and clothing. "Whatever you think of this food now," he said, "the days will come when you'll ache for it, I can tell you. You'll get this for breakfast, if you're lucky, and all day long while you work like monkeys pulling the sledges you'll be longing to feel it warming your bellies in the evening, when you camp. That's if you've got enough left to eat."

Joyce left them by the fire and foraged about the hut. The stables that had held the ponies were under ice; probing through the snow he found pieces of underwear for Gaze and Stenhouse, who had suffered the worst soaking. He then found what must have been intended, he said, for "a celebration banquet in 1912 that never came off." The stash included a box of stale cigars, which he offered all round, a pack of cigarettes and a bottle and a half of green spirits, which they decided was crème de menthe. He also found two cartons of dog biscuits, which he remembered helping to unload from *Discovery* in 1902. They were still quite fresh, so he made tea and the men chewed the dog biscuits and listened to the wind starting to yammer at the hut. Soon it rose to gale force, and then to blizzard strength, so they pulled a wall of cases between themselves and the door and sat facing the blubber fire, clutching their knees. With their backs against the boxes they dozed the hours away.

Joyce would not risk the ice under wind, so they did not get back to the ship until January 21, having been out three days. Meanwhile, Mackintosh was worried. His chief officer and five men were absent, and he was fretting to get the loaded sledges on the Barrier so that he could get several parties moving south within a few days.

Before this could be done, however, the provisions had to be weighed and bagged, and the fuel allocated. Mackintosh had decided that he would direct all the depot-laying himself, leaving Stenhouse aboard to take command in his absence.

When Joyce and his party returned, he found matters settled. Joyce did not like the haste. Joyce felt that some time should be set aside for the men and the dogs to become fit for travel on the shelf. Even though the season was getting on and they would undoubtedly meet some difficult weather, it would be best to prepare properly, perhaps leaving the depot-laying work until early the next summer.

Mackintosh dismissed this. "Look! Let's face up to it. We're a month behind now from the delay in Sydney, and the Boss expects me to lay a big depot down at 80° South in case he gets across from the Pole to the Beardmore this year. He could do it, so there's nothing else for it. We have to get the food and fuel down there."

The nature of the ice shelf in late summer burned in Joyce's mind. Captain Mackintosh, courageous and determined though he might be, had not been beyond the Bluff on his one journey with Joyce in 1908. At twice that distance, 80° South was farther south than the place where Scott and his companions had died in mid-March 1912. Mackintosh wanted to take parties of sledging tenderfeet down there, and they would be hauling not only their own supplies, but also supplies for six other men.

Joyce also knew the dogs would be crucial. "I fear the dogs are not acclimatized, Mack," Joyce said. "I've fixed their harness, but they're not ready to go. They've been cooped aboard ship too long, deluged with cold sea water, and they are just not fit for hard pulling."

Mackintosh swept aside Joyce's arguments. The 80° depot had to be laid down this season whatever the cost. Shackleton and his party might have made a quick landing and could conceivably march across the continent in three or four months, staking their lives on the depot being in place. Mackintosh would hear no further argument: He would take *Aurora* through the loosening ice as near to Hut Point as possible, and make all preparations for the journey South.

Ernest Joyce supervised the bagging of provisions. No man aboard other than Mackintosh had any experience in the technique of sledging: its perils and pitfalls, the demanding hard grind through the snow, and the gnawing hunger that attacked both mind and body. Food was as critical as fuel, he declared, as they worked on allocating the supplies—a task which had to be done with precision. Each bag of provisions had to last three men a week, with one member assigned to cook each week. Too much food would mean pulling unnecessary weight, while too little food could mean starvation in the cold.

"Sledging is no game," Joyce warned. "It's long hard work in the cold by hungry men, even starving at times. Suppose you're careless in weighing out those weekly rations; imagine out there after a day of hauling through the snow, the men come into the tent and there's no food left. The poor devil who's cook for that week of short rations would have more than his fortune told."

They filled calico bags with the allotted weekly supply: the main staple of 10½ pounds of pemmican, with 7 pounds of sugar, 2 pounds of oatmeal, 21 pounds of hard tack biscuits, 1 pound of tea, and less than 2 pounds of chocolate, plus 10 pounds of fuel oil and the luxury of 10 ounces of a dried milk product. Sledging equipment—tent, sleeping bags, snow sheet, poles, axes, ropes, a medical box, and the sledge itself—meant a drag of another 200 pounds on the hauling lines. There also was the weight of seal meat and biscuits for 18 dogs. And, of course, on the outward journey they would carry supplies to build the depots for Shackleton's overland party.

By the evening of January 23 the men were packed and ready to begin sledging operations. In the meantime Mackintosh had butted *Aurora*'s blunt nose through the pack ice and had secured her with grappling anchors to the ice front nine miles from Hut Point. That evening, Joyce drew a ration of hot water from the engine room and spongebathed before donning his issue of long woolen sledging underwear; this was to be his last bath and change of clothing for two years.

At breakfast next morning, Joyce discussed the sledging plans with Mackintosh: Joyce was to break trail with two powerfully built Australians, meteorologist Keith Jack and Irvine Gaze. Mackintosh would follow with Ernest Wild and Spencer-Smith, and then would come two other parties of three, one of them testing out the motor sledge Shackleton had agreed to try in the southern snow. Mackintosh called all these men together for a briefing and for advice from Joyce. The veteran campaigner told them of his experiences with the treacherous ice shelf, and advised them on how to guard against hidden crevasses and how to deal with frostbite and snow blindness. "Take good care!," he cautioned. "Never travel on the ice without first putting on your snow goggles. Never, never! True, we have something in the medical box that relieves the pain—but I tell you, I know of no agony that is so intense. So don't neglect that precaution."

The new sledgers were keyed up for their coming adventure. They gathered at the ship's side as Joyce hitched his dog team to the first sledge. The animals were untrained and gave some difficulty, and the men were calling out rough advice, jokingly covering their own lack of expertise. "They have yet to learn to work as a team," Joyce told them. "That's what you fellows will have to learn, too."

It was routine to inspect the loading carefully, to make certain it was fast. There was a calculated weight of 1,200 pounds, a half-ton to be dragged through snow and over uneven ice by three men and a team of nine disagreeable dogs. If the cargo spilled in packets it would be more time-consuming to repack than to right a capsized sledge. Joyce walked along the line of excited dogs as they snapped at one another and bared their fangs. He learned their names: the strong leader, Nigger, about 100 pounds, with a big noble head, and Gunboat and Duke, then Scotty, Hector, and Dasher, and behind them Tug, Briton and Pat. They gave some trouble at first. With Joyce, Jack and Gaze pushing the heavy sledge and the animals all trying to run in different directions, the journey got underway. The rest of the ship's company called parting words, and then yelled and cheered and waved their arms as the sledge and crew dwindled to a smudge on the bay ice.

The dog team quickly fell into a unified trot, working as though some inherent memory had been aroused in their brains. They seemed to know they had been set a target ahead, to be reached as quickly as their strength would allow. The men would see this aspect of the dog's nature again and again on the ice, and it always aroused admiration and attachment among the men who slid, rode, or trotted behind.

The three men covered the nine miles without mishap and reached Hut Point within three hours, the best run they were to have for many weeks. The dogs were tethered outside the hut in the snow, and Joyce walked the slope of Observation Hill, as he had done in 1902. On the hill stood the cross erected by Captain Scott's sorrowing companions just two years earlier, its crosspiece carved with a line by Lord Tennyson, which had been found written in a book of poems carried by Scott on his journey: "To strive, to seek, to find, and not to yield."

Joyce looked south from near the site of the cross and saw danger marks of dark grey and black beyond Cape Armitage; he recognized them as a sign of thin ice. They would have to avoid that area by keeping well out to the west, he decided, if they were going to reach the low lip of the Barrier without trouble. Men and dogs fed, they camped down early that night, content with a good start and knowing that a night under cover, no matter how rough, would stand them in good stead and allow an early getaway in the morning.

Their sleep was disturbed, however. A rumpus in the early hours had them all awake; the dogs were barking and snarling and yelping. Growling at the disturbance, Joyce found they had bitten through their tethers and had gathered in a circle to fight for the right to leadership, a result of the wolf strain he had seen manifest on his first Antarctic voyage. One dog already lay dead, blood from its ripped throat running scarlet into the snow. From now on they would have to remember to tether the dogs adequately at the end of each day of travel.

Over the next several days, bad weather delayed their plans for getting to the Barrier surface. Joyce was so concerned at the delay and the poor going that he sent Keith Jack back on foot to warn Mackintosh of the conditions, and to say that he would find a passage westward across the bay ice and erect a cairn to mark the turning point.

Jack expected to find Mackintosh, Ernest Wild and Spencer-Smith all camped at Hut Point, since they had been due to leave the ship the day after Joyce's party. Instead he returned to Joyce's camp southwest of Cape Armitage later that night to tell Joyce that Mackintosh's party had only just arrived at the hut after losing their way from the ship. He related how Mackintosh and his two companions had run into a whirling snowstorm after leaving the ship and had tried to battle on. The visibility deteriorated so badly, however, that they eventually made camp where they stood. The next day, when the air had cleared, they see that they had been marching directly toward the western mountains, and had slogged for 18 miles to cover the much shorter distance to the hut.

Joyce, Jack and Gaze erected the guide cairn, but they still found the trail to the Barrier to be heavy going. The new snow was so soft it dragged on the sledge runners like glue, causing strain on the men and the dogs so that they were compelled to move in relays. They would unload half the sledge cargo and carry it forward, then come back for the rest—a process that had them covering three miles to advance one. Wearied from the labor of hauling their stores and equipment up 40-foot-high snow slopes, Joyce and his two Australian comrades reached the surface of the Barrier on the night of January 30 and camped on the ice shelf to wait for Mackintosh. Joyce noted the struggle in his journal: "When one realizes the edge of the Barrier is only seven miles from Hut Point . . . and this distance covered in three days, well, it is far from easy work."

Mackintosh and his two men were a day behind. They had covered little more than two miles over 12 hours, with increasing labor. To try to overcome the terrible drag of the soft surfaces they started walking in the colder air at night, but they still had to relay their sledge load. Sitting in their tent as Wild cooked the hoosh, Mackintosh wrote in his diary: "I feel somewhat despondent . . . we are not getting on as well as I expected nor do we find it as easy as one would gather from reading."

Mackintosh hoped that the surface would be better for travel once they climbed to join Joyce's party on the Barrier, but those hopes were not fulfilled; there was even worse to come. He was beginning to worry now about completing his undertaking to lay the depot at 80° South that season. Frustration with the conditions showed in Mackintosh's diary after his party's first night of struggle across the plateau: "Surface too dreadful for words . . . we sink into it, snow up to our knees, the dogs struggling out of it, panting and making great efforts."

Six other men followed the Joyce and Mackintosh parties onto the surface. Richards and two companions drove the motor sledge for a brief and difficult passage across the bay ice, but had to abandon the contraption short of Hut Point when the clutch burned out. With the other party of three, they continued forward on foot.

Finally, all 12 sledgers reached the point known by Scott as Safety Camp. Here they found bamboo poles still standing in the snow, and three feet down a bag of oats intended for Scott's unfortunate ponies, along with two cartons of dog biscuits—a find more precious than Mackintosh then knew. Richards and Spencer-Smith saw another object of interest: digging away with ice axes, they uncovered a defunct motor sledge from 1911, still with its petrol tank half-filled, and as useless as the machine they had left near Hut Point. The supporting parties returned to Hut Point, while Mackintosh and Joyce and their men faced the journey south.

At this point, Mackintosh assumed charge of the depot-laying over the more experienced Joyce. He had already left the ship, vital to their future safety, in the hands of officers with no knowledge of the tempestuous nature of the Antarctic climate, and no experience with the behavior of sea ice or polar storms. Now, on the hostile surface of the ice shelf, with only his brief sledging experience of 1908 to guide him, Mackintosh made decisions that would have dire and tragic consequences in the following season.

Crew eating on deck

Against Joyce's advice, Mackintosh pushed unfit dogs beyond their endurance. He soon noted the strain on his team, and wrote in his diary: "Decided to make a shot at traveling with the whole load. It was a back-breaking job. . . . We managed to cover one mile. Even this is better than relaying . . . the dogs being entirely done up, poor brutes." Yet the very next day he threw a challenge to Joyce and the two Australians that he would race them to the Bluff, the prize for the winners being a magnum of champagne once they were back in civilization. Later that night he recorded that "if the dogs do not pull together we cannot move. Sledging is real hard work; but we are getting along."

For six days and nights the two parties thrust ahead, pushing against the plateau winds with their heads down, the drift clogging their goggles, other times huddled in their bags for a whole 24 hours while a blizzard screamed around their tents, the scene a whirling white chaos, the dogs marked only by heaps of snow with a hole for breathing. "Every mile traversed is monotonous," Joyce complained, "going blindly ahead, advancing slowly, covering the mileage. . . ." He added praise for his two companions and the way they had settled into the toil of sledging, noting that "they are two splendid mates and an excellent sample of Australians."

The sledgers' day started at 5 each morning with a pint of hot pemmican and the agony of forcing their feet into rigid finneskoes, the fur always frozen solid from the previous day. Then it was out in the driving wind to dig out the dogs and feed them, avoiding the angry, snapping fangs, then break camp and load the sledge and push, push, push. Joyce described this as "grind, grind, grind . . . the dogs behaving splendidly, but I think it all too much for them." After 16 days of strenuous hauling, they finally arrived at the Bluff, two days ahead of Mackintosh, Wild and Spencer-Smith. There, Joyce and his men gloated over the prospect of drinking a magnum of champagne they would never receive.

The two parties joined in building a tall cairn to mark the deposit of supplies. Joyce remarked that they could not be certain the location met the bearings that Shackleton had specified. The western mountains, White Island—Minna Bluff itself—and Mount Erebus were all hidden in the shroud of flying drift and ice haze. Perhaps they could check this later.

"Not so sure of that, though," he added. "I don't recall any travelers meeting good weather at this place on the shelf. Maybe there is some current of wind from the polar plateau that sweeps along the arm of the Bluff which causes the disturbance."

They cut the blocks of hard snow with their spades and then piled them to a height of 12 feet; a black flag was lashed to a long bamboo pole and set atop the mound, some 20 feet above the surface. All in all, they agreed, it was a good mark for Shackleton's party.

Mackintosh declared himself satisfied upon reaching this objective. But the achievement proved to be a pyrrhic victory: The dog team, which had striven so hard in the weeks since they had left the ship, now lay in a line, unusually quiet. One dog did not move at all; the men found that it had curled itself into a ball and died silently in the snow. Faces furrowed by the knifing south wind, their eyes reddened by snow glare and gaunt from travel and hunger, the men stood over the carcass, sorrowing as at the loss of a comrade. Joyce gave the remaining dogs an extra feed that night. Then, after the men had eaten, he went to Mackintosh's tent to air his misgivings.

They sat in the green light from the canvas as the primus melted snow for their tea, and Joyce argued that the dogs should do no more work. "They've had too hard a time," he said. "They're caved in and we'd be mad to take them any farther."

Mackintosh, however, was grimly determined to continue. Unhappy with the death and the loss of pulling power, he had to—he was bound to—weigh the lives of animals against the lives of men. Shackleton's order had been explicit: lay a depot of supplies at the 80th latitude that season. "That order will have to be complied with," he said. "We have no choice."

Shackleton's wish for a substantial depot at 80 degrees south was based on the vain hope of crossing the frozen continent that first season. Joyce knew from experience this was not sound reasoning, but he recognised that a depot of plentiful food and fuel at that spot on the vast ice shelf could save the lives of men worn down from fighting their way north on that last gruelling stretch. Also, the depot would ease the initial sledging burden in the coming summer of laying deposits of supplies across hundreds of miles to the foot of the polar plateau, as well as being a sanctuary on their return to base. But there was the question whether the dogs, yet to be hardened to severe Antarctic travel, should be sacrificed to achieve a depot at 80 degrees South.

Joyce, the veteran sledger, went on arguing, basing his views on his experience during seven treks across the ice shelf. He reminded Mackintosh that they would be coming back in late March, and how at that time, in this very place, Scott and Bowers and Wilson had died, unable to travel.

"I understand you have to lay this depot," he said. "But please, Mack, don't take the dogs any farther. We'll need them much more next season when we have to go through to the Beardmore. We can take supplies down to the 80th, but I fear the dogs won't survive much longer. Send them back!"

Mackintosh compromised, and rearranged the two parties. Joyce and Mackintosh would go south with Ernie Wild and take the strongest dogs with them. The other dogs would go back north with Spencer-Smith, Gaze, and Jack. This meant the weakest dogs would be pulling a light sledge, and a week of provisions should see them through to Safety Camp. There would be little strain on the animals. And so it was. Joyce disagreed with the decision, but had to comply, for Mackintosh now asserted his authority. There would be no more discussion on the matter.

The two sledges were reloaded immediately, and the two parties broke camp and said their good-byes. The returning group headed north, the wind at their backs, the men leaning into the sledging harness pulling along with the five weak dogs. They moved the light sledge so quickly that they soon vanished into the white haze, with Spencer-Smith's voice coming back clearly as he called encouragement to the team.

Mackintosh at once turned his team of nine dogs to the south. It was almost mid-February, and with little more than a month of traveling weather left in the season they still faced a slog of 200 miles. For the first half of that distance they would be hauling a heavy sledge, loaded with supplies for Shackleton's overland party as well as supplies for their own needs. And with each mile that passed under their burden, Joyce's misgivings grew stronger.

Two days after the two groups separated, with sudden polar savagery, a blizzard burst over the small southern party and they were tent-bound for 24 hours, bundled in their sleeping bags for some fragment of warmth while the banshee howled about their camp. Then, with the typical astonishing atonement of the Antarctic, came a beautiful day— a calm day of sunshine with wonderfully clear visibility. The air was so clear they could see the Bluff standing sharp, and in the far north, more than 100 miles distant, the stark cone of Mount Erebus, its hidden craters throwing up columns of steam and yellow clouds into the high sky. The dogs were buried under the snowflakes, showing their positions only by the breathing holes fashioned by their warm breath.

From then on they all worked at hauling in 10-hour stints, making an average distance of five miles each day. On the afternoon of February 19, however, they struck the porridge snow again, sinking at places to their waists, so that when the haul ended the men were soaked through with water and the sweat of their exertions. They spent an exceptionally cold night in their bags, gaining little sleep because of their violent shivering.

The following day, on the evening of February 20, they took their bearings and found they had reached the 80th latitude. Joyce noted sourly in his diary that they had been out a month and had averaged only five miles a day—prompting the prediction, "To lay the depots to the Beardmore we will have to double that mileage." It grew much colder overnight, and in the morning when they went out to check their bearings against the mountains, Mackintosh had to pull out his whiskers from where they were frozen to one of the instruments.

The work the men were doing, building snow cairns to guide the overland travelers to the major depot, seemed to enrage the elements. The worst blizzard of their journey now came down upon them, and Wild and Joyce fell victim to frostbite. This was a penalty for assisting the dogs. On February 25 Joyce noted, "The blizzard still raging . . . the wind so great, it is almost impossible to lean against it; the force is close to 100 miles an hour. It is a miracle how the tent stands the strain. The dogs are out of sight, completely buried."

Joyce called on Wild to assist in the long, chilling job of digging the animals out. "It took us over two hours to release them. They appeared very weak and we gave them a good supply of biscuits." He found a mystery in the nature of these creatures: "If a blizzard springs up, the drift covers them and after a time they are completely buried with no chance of freeing themselves . . . with temperatures down to 30° below the snow becomes compact . . . what chance have they? This seems against the laws of nature; if human aid were not there to help, where would they be? Antarctic conditions must be quite different from those in their natural Arctic home."

As he wrote these words, the gale winds tore at the tent so fiercely the men expected that any moment it would be ripped to pieces. It was so cold they shivered in their bags until morning, when the wind abated. Outside, the dogs were again completely buried. While digging out the animals, the men found that two more dogs had died. That left seven dogs, which were allowed to run loose in the snow and to gain warmth from exercise, while the sledge was dug free and the men went into the tent to prepare warm food. As they ate, the men heard long mournful wolf howls. Fearing further disaster, Joyce went outside to find the unhappy creatures all seated on their haunches with their noses held high, crying their misery to the bleak sky. "Poor fellows," he said, "these blizzards are a trial to man and beast."

For two more days the party was pinned down by the fury of the blizzard. The fine drift was blown into every crack of the tent and the men's clothes and with a seeming malevolence the temperature rose from 30° below to freezing, so that their bodies melted the drift, soaking their underwear and socks; the sleeping bags were now coated

with ice, which made them three times their normal weight. Mackintosh made a note: "Outside is a scene of chaos. We long to be off but
the howl of the wind shows how impossible it is. I am afraid the dogs
will not pull through. We have a week's provisions and 160 miles to
travel. . . . We will have to get another week's provisions from the
depot, but don't wish it. Will see what luck tomorrow."

The food situation was grim the next day. Mackintosh wrote, "It is a
rotten miserable time. We are reduced now to one meal in 24 hours. . . .
It is bad enough to have to wait, but we have also the wretched thought
of having to use provisions we have already depoted, for which we have
had this hard struggle."

The weather cleared the following day and Joyce and Mackintosh
went to raid the depot for another week's supply, leaving a week's food
for six men and enough biscuits and oil for two weeks. The sun was out
while they did this work, and Joyce observed his companion closely,
noting, "Poor Mack, he is feeling the strain." Back at the tent, Ernie Wild
laid their ice-laden sleeping bags in the sun and made a pot of hot
hoosh for the men. The sun seemed also to enliven the dogs, but Joyce
observed that the barking that used to mark their feeding time had been
blown away by the blizzard winds. The team was apathetic, and showed
none of their usual joy when turning their noses to the north.

They had clear weather on the last day of February, but found little
cheer in this. The dogs were growing very weak. Joyce was stricken with
snow blindness and had to give up his task of steering their passage
through the white waste. Then, on March 2, when a wind came on their
backs, they fashioned a sail from a snow cloth and the dogs were
allowed to totter along behind. Their condition was now pitiful. Two
more died quietly; soon the men judged that death would be a kind
release for another three. The animals were in such a state they soon
collapsed in the snow. Mackintosh wrote, "They are all lying down in
our tracks. They have a painless death. . . . They curl up and fall into a
sleep from which they will never wake." Joyce managed to keep alive
just one canine mate. "It is a sad blow. There is now only one survivor:
Pinkey." Three days of crushing toil followed; Joyce noted that Wild

was suffering from frostbitten feet, and that he "and Pinkey were having a busman's holiday, but a cold one, riding on the sledge."

He still hoped that they might get Pinkey back to the hut, but the temperature fell so low in the afternoon that Pinkey fell and died. Joyce mourned the loss: "We are sad . . . On polar journeys the dogs seem almost human. One never feels lonely when they are around."

The blizzard came back that night, and the three men sat in the quaking tent doctoring their frostbite. Mackintosh was suffering from blistering of his face and hands. Ernie Wild's feet, Joyce noted, were "raw like steak." He admits to his own condition with the observation, "One does not feel inclined to write diaries when the hand is so badly blistered. . . . It has been one abominable, long struggle. And to make things more unpleasant after long marches—sometimes 10 hours on end—no sleep at night . . . the strain is near breaking-point."

They finally reached the Bluff on March 10 and, blessed with clear skies for a few hours, were able to pick out the bearings that Shackleton had requested for the Bluff depot: a line drawn with the center of White Island and Erebus and crossed with a line through a peak on the Bluff with Mount Discovery. Their sighting showed the deposit they had left on the outward trek to be four miles too far to the east.

Now that they had the correct site, they faced the task of trudging an additional eight miles, dragging all the stores and fuel that had been left where the black flag fluttered in the wind to where they now pitched their tent. They had been on the move for nine hours without respite or hot food, but they did not wait now, since the weather was treacherous and their starvation diet had depleted their ability to resist frostbite. They marched to the old depot with an empty sledge and carted all that was useful back to their camp, an additional trudge of five hours. That done, they heated their hoosh in utter darkness and crawled into their ice-coated sleeping bags. They were so exhausted they did not hear the blizzard that rose about them in the small hours of the morning.

It wasn't until two days later that the wicked weather gave them a few calm hours in which to build Shackleton's new depot. It rose to more than 20 feet, with three masts and flags that could be seen in clear air for many miles. Lodged in the great cairn of snow were provisions for six men for 10 days and four weeks' supply of fuel. For themselves they took food and fuel for only a week, and then headed for their next objective: Safety Camp, some 50 miles to the north. It was, in Joyce's phrase, a "tiny speck upon a frozen sea," but it loomed in their minds as a wonderfully welcoming target.

The next days were times of greater suffering and struggle. For Ernie Wild each step became "a ball of fire"; for Mackintosh the time brought a raging toothache on which, innocently, they put a cotton wool pad soaked with methylated spirits; the spirits had taken on the temperature of the air, and at the 80th latitude were like boiling water. Joyce noted that "Mack's Billingsgate language was supreme! Wild and I indulged in our first laugh since the dogs died, although when we laugh it hurts as our faces are a mass of blisters."

Pathetic against the vast white scene around them, the weakening trio struggled northward, day after day, with each day bringing shortened steps and reduced food. On March 21, with close to two months of unceasing toil and cold behind them, the men were down to half rations: half a cup of pemmican and one biscuit per day.

Reduced blood flow brought worsened frostbite. After a physical "overhaul" in which each man was examined for the blistering of frost, Joyce recorded, "We are three old crocks." They were staggering along, "just crawling three miles in ten hours. Our food, biscuit crumbs and cocoa." The temperature was 50° below zero.

On March 24 they had their last meal of "crumbs and cocoa" and were underway at daybreak, with Wild limping on swollen, raw feet. "Impossible for him to be drawn on the sledge as we can just crawl . . . struggling on and on, the scales weighing in the balance . . . I caught a glimpse of the depot flag . . . Safety Camp, on the verge of the borderland."

Hurriedly they put up the tent. Wild went inside to start the primus while they opened cases of food from the stores they had left on the outward journey. Wild called out to them, anguished: The right side of his neck and face had frozen, badly bitten by frost. "I had never seen anything like it," Joyce wrote, "but with the aid of the warmth of our hands we got the circulation going again." Mackintosh was more graphic: "This was the last piece of his face left whole—nose, cheek, neck, all with bites. The ear was a pale green." When Wild's fingers changed color with frost, he impulsively held his hand over the lighted primus. "The agony brought tears to his face." But soon the warmth from the hot food was pumping blood through their bodies, and they were ignoring the cautionary rules to eat sparingly after starving. Joyce observed, "A starving man has little conscience when the crossroads meet."

There was only a good day's march left to the Barrier Edge and the ice crossing to Hut Point. Nevertheless, they suffered a night full of pain and disturbance, with little sleep—a "woebegotten night," Joyce termed it—because of their throbbing frost blisters. In the morning they collapsed the tent and packed the sledge, but left it standing in the snow—a millstone to be recovered at some later time—and set off to make the hut that day, a day of blessed relief.

But though they were out of the clutch of the ice shelf's savage climate, the summer winds and currents dashed their hope of a quick and easy crossing to the hut. The water of the Sound was now clear of ice as far north as they could see from the Barrier's edge, and their only way to shelter was across the perilously steep ice-clad slopes, over daunting slippery inclines—this with poor Wild hobbling.

Three bedraggled, limping wretches, they clawed their way onward. In desperation at the end, they slid on their bottoms down an icy ride, stopping scant feet away from a precipitous drop. Then they were at the hut, and the biologist-cum-doctor John Cope was there with a blubber fire burning under the steel plate, a welcoming beacon to the weather-beaten travelers. It was a moment that Ernest Joyce would always remember, when they crowded round the primitive stove, seeing the ice fall from their frozen beards and cracking, jumping, melting into droplets that sizzled and vanished as steam.

Their afflictions did not vanish so quickly, nor as easily. The mark of the ice shelf stayed on them for many days. Cope was gentle when lancing the large blisters that made their faces almost unrecognizable. "They must wonder what tribe of Eskimos we come from," Joyce joked. Ernie Wild lost the top of one ear, and part of a big toe was amputated.

Two other men now joined them: Hayward and Keith Jack. They had come to recover an abandoned sledge, and they too were trapped by the retreating ice and could not walk back to Cape Evans. Now there were six men at Hut Point, facing incarceration in squalid conditions for some weeks until the winter ice grew thick enough for them to travel the 13 miles across it, skirt the five-mile-wide projection of Glacier Tongue and its crevasses, and come inshore to the Scott base hut. And for these six men there were only three sleeping bags. For reasons unknown to them, Stenhouse had landed no equipment, stores, or fuel here for the returning parties. The three reindeer bags that had served Mackintosh and his two companions to the 80th latitude and back were still on the sledge atop the Barrier.

It was turn and turn about: three men in the bags, three hugging the stove, in air so cold that water froze within a foot of the burning blubber. They tried to laugh at their predicament, but found it too painful with their cracked faces. However, the three patients were soon able to move about. With bandaged fingers Joyce continued to make entries in his diary: "Living the primitive life. No soap, no towels, no wash, no shave. The blubber stove throws out its reeking fumes when it is replenished."

When the sun went down for winter, they ran out of seal blubber and turned for fuel to the small observation huts Scott had erected there in 1902. Those huts' historic planks were broken into kindling, which kept the men alive until new seals were sighted on May 9. Five of these, flensed and butchered, provided fuel and food for another 10 days.

A 100-mile-an-hour gale flung rivers of snow from the Barrier and sent the temperature tumbling to 30° below. When it abated, Joyce and Wild tried the ice; Wild went through into water and returned with his greasy clothing frozen stiff. On June 1 Mackintosh went out to retest the ice with the irrepressible Joyce, and the two men were encouraged enough to schedule a departure for Cape Evans.

The six men started out the next day, pulling a sledge in moonlight. Soon this light was extinguished by clouds, and the party was forced to feel their way forward until, passing the upheavals in the ice fronting Glacier Tongue, Ernie Wild's sharp ears heard faint sounds. A grin on his cracked face, he said, "I can hear the dogs barking."

The sound came to them clearly as they crossed the remaining five miles of ice, the five dogs at Cape Evans growing more excited, and making enough noise for 20. The noise brought the inmates of the hut out into the darkness, to wait on the shore to welcome the newcomers. In the midst of that greeting, as the returning men walked the last 30 yards over the beach of frozen shingle, still wearing their snow goggles against what seemed blinding light from the acetylene lighting in this "palace of luxury," not one of the six men from Hut Point noticed that the ship was not there.

* * *

The same moon that had lit the ice for the first hour of the crossing from Hut Point also shone in the Weddell Sea, on the desolate situation in which Ernest Shackleton was trapped. "*Endurance* is in the grip of the icy hand of winter," he wrote. Amid grinding pressure ice, with big floes lifted up on end, he and his 28 men and the ship were menaced by the movement of the pack, which was carrying them closer to the side of a huge iceberg. The berg seemed to be aground: It held its position against the drift of the ice masses.

During the next 24 hours the ship inched closer and closer to the ice wall. Shackleton noted that ". . . *Endurance* moved steadily toward the berg. We could see from the masthead that the pack was piling and rafting against the mass of ice, and it was easy to imagine the fate of the ship if she entered that area of disturbance. She would be crushed like an egg-shell amid the shattering masses."

With the sun's fight gone for the rest of the southern winter, he recorded that "one feels helplessness as the long winter night closes upon us. By this time, if fortune had smiled upon the Expedition, we would have been comfortable and securely established in a shore base with depots laid to the south and plans made for the long march. . . . Where will we make a landing now? Time alone will tell."

Time did tell—but the crew was never to make the landing the Boss sought. The drift of the Weddell Sea pack shifted and carried them away from the stranded berg and back northward for hundreds of miles, with no hope of escape for the ship. Like the men at Hut Point and Cape Evans, they were compelled to hunt the seals (plus a few emperor penguins) for fresh meat and use their blubber for heating, in order to eke out the dwindling supply of coal. They also suffered bludgeoning by blizzards from the polar plateau, so that the doomed *Endurance* became ice-crusted and, in Shackleton's words, made "to tremble under the attack."

Meanwhile, the Antarctic winter struck over McMurdo Sound with equal savagery. By then the men from Hut Point were ensconced in the Scott hut, still recovering from the rigors of sledging on the ice shelf. But they now confronted a fresh crisis, as grave as the one that faced Shackleton and his companions. And ahead lay more journeys across the ice—trips that would be far more difficult than their most recent one in terms of loads hauled, distance covered, and human cost.

Captain Aeneas Mackintosh

<hr>

C h a p t e r   3

Marooned

The apprenticeship of Dick Richards, the stripling of the Ross
Sea party, to the rigors of sledging was rounded off by a brief
introduction to the primitive existence at Hut Point. While
Mackintosh was driving the flagging dogs through the drift,
bent on reaching the 80th latitude, Richards and his sledge mates had
come back through Safety Camp to find the ice had gone out at Hut
Point. Furthermore, the ship that was to have taken them back across
to Cape Evans was nowhere in sight.

This isolation was not entirely unexpected, though it did cause
some uncertainty among the young men. They knew that Shackleton
had been strict with his orders for the wintering of *Aurora*. No place
south of Glacier Tongue, on any account, he had said, recalling how
Scott with *Discovery* had been icebound at Hut Point for two years. So
Stenhouse, left in command of the vessel while Mackintosh was sledging south, had been assigned to seek a winter berth of greater promise.
The cold, hungry men at the old hut assumed that the ship was still

away on this mission, so they settled down to life around a blubber fire in a shed half-filled with ice, with little food left—Joyce, the ace scrounger, already had combed through the place.

They caught a few seals, ate their meat and burned the blubber in the stove, and so kept warm and fed for a day or two. Then, from Observation Hill, they saw the ship's crow's nest jutting above the headland at Cape Evans. They hastily lit a fire with blocks of blubber to make black smoke and attract attention. Within hours the vessel took them off and back to the comfort of the big hut, where they were able to enjoy a substantial meal and to hear of the ship's doings.

Aboard *Aurora*, Chief Officer Stenhouse and the crew had spent weeks of discomfort, difficulty and frustration that had ended finally in disappointment. Long hours spent on the little canvas-screened bridge with only snatches of sleep; days of enduring storm winds and heavy seas, with green waves breaking over the blunt bow and ice floes crunching along the ship's sides; dodging icebergs in the dying light of summer—it had all been in vain. At times the great katabatic winds that fell from the polar plateau and swept the flat ice shelf had come across the Sound with such force that the ship had been blown backwards, the 98-horsepower coal-fed engine powerless to hold the vessel in position. But they had found no berth north of Glacier Tongue, and so had steamed back to Cape Evans. From there, on March 11, 1915, the men on the ship had seen the black smoke on the height above Hut Point, and sailed the thirteen miles to take Dick Richards and his companions aboard.

Complying with Mackintosh's strict order, Stenhouse at once took the ship back to Cape Evans. He was afraid that a sudden drop in temperature could lock her into this place, and he reasoned that if the ice came in, the other returning parties would make their way across the sea ice to the new Scott hut. Richards, Gaze, Jack, Hooke and the others welcomed the rough conditions on *Aurora*, and for the first time in weeks they sat down to a hot meal of variety and substance. As the ship dropped anchors off the Cape Evans beach, the men climbed into their blankets and fell into the deep sleep of exhaustion.

In the early hours of the morning, officers and crew were given fore-warning of the disaster to come. The first intimation came to Dick Richards through the fog of deep sleep: He heard a pounding of boots, then the raw Scots voice of the bosun, Scotty Paton, yelling to the doz-ing chief officer, "She's away, sorr!" The swell was lifting the deck beneath the stirring men, and then the rise and fall of the ship brought them topside to peer through the winter darkness at the rocky head-land, perilously close to the now-drifting ship, which had torn its anchors loose from the seabed. The hands fought to raise the two anchors, which still hung from the front hawsers; meanwhile, a mist swallowed the ship and a heavy sea ran beyond the headland.

Stokers in the engine-room hurriedly raised steam to try to pro-vide enough thrust to turn the ship's head into the wind and the waves. The hours went by as they tried this operation again and again. Each time the sea and the wind took command and *Aurora* fell back, side-on into the path of the rising seas. Sleepless and wearied after 12 hours of struggle, Stenhouse ordered the engines to stop and the old wooden sealer was allowed to wallow, rolling side to side, prey to the elements. Soon her weather side was heavily coated with ice from the flying spume, and the tired men chipped the thickening ice from the ship with hammers and chisels to avoid the danger of cap-sizing under the growing weight.

The storm lasted a full day. As it finally moderated, *Aurora* steamed slowly back to Cape Evans, her stem crushing ominously through newly formed ice. Stenhouse decided at once to put the ship into position at Cape Evans for her winter moorings. Several factors led to this decision: The sun had gone below the horizon at the end of February, and it was clear that ice could form quickly and capture the ship if she was taken back to Hut Point—just as it seemed certain that very soon there would be ice all round the moorings some 40 yards from the beach at Cape Evans. The last chance of ferrying anchors ashore by boat would soon vanish, and Stenhouse wanted to tie the vessel into solid land rather than depend for anchorage on ice in the bay that could blow out any time with a savage blizzard wind. No time was lost, and the work of securing *Aurora* for the winter began on the morning of March 14, with a longboat ferrying two heavy anchors to the shore. There, the anchors were sunk into the gravel with their stocks upright and then iced in with sea water.

The ship was now stern on to the shore. One by one, seven steel hawsers were paid out from the bollards and shackled to the anchors buried in the frozen gravel. Forward of the *Aurora*, Stenhouse dropped his two heaviest anchors on some 70 fathoms of cable down to the sea bed. As the sea ice thickened it became possible to snake a heavier cable to one of the anchors ashore, giving additional attachment to the port side bollards amidships. This done, it was possible to increase the tension on the hawsers and draw the vessel closer to the beach, giving increased bite to the forward anchors.

Stenhouse was now complying with expedition plans for the wintering of the whole Ross Sea party. These called for using the ship as the main base, while maintaining a small group at the Cape Evans hut to carry out the various studies that Shackleton had outlined in the plans announced in Great Britain. These included measurements of wind velocities, temperature readings, and observations of wild life.

The men ashore would also kill seals and other creatures to supply fresh food in order to prevent scurvy—and to supply fuel for heating. Some ten tons of coal, bagged in the ship's bunkers by the men, had been landed on the beach, along with a hundred cases of fuel oil. The toiling men resisted the chief officer's insistence that this load be dragged high on the shelving gravel towards the hut, however, and as a result the fuel would never be used. It vanished with the flooding of the beach when the ice was blown out—which had happened before the final winter moorings were made. That meant that gathering seal blubber was to be an essential and regular part of the work of the small shore party, along with the four-hourly meteorological readings from the anemometer located on a small rise some 80 yards from the hut.

Once he was satisfied that the ship was safely moored, Stenhouse detailed the party of four that was going to work ashore. They were the chief scientist A. Stevens, Spencer-Smith, Gaze, and Dick Richards. This move was made on March 23. Since the ship was so close to the shore, little thought was given to landing equipment; no food, no fuel, no clothing was put ashore.

Richards later recalled walking along the incline of the beach to the historic hut, entering its portals and remembering how the tragic death of Scott and his companions had been front-page news across the English-speaking world, "We were inquisitive, agog to poke into every dim recess in the hut. How fortunate that was for us later; for as well as finding much to interest us we came on discarded clothing, some gear for sledging and some general stores that were to prove most valuable."

To enter the hut, they had to pass through a double entranced porchway with two doors before reaching the main area to keep out gusts of cold air. This was one of the features they marvelled at, after their experience with the much less luxurious Scott shed at Hut Point. The floors were also insulated and covered with linoleum. There was a ruberoid lining to the walls and two stoves, one each for heating and cooking. There were accessible bunks in tiers of two, and outside were snow-lined corridors, one of which could be used as a lavatory. There was a separate dark room for photography, a spacious area for laboratory work, and a partitioned cabin that had been Captain Scott's personal province. The windows were small, but in the Antarctic winter that mattered nothing to the four men. They reveled in the lighting, which utilized flexible connections fed from the portable acetylene generator that stood in the double-entranced porchway.

It was all new to them on March 23, but it was to become extremely familiar. Dick Richards would recall how Mount Erebus dominated the outdoor scene, its crater sending steamy vapor into the sky. He remembered with clarity how its ramparts ended with the snout nose of a glacier that dropped steeply some 80 feet to the sea. Beyond that was the black mass of Cape Royds, which Shackleton had used during his 1908 trip, when Scott refused to allow him to use the building at Hut Point. And then there was McMurdo Sound—in winter a sheet of shining ice, with captured icebergs standing against the backdrop of the western mountains.

During the first period of their existence in the hut, however, the four men had little chance to admire the scenery. The Antarctic winter night was upon them, and they went outdoors only when it was essential to do so. Moreover, the chief scientist, Stevens, had planned a busy schedule for them. There were numerous instruments to be improvised, including a makeshift cloud chamber for counting dust particles, so hands and minds were kept busy during the dark days.

The men lived comfortably enough in the insulated hut, but their real home was the ship down by the beach, just a short walk across the ice. The ship offered broader companionship, as well as access to personal possessions and the cache of stores for the whole expedition.

The following weeks brought a succession of bad blows from the ice shelf, a string of blizzards that howled and beat around their shelter and roused some anxiety among the men. There was movement in the ice that held *Aurora*. Cracking and breaking of the sheet some distance out in the Sound saw occasional areas of an acre or two come away. But the party's anxiety was allayed by Stenhouse's conviction that the ship was safely moored for the winter. He was so convinced of this that he decided no stores and none of the special scientific equipment should be landed until Captain Mackintosh and the sledging parties came across the ice from Hut Point. He held to this view even when, in mid-April, a heavy gale swept the Sound, parting two of the hawsers from the stern of the ship.

The ship was safely tied up to the shore, he said. And so it was, until the night of May 6, 1915.

The wind had been strengthening since the afternoon. After their evening meal, the four men in the hut sat at the long mess table that Scott and his men had used. Outside, they heard the bluster grow to gale force winds. Irvine Gaze and Stevens went early to their bunks. Spencer-Smith, as ever, was reading a book by the light of the acetylene lamp. Young Dick Richards had had a long day. Now, warm and fed, he also wanted to climb into his bunk. "I'm tired," he told Spencer-Smith, "but I've got to stay up to take the weather readings at eleven and again at three in the morning."

Spencer-Smith smiled in his gentle way and urged him to go to his bunk. "I'll take the eleven o'clock task for you, Richie. You can get a few hours sleep and do the chore at three o'clock."

Dick Richards went to bed, and woke later to the sound of wind buffeting the hut and the swish of hard snow across the roof; the gale had grown to blizzard force—but the 3 a.m. reading still had to be taken. He donned his heavy weatherproof coat and went outside. He found the moon shining through broken clouds above a racing blanket of snowdrift about twice the height of a man.

The entrance door to the hut faced the shore, and the step on which he stood was some 20 feet above the ice level. From here he could see the ship in normal times, and with this drift blanket he knew he should be able to see the topmasts clearly, especially in the moonlight. So he stood a moment in puzzlement, for at 3 on this morning, May 7, there were no masts to be seen.

Startled as well as concerned, Richards trod hurriedly down the shelving beach, a 30-yard journey accomplished in seconds. He found mute evidence of some irresistible force at work. The two fixed anchors were still in place, but their stocks were bent seawards—and the hawsers that once held the *Aurora* lay broken and twisted across the beach. The open water showed black in the night where the ship had lain in thick sea ice. It was as though some awesome hand had plucked her from her moorings and left the steel strands dangling like broken threads of cotton on the shore.

Richards ran back up the beach carrying the news to his three companions. Bursting into the hut, he yelled to the slumbering trio, "She's gone. The ship's gone. The wind has taken her out!"

The full import did not strike them immediately. At first the men took the fact of the missing vessel as just another setback, nothing more. They made a hot drink and talked the hours away. They recalled coming back from Hut Point to find that *Aurora* had been blown down the

Sound. That recollection was reassuring: When the engine was rigged and the boilers fired and the wind dropped, she would come steaming back, and they would stand on the beach and cheer her arrival.

There was a chance she might be signalling them even now; so they spent hours bent over the small wireless receiving set, hoping and listening for a Morse message that Lionel Hooke might send with the old Mawson equipment aboard *Aurora*. They heard nothing. They decided next to climb the lower slopes of Mount Erebus. From there they peered into the winter blackness beyond Cape Royds for a glimpse of the topmasts or the smudge of the crow's nest, or perhaps a lamp swung in the rigging. All to no purpose.

Two days after the ship had vanished, there came the fiercest blizzard of the winter. It was a madly battering gale, which at times registered a force above 125 miles an hour on their small recorder. They sat in the hut knowing that *Aurora*—helpless without engines, caught in that tearing wind either somewhere down the Sound or out in the storm-torn Ross Sea—was in terrible danger. For three days the berserk blizzard hammered at the island, until, unwillingly, the men concluded that the ship would be unable to return before the next summer. Their unspoken fears were that she had foundered, taking with her their companions and their only hope for relief.

Irvine Gaze put the matter bluntly one morning as they sat at breakfast in the hut, "We won't see her back this year—if ever. We have to face it. We are marooned."

Four men alone in a hut trembling under the attack of the Antarctic blizzard could do little other than consider their predicament. Their only clothing was what they wore, plus a few items of underwear in their bags. No stocks of food had been landed, and the coal and oil they had dragged up the beach had vanished in the same way the vessel had gone, with the ice, somewhere down the Sound. Along the passageway of encrusted snow on the east side of the hut they found the floor was formed of wooden cases. Laboriously hacking down into the ice, they found these to hold mainly tins of jam. They searched for other food and found a discarded pile on a foothill to Erebus, containing enough flour and oatmeal to last a few men a year or more. There was also pemmican in several boxes, but there were only a few tins of meat. They found no soap, no tobacco, no luxuries of any kind. Their medical supplies were limited to the contents of one of the small emergency boxes carried on a sledge.

The gales and snowstorms now became more frequent and limited their searching. So the days of May dragged by slowly, bringing increasing doubt. The seaward scene was bare and bleak without the sight of the ship and its comforting assurance of a return to civilization. The voices of *Aurora*'s crewmen no longer floated to them across the 40 yards of ice; outside the hut the sound of the moaning wind, the swish of hard snow, and the dogs crying into the dark deepened the four men's sense of isolation.

But they had work to do. When weather permitted, they went in search of seals, cutting strips of their blubber into blocks for fuel that was added to a meager stock of coal they had found; the seals also supplied fresh meat to ward off scurvy. In addition, the men maintained the regular recording of weather patterns, wind velocities, temperatures, and dust collections; they spent hours in the hut working to assemble makeshift scientific instruments to help make these observations.

They gained comfort from this activity, and were tired enough from it to sleep well. The days ran into one another with a sameness—until the night of June 2, a night of reunion, with the dogs straining at their tethers, barking into the winter darkness beyond the shore. Six figures emerged from the south, dragging a sledge up the beach. They were haggard, dirty men, their faces black from weeks of hugging the blubber stove, beards matted, skin showing here and there the scars of recent frostbite, their clothes reeking of the smelly fat of the seals that had saved their lives. So Joyce and Mackintosh and their companions from the first sledging journey came to the hut, to the palace they had dreamed of reaching, to find the light so bright from the gas burners that they had to pull the snow goggles over their dark-conditioned eyes. They were greeted as returning heroes, champions of great feats out in the wastes, brothers in adversity. At first the grave news was withheld from them. As chief officer of the hut, and thus host, Stevens insisted on plundering the best food he could find and cooking them a sumptuous meal, with an art that was to mark other such efforts later.

Their meal was merry and bright and the food enjoyable. The doings of the six just back from Hut Point were related with gusto. Then the news of the vanished ship could be withheld no longer, and 10 men sat silent for moments at the long mess table. Captain Mackintosh was appalled; his one bleary eye stared in disbelief, and dismay was written across his face and in the slump of his shoulders.

Stevens, ever formal, made his report. "It was considered onboard that the ship was secure, though I believe there was some anxiety. The anchors had held badly before, you know, and the power of the ice pressure was uncomfortably obvious. We have kept a lookout since she went, but nothing has been seen or heard of her. The coal and oil landed on the beach have also gone out with the ice—and only small, indispensable supplies were put ashore with us, I'm afraid."

The joyful reunion was dulled by these tidings. Well-fed but depressed by the situation, the men doused the lights and crawled into bunks to seek uneasy slumber. Joyce grumbled to himself of his "amazement" that no gear, no clothing, no food had been put ashore, either at Hut Point or here at Cape Evans; but he thanked Providence that they had at least returned from 129 days of hellish privation and toil on the shelf. However, he confessed to being "bothered, bewitched, and bewildered" by the ineptitude, the lack of foresight, and the "worst calamity," no tobacco! He mused before sleep, "One can forgive and forget many indiscretions over this soothing weed."

Captain Aeneas Mackintosh now faced the gravest challenge of his career; not even the loss of his eye not many miles north of here in 1908 had been so painful a blow as the loss of *Aurora*. For indeed, he had to consider her lost, though he would not speak the words, and could barely conceal his deepest fear in his diary, where he wrote, "I

Aurora iced up

dare not think that any disaster has occurred." He had, nonetheless, to prepare his mind and plan his operations against that worst case. The ship had been gone a whole month now, and he knew that rerigging engines and steaming back could have been achieved by that time. She was gone—that had to be accepted—along with their vital equipment, including the sledges, cookers, sleeping bags, and the special windproof Burberry outer-garments and the Jaeger underwear they would need for that long haul down to Mount Hope at the foot of the Beardmore; along with the food they would need and the supplies they had to carry for the overland travelers; along with the footwear, and the tents, and the fuel, and those crucial primus stoves they would have used to melt the snow, to heat their food, to stay alive on that long journey south. Yet Mackintosh and his men still had to make that trek if they were to keep their commitment to the men of Shackleton's party.

Meanwhile, the assurance of a passage home from the white southlands had vanished with *Aurora*, and so had the support of her crew and the comfort of her shelter. Mackintosh, however, as leader of the expedition, had to show a cheerful face to his men and help them come to terms with their situation as Antarctic castaways.

It was a few days before he could commit his thoughts to paper, and then he was generous enough to lift blame from his surrogate commander, the chief officer he had left in charge of the vessel. "Taking everything into account it was quite a fair judgment on his part to assume the ship would be secure here. The decision of Stenhouse to make this bay the wintering place of the ship was not reached without much thought and consideration of all eventualities."

The Captain also recorded in his log that he had been partly the cause of *Aurora* anchoring at Cape Evans. Mackintosh had passed on the warning from Shackleton not to moor farther south than Glacier Tongue since "that was the area of the bay in which Scott had been snared in *Discovery* for two whole years." And in his search for a shelter from the blast of southerly blizzards Stenhouse had indeed gone south. "He had already tried the Glacier Tongue anchorage, and other places, but at each of them the ship had been exposed in positions of danger. When this bay was tried the ship withstood several bad blizzards . . . the accident proved, yet again, the uncertainty of conditions in these waters."

On June 26 Mackintosh gathered the men around the table, and in a free dicussion of their predicament he showed his doubt of early relief: "We have to face the possibility that we may have to stay here, unsupported, for at least two years. We cannot expect rescue before then, and so we must conserve and economize on what we have; and we must seek, and apply, what substitutes we can gather. Our first task is to survey what we have—we shall not begin work for the sledging operations of the summer until we are more certain about *Aurora*."

Captain Mackintosh's demeanor, his boldness and cheerfulness, now evoked both admiration and sympathy. Joyce himself recorded how the Captain was going "great guns, stimulating us all, keeping us cheerful and bright." Joyce knew that Mackintosh had borne many burdens in this command. He had already noted in his diary how poor Mackintosh had been plagued by Shackleton's refusal to send money for operations in Sydney, where "funds were short, the ship had to be docked and overhauled, and a considerable amount of stores had to be purchased." Now those burdens had grown far heavier, and Mackintosh seemed to bear them well.

Captain Mackintosh and the veteran sledger Joyce sat with Stevens at the small table in the partitioned cubicle where Captain Scott had once found seclusion. They pored over an inventory of the stores and supplies that the present party had uncovered on their survey of the Cape Evans site. At once Mackintosh declared their principal and immediate hardship was a lack of fresh clothing and a complete lack of soap.

The six men who had just arrived from Hut Point, himself included, still wore the clothes they had worn upon leaving the ship on January 25. That clothing had now endured the wear and tear of five months, of camping on the shelf, of the rip of blizzards, and of weeks of soaking up seal fat while hunting and burning the blubber in the crude stove at Hut Point. The hunting of seals, followed by the flensing and chopping of strips of blubber into chunks to feed into the stoves along with their scanty supplies of coal, still went on day by day at Cape Evans. It was lucky, they felt, that in the cold their smell did not increase beyond the limits of tolerance. "I cannot imagine a dirtier set of people," the Captain remarked.

Yet the men found some relief through their ingenuity and initiative. The lavish Scott expedition had abandoned many things that now lay buried beneath blankets of snow. Ace scavenger Joyce and a team went to work excavating a hillock at the back of the hut; they found an assortment that Joyce tagged a "very poor line to offer in Petticoat Lane."

It was to be their greatest find of the mission. There were old sleeping bags that the Scott men had thrown away, along with discarded socks and underwear and parts of rugs for the ponies. There was also a supply of canvas from a vast tent, which Richards guessed would hold some 30 men; it had been provided by Scott against the possibility of the hut burning down. They went on searching and came upon three sailmaker's sets of palm and needles with cards of twine; spare bits for the cooker assemblies and parts; jet prickers for primus stoves; two old tents and poles; two well-used primus stoves; cans of petrol for the defunct motor sledges and fuel for the primus heaters.

There were cases of "less-than-fresh" pemmican, and some oatmeal, cocoa, and sugar, along with dog food and biscuits that had survived the southern winters. They came on evidence of the good living that had marked the hut during Scott's stay: a few boxes of chocolates (some "with delicious liqueur centres"), and tins of cakes wrapped in foil. There was no soap, however, and there were no medical supplies.

Referring to the assortment they had collected, Joyce wrote, "It will have to be turned into sledging gear, garments for nine men for at least six months" sledging, in the conditions one must overcome to lay the depot at Beardmore Glacier . . . at temperatures as low as 60° below."

With Ernie Wild he opened Joyce's Famous Tailoring Shop, "sledging equipment being my special department." They took the shears to the great canvas tent; they measured each man and spent the days with sore thumbs, cutting the patterns for trousers, not tailored, but "simple, like sailor's bags." They sat through the long hours stitching with palm and needle so that within a week or so each man in the hut had a new set of canvas trousers. Joyce knew these would be purgatory to wear on the trail—"they would soak the moisture and freeze stiff"— but it meant the blubber-rich clothes would be available for "dry cleaning." This involved soaking each of the 10 pairs of fat-drenched sledging suits in pans of petrol and then hanging them on a line in the rare sunshine to dry out—not to be worn again until the sledging season began in September.

Despite Mackintosh's decision not to prepare for the coming season until they were certain that the *Aurora* would not come back, Joyce voiced the opinion that the laying of depots for Shackleton's transcontinental party was their first consideration. "That's what we're here for, and that's what we must work for," he declared.

This determination led to an assessment of what depots could be laid down across the Barrier from the spring onward. The snows about the Cape Evans site were thoroughly probed and raked over for every case of discarded food, every scrap of dog fodder and every tin of jam and meat—though they were never to be free of the need for harvesting seals and other wildlife for food and fuel. In all, Mackintosh calculated they would have around 4,000 pounds of supplies to drag across the ice to build the southern depots.

Joyce contested this, saying he thought a total weight of 3,000 pounds would be sufficient. Joyce argued that these hundreds of miles would all be man-hauling. There were only five dogs now left alive, and of these only four could work. They would be more hindrance than help, he said, and would not be worth the extra weight to be carried in food; they would be too slow for the men and the sledge would run into them.

During the remaining days of June and on into August they polished their plans for the journey. The final scheme was drawn into chart form and displayed for comment: three teams of three men would haul the loads, with the scientist Stevens remaining at Cape

Evans, both because of his ill health and in case the ship should return. The three teams would carry the total load in stages across the 13 miles of ice to Hut Point. From there they would make four separate relay journeys transporting the total weight to Minna Bluff, on the Barrier, in order to build the big depot from which the other southern depots would be supplied.

Loads from that big depot would next be moved in two further stages, to 80° South, and to 81° South. The men would then make the last big thrust to the rim of the polar plateau and lay the critical depot on Mount Hope at the foot of the mighty Beardmore Glacier. This final objective was close to 83° 40' South, almost 100 miles farther than Scott, Wilson and Shackleton had reached in that first traverse across the ice shelf.

To perform this demanding task within the short sledging season and to avoid the blistering gales they knew would arrive in mid-March, Captain Mackintosh set the starting date as September 1. Joyce noted that September was the most difficult month for sledging, with still-soft snows of winter overlaying the ice.

The preparations now intensified. Ernie Wild and Joyce attacked what remained of Captain Scott's emergency marquee and sliced materials for nine sledging blouses, cut with parka hoods, to shield the men's heads and faces. Then they worked on the old sleeping-bags, slicing the fur into sledging boots—the finneskoes they would need for trudging south. Nearly 40 pairs of finneskoes were cut and sewn by the two men. The overshoes of canvas, however, were passed out to each man to sew on his own, using those same palm and needle sets left behind by the Scott mission.

Wild and Joyce then set about cutting and stitching the food bags, some 500 calico bags with string-tied necks that were to be filled with sledging rations. As these became available, Richards and Keith Jack did the meticulous weighing and packing of the critical food allotments.

The precision needed for this task was obvious from the daily allowances per man: 1/2 pound of pemmican; 1 3/4 ounces of oatmeal;

5¹/₃ ounces of sugar; ²/₃ ounce of dried milk; ¹/₄ ounce of tea; 1¹/₄ ounces of chocolate and 1 pound of biscuits. For a three-man team this ration meant that a single week's food weighed nearly 50 pounds. Added to that was a week's supply of fuel: a gallon of kerosene and a small bottle of methylated spirits for igniting the little primus.

The man-hauling they would be doing made the weight reduction a vital factor. Richards noted that "the diet was designed to give us just enough energy and body heat for efficient work . . . but we were always hungry." And the gruelling experience that awaited him on the ice shelf produced other dietary symptoms. "The body lost condition. After three months the signs of scurvy showed. After five or six months on this food a man got desperate and was near to death."

More than any other commodity—more than soap, fresh clothes and baths—the men missed their tobacco. Joyce wrote in his log: "If only a case of tobacco had been landed! What an oasis in this wilderness— a pipe makes all the world akin." They tried many substitutes—dried tea leaves, coffee grounds, even shreds of dehydrated vegetables. "And then," Joyce wrote, "the inventive genius of Ernie Wild asserted itself. With exquisite care he blended tea, coffee, sawdust, a few species of herbs—and he called his creation Hut Point Mixture."

The coughing that greeted the smoking of Wild's blend in the hut, plus the reek in the nostrils, did not daunt the smokers. Hut Point Mixture, Joyce noted, "survived the gamut of criticism". In fact, it became the standard smoke for the marooned men, and was looked upon as a delight to be savored after the day's activities.

Captain Mackintosh watched the men in his charge carefully, and was pleased at their demeanor and the way their stated common objective of laying the vital depot at Mount Hope had brought a new purpose and unity to his party. "Everyone is taking the situation philosophically and all is going smoothly. Wild . . . a cheerful willing soul, is working with Joyce. Richards has taken over the keeping of the meteorological log. He is a young Australian, a hard conscientious worker, and I look for good results from his endeavours. Jack, another young

Australian, is his assistant. Hayward is the handyman and Gaze—another Australian—is working with him. Spencer-Smith, the Padre, is in charge of the photographic work, and, of course, assists in the general routine."

That routine helped them get through the winter days of darkness. They all had set hours of work, rising for breakfast and working until the time came for what the Australians called their "counter lunch." Then on again until early evening, while Stevens, often in the role of chef, found new ways, and new additives, to make their diet of seal meat and dried vegetables more palatable. He always seemed able to please, and Joyce noted that "our appetites need no cocktails to assist in creating a desire for our dinner." After the evening meal, with their pipes of Hut Point Mixture burning, discussion inevitably returned to the months ahead. Veteran sledger Joyce warned them again and again that "we will surely know something about depot-laying on the ice shelf when all this is accomplished."

It was during their discussion of the prospect of slogging dozens of miles through deep snow while transporting a load of almost two tons that the subject of the motor sledge arose. What a disappointment that had proved to be, lasting no more than a single trip to Hut Point! And yet it had made that journey. Could it be done again? That was the question. Couldn't they repair this machine, if only to replace the work of a team of dogs for 13 miles across the ice to the old Discovery Hut? Wouldn't that save a great deal of human effort? Like the contraption of Scott's that they had found on the Barrier, it now lay abandoned under a coat of snow, with the petrol still in its fuel tank, but unable to move.

"No use," said Dick Richards. "The leather clutch plate is burned out."

Then Stevens remembered that, for some reason he could not fathom, a spare clutch plate had been landed with the very few items of equipment brought ashore from *Aurora*. They could repair the sledge! Mackintosh at once detailed a party to trudge to Hut Point and drag the defunct sledge back for repair. He gave the repair job itself to Richards and Irvine Gaze. "See what you can do," he requested.

The two young men faced difficulties in dismantling the clutch assembly, since the proper tools had been left in the ship. They spent many hours improvising; then, when they finally took the assembly to pieces, they found the leather clutch plate was held in place by 33 bolts, and that the holes for these bolts had not been drilled in the replacement part. They had no drilling equipment for this task, but they surmounted this problem by heating large nails in the flame of a petrol blow lamp that Scott's men had left behind on the workbench.

By dint of this effort they managed to reassemble the clutch, restart the engine, and then drive the cumbersome motor sledge. It moved over the ice well enough—but it proved to have too little pulling power to be of any use during the big journey ahead.

The first glimmers of light began to show in the northern sky as their sledging preparations went ahead. Mackintosh got in the habit of walking each noon to the hillock behind the hut, to scan northwards beyond the snout of the glacier and the black bulk of Cape Royds. As daylight brightened he could see open water out in the Sound. When he related this to his companions, it roused new conjecture about *Aurora*. With open water, why had she not sailed back to Cape Evans? What disaster had overtaken her?

There was much heated debate on this question, some members of the party seeking to blame Stenhouse and the crew for carelessness, or even for being uncaring. This was natural, the matter being of such great importance to the castaways. Not only were they marooned on the frigid island, they also faced one of the toughest sledging assignments in the exploration of Antarctica with no support, niggardly resources, and makeshift equipment. If by some miracle *Aurora* was to come sailing back in time, the forbidding task of slogging their way down to Mount Hope at the foot of the polar plateau would be facilitated by the efforts of more men and decent equipment.

Speculation about what had happened to the ship led the pessimists to clash with the optimists. The wiser heads, such as Joyce, offered a realistic explanation, based on experience.

Twenty years ago, Joyce recounted, the first ship to spend a winter drifting and trapped in a field of solid ice in the Antarctic was the Belgian vessel *Belgica*. The ship was part of an 1895 expedition sponsored by the Belgian government, and there were some notable men aboard, including Roald Amundsen and an American surgeon, Dr. F. A. Cook. (Cook had been with Peary in the Arctic and was to win some notoriety by claiming to have reached the North Pole.)

While expedition leader Carstens Borchgrevink was still in Melbourne, planning the first expedition ever to winter on the Antarctic mainland, the captain of *Belgica*, a naval officer named Lieutenant de Gerlache, took the ship into pack ice off Alexander Island, near the foot of the Antarctic peninsula. Joyce told his mates what had happened next: "I remember occupying a seat next to Dr. Cook at a luncheon some years later, and he told me what happens when a ship gets caught in the ice, as the *Belgica* was. They spent 13 months in the trap before she broke free, more than a year of great storms and cold and ill health. They were overcome by a kind of creeping lethargy, which the doctor called 'polar anaemia,' and which you might reckon to be nothing other than scurvy."

Dr. Cook had published the English version of the account of the *Belgica* expedition, and had written of the hatred generated among the men for the makers of the tinned food they had to eat—but also of how, despite this, they all detested the lifesaving seal meat. Even the good doctor shared this aversion, writing that "If it is possible to imagine a piece of beef, an odoriferous cod fish, and a canvas-back duck all roasted in a pot with blood and cod-liver oil for sauce, the illustration will be complete." The seal meat that could have saved them from severe illness and suffering was thus rejected. One officer died during the ship's icy imprisonment.

"If *Aurora* is in a similar plight," Joyce continued, "then it will be useless to depend on her for sledging equipment. We will have to make do with the remnants at our command."

Joyce listed some of the things they now had for their journey: three old tents that had been patched, "making them reliable as possible," but that had seen better days and would have to be treated with great care; cooking equipment, which had been overhauled, though the primus stoves still gave him "grave concern." All three had seen service with the Scott expeditioners, and they worried that there were no spare parts for the stoves. "A primus is the principal item of equipment on a sledging journey," Joyce said. "It is the only means we have of melting ice for drinking and for cooking. If it fails, it is not difficult for one to conceive what the results would be."

On the credit side were the sledges and ropes and harness. These had all been repaired and spliced and were generally "in good trim." There was other cause for optimism as well. In mid-August, about 10 days before the sun's rim lit orange fire along the horizon and paled the rose glow from the crater of Mount Erebus, Mackintosh decided to make a sortie to the old Shackleton base at Cape Royds.

It was a direct journey of some 10 miles each way, but since the sea ice would not bear men or a sledge he took a laborious and demanding route over the precipitous coast line. Mackintosh took the methodical Stevens with him, to help take inventory of what might be found useful at the former base. Their route required climbing to the lip of the mile-wide Barne Glacier, treading their way through badly fissured ice and across deep crevassed areas and then negotiating the slippery sides of rocky Cape Barne. From there the sea ice was strong enough to take them the rest of the way to the 1908 hut.

Walking to the hut from the anchorage, Mackintosh found that the gales had torn the door from the porchway. He and Stevens dug through the compacted snow of several winters with a shovel they saw sticking out of the snow. In the hut they saw a small hill of snow and ice that had entered through a roof ventilator that had somehow been forced open. While Mackintosh cleared this away, Stevens lit the stove and heated some pemmican—the first food they had since leaving Cape Evans eight hours before. Stevens found cause for merriment as he started this chore; posted above the stove was a handwritten notice calling on all users of the hut to wash clean the dishes and plates they had used before leaving.

They searched the hut and came upon a small treasure trove: a box of cigars, along with a single tin of Navy Cut tobacco and some bars of soap. Outside were a few cases, though nothing like the profusion Scott's men had left behind at Cape Evans. In these they discovered tins of meat, bags of flour, dried vegetables and other eatables, which would last a few men months when combined with the supplementary diet of seal meat. There were some oddments of old discarded clothing, but nothing that could be useful on the long haul south.

Mackintosh and Stevens returned to Cape Evans two days later, thanking their stars they did not stay at the 1908 hut any longer, since they just escaped a wild snowstorm. Mackintosh and all his men handed round the cigars and tobacco, the stumps of the cigars going into Ernie Wild's pile of Hut Point Mixture. But they had more to be thankful for than for the tobacco: There had been drama at the Cape Evans hut; disaster for the whole party had been narrowly averted.

It began when the men had noticed a leak in the acetylene gas lighting system, and someone (unnamed) had searched for the location with a lighted candle. This foolish action had the predictable result. The sudden explosion caused a sheet of flame, and almost at once the dry wooden frame of the hut began burning. Luckily, a pan of snow had melted on the warmth of the cooking stove; this water was used to douse the fire, thus averting an awful disaster. Without the hut they would have been left at the mercy of the winter blizzards without shelter, for Scott's emergency marquee tent had by then been cut into the trousers and blouses that the sledgers would wear on the Barrier.

* * *

When daylight spread across the Weddell Sea that same southern spring, it lit a forlorn scene: *Endurance* set amid the pitiful igloos of the crew's Dog Town, still captive in the ice, but now prey to the new threat of huge growlers and floes breaking apart in the summer thaw. Ernest Shackleton confided to his diary that "the pressure continues, and it is hard to see the outcome." Yet he noted that all hands were cheered by the indication that winter darkness would soon end.

The first day of August, however, brought the shadow of coming events. A strong southerly gale produced warning sounds from the ice, and the ship listed some 10 degrees under the pressure of the crunching floes. Shackleton, alarmed, had all his dogs brought aboard from their snowy homes and housed in wooden shelters on the deck, in rough kennels that he had all hands work on under the direction of the carpenter.

The major concern at that juncture was the ship's rudder, which he saw "was being attacked viciously" by the moving floes. Massive hunks of ice were being forced under the keel, and it looked as if the vessel was to be made "a plaything of successive floes." *Endurance* lifted bravely when the movement came from beneath. She had been stoutly built to withstand icy conditions, but the effects of the pressure all around her were literally awe-inspiring. Shackleton wrote, "Mighty blocks of ice, gripped between meeting floes, rose slowly, until they jumped, suddenly, like cherry-stones squeezed between thumb and forefinger. The pressure of millions of tons of ice was crushing and smashing inexorably. If the ship is once gripped firmly, her fate will be sealed."

Sledge party

Chapter 4

Battle to the Bluff

W inter's dark was finally banished from the dismal scene at Cape Evans on Sunday, August 22. For almost six months the Antarctic night had shrouded the lives of the 10 castaways. Now, suddenly, the sun rolled along the horizon to herald the birth of the season of twenty-four-hour daylight. All at once the waters of McMurdo Sound were licked with gold, and the line of the noble Western Mountains stood stark against a canopy of green and cobalt, the angled light glancing from glaciers and bouncing from the steep white-pink slopes of Mount Erebus directly into the eyes of the rejoicing men. They had longed for this day of light through endless hours of darkness, longed for it week after week, each marked by blizzards and screaming winds, snow, cold and crisis.

The Reverend Spencer-Smith, beaming to match the new sun, called his "faithful flock" together to give thanks to God for this blessing. They crowded into the alcove in which Scott's famed photographer, Herbert Ponting, had set up his darkroom. The new photographer,

Spencer-Smith, had set aside a corner of that small space for his "tiny altar adorned with two brass candlesticks, so they could lift up their hearts and minds in thanks to the Almighty."

The ceremony had other significance as well. It came during the final days of preparation for the long southern journey. "The sun is back in all its glory," Ernest Joyce wrote. ". . . Richards and Jack have completed bagging the stores; our house is in order and all hands are ready for the ordeal."

The months of winter had been a challenge to mind, spirit and body, with the tasks allotted to each man filling the hours. When August ended, Richards was to describe this period as "the end of their busiest of the whole mission." In the final entry Mackintosh made in the journal he left at the Scott hut, he wrote that all the secondhand gear had been patched, sewed and overhauled; that every man had been "up to his eyes in work"; and that they were woefully short of protective footwear. "Tomorrow," he added, "we start for Hut Point."

Mackintosh himself made the start, leaning into the sledging harness together with Ernie Wild and the gentle Spencer-Smith. It was the morning of the first day of September, which Joyce had frequently observed to be about the toughest month of the whole season for sledging across the ice shelf. The other seven men helped drag the heavy sledge, with its load of 600 pounds, down to the sea ice, then stood and cheered and bellowed good wishes as Mackintosh, Wild and Spencer-Smith set off to skirt the icy face of Glacier Tongue on their 13-mile haul to the old Discovery Hut.

There were only three tents available to the marooned men: the one from *Aurora* and the two left by the Scott expedition, which the "old salts" Wild and Joyce had patched and repaired. It was one of the latter that Mackintosh set up on his first trek to Hut Point. Bad weather slewed in from the Barrier, so he made camp overnight and then left the tent standing as a halfway stop for subsequent parties hauling their cargoes to the starting point.

During the whole month of September the entire team labored in blizzards and biting cold to shift the sledging foods and fuel across the sea ice to Hut Point. Sometimes the men went in groups of three; later nine hauled the three sledges linked together. They met with typical September conditions, with temperatures as low as 60° below freezing.

They began suffering from frostbite even before they set foot on the ice shelf. Irvine Gaze, rugged as he was, could not take part in the initial depot-laying because of the state one of his feet was in. If Gaze was to take part in the arduous sledging that lay ahead, he would need to rest to allow his foot to recover, so Mackintosh sent him back to Cape Evans. John Cope took his place in the harness with Keith Jack and Hayward, though up until then the biologist had been considered to be in the poorest health of the group.

Joyce was pleased that Irvine Gaze would be looking after "his dogs." He thought, even at that early stage, that the sled dogs would be needed when the real slog started south from the Bluff, and the man began the work of laying depots every 60 miles. During the latter days of winter Joyce had been deliberately toughening the animals, feeding them well and taking them on excursions to haul in the heavy seal carcasses that had been harvested and left to freeze stiff on the ice. The men might well need the few dogs, he now reasoned, because there was doubt and some apprehension in his mind regarding the weight of the stores they were to haul.

"Under ordinary circumstances," he reflected in his diary, "with so poor an equipment, one would not consider—not for a second—such a journey as we have to make. The Bluff depot would be the limit of our mileage. If any old Arctic or Antarctic explorer reads this log I feel certain they will agree with my remarks."

Joyce's doubts had been fed by the month of work hauling supplies across the bay ice to Hut Point. Those days of struggle had been plagued by gales and snowstorms so thick he sometimes couldn't see to steer; he and his companions could easily have lost their way on the short journey from the half-way tent to the hut. They were already wearied before a single pound of food had been taken onto the ice shelf. He commented that some in the expedition were suffering badly from cold: "Most of us wore the canvas trousers made from Scott's old tent, and they froze on us like boards. . . . However, we had the consolation that this had saved our Burberry garments for the work on the Barrier."

The slavery of ferrying the thousands of pounds of dried food and fuel across the bay ice to Hut Point and Safety Camp was such a grueling experience that the men were glad when a 60-mile-an-hour blizzard came roaring over the old hut from the south, delaying the projected start of their first journey to the Barrier. Instead they rested and fed themselves. On the first day of October Joyce became chef, and with a big blackened ship's frying pan, he cooked up hunks of seal meat. He was astonished at how quickly it was devoured: "pan after pan was emptied, some 15 pounds of meat or more . . . for breakfast!"

The blizzard gave them rest for four more days, then relapsed into two days of calm, allowing the first full cargo to be hauled to the desolate spot Captain Scott had named Safety Camp. The camp was reached by sledging straight south for a mile, then turning eastward through the ice hills around Cape Armitage for six miles further. There it was possible to climb the snow hills onto the edge of the ice shelf. Scott's bamboos still stood above the snow, marking the path toward Corner Camp, another 20 miles to the east.

In the second week in October, the weather finally relented enough to allow the men to drag a major load to the Barrier surface. They were all roused from their sleeping bags soon after 5 that morning, and didn't reach Safety Camp until after midday. Nearly eight hours of toil were rewarded with hot tea and a few biscuits. More hours of work followed. Mackintosh supervised the loading of each sledge with what he calculated to be the equivalent of 200 pounds of weight per man. This meant each three-man team had 600 pounds to drag to the Bluff on its sledge. This done, they set off at once across the shelf surface toward Corner Camp. By 6 that evening they were exhausted, and had traveled a mere half-mile. In his tent that night, with Cope and Joyce, Richards noted they were all "tired and dispirited." Joyce commented that, with the soft surface of the snow making the going heavy, they were toting too much weight per man. "We're going to have to relay; no doubt about that," he told Richards.

They were out of their sleeping bags at 6 next morning, and again Mackintosh had the nine men haul all three sledges in a chain. Joyce labeled this a "farce," and at the lunch break he protested to Mackintosh, after which they reverted to three-man teams hauling separate sledge loads. This approach yielded little success. The diaries for the night of October 10 noted that the men had slogged less than two miles in the five hours before lunch, and had encountered even worse going in the afternoon. As a result, they covered only three miles the entire day. Richards, Cope, and Joyce brought in the last sledge and were so exhausted that Wild and Hayward came out to help them into the camp. "In all my experience in the Antarctic," Joyce complained, "I have never come across harder pulling!"

They crawled into their bags that night, their underwear soaked with sweat that quickly turned to ice, and spent restless hours with the temperature dropping to 36°C below freezing.

The party got under way again at 8 the following morning. Once more each step was a laboring, short lunge forward, with the body straining against the deadweight of the dragging sledge. But this time, after toiling for a hundred yards Joyce brought matters to a head, yelling into the wind to Mackintosh to halt "this farce." He told the Captain that the sledge loads would have to be weighed and the situation reviewed. Angry that their strength was being sapped before they had even covered the first few miles, Joyce declaimed, "It is impossible to proceed on the lines we're going. You will have all hands on the sick list before half the sledging season is over."

He reminded Mackintosh that they had discussed the weight each man would pull when they were planning the operations together back in the hut at Cape Evans, and it had been agreed that the limit would be 174 pounds per man *at the start of the journey.*

The tension between Joyce and Mackintosh was plain as Joyce started to weigh the sledge load in front of the other men. He then announced he had found the minimum each man was lugging was not 174, but more than 220 pounds.

"I tell you, Mack," Joyce said, "you are mad to think we can get along with these loads under these extreme conditions. In the first place, we haven't got the physical capacity among these men. And, second, our clothing, equipment, and the way we have lived during this last winter is against us. Take my advice, lower the weight limit so we make five trips to the Bluff instead of four, and in that way you may save the men. Remember, you'll get the best out of the men if you study them. If not, you'll have them laid up, with no depot laid."

The veteran sledger carried his anger into his tent. He told Richards that Mackintosh was not going to take his advice: "He is too pigheaded to listen. He will go on in his own way, but he'll regret it later. I'll have another go at him in the morning."

The morning, however, brought a whirling drift that thickened in the teeth of a strong gale blowing down from the mountains, making travel impossible. Just the same, Joyce went to Mackintosh's tent to argue his point of view, still incensed at what he saw as folly, and anguished at the harrowing demands being made on the men.

It was an argumentative meeting, but a sad one. These two men were bound together by the same mission, and for all their difference of attitude they were members of a small party on the fringe of a vast hostile continent, committed to putting down precious food and fuel for the handful of travelers they expected to come across the wilderness. They were companions now unhappily at odds with each other as to how they should honour their undertaking. Joyce could not forget the bodies of the dozen or more dogs that, because of overwork, lay dead in a string between Cape Evans and the long arm of Minna Bluff, 70 miles to the south. Now he feared the same might happen to the men.

"Mack, whatever happens, as long as I breathe, we shall lay the depot for the Boss at Mount Hope," he assured the Captain. "But you are asking the men for a physical impossibility. They are pulling too much weight, too early in the season."

With the tent canvas flapping against the poles, Mackintosh finally made a concession. He would take 60 pounds of weight off his sledge, he said, and press forward on his own with Wild and Spencer-Smith. Joyce could take charge of the other two teams and make his own decisions on sledging weights and pace of advance. "You come on behind us. We will see you at the Bluff," he commanded.

They followed that system of marching in the coming months, during which leadership slipped from the grasp of Aeneas Mackintosh and was never properly regained.

Many years later, when Dick Richards recalled those days with Joyce and Mackintosh, it was always with a sense of distress. He believed that the appointment of Mackintosh to command the Ross Sea party, while it "redounded to Shackleton's credit as a man who kept his promise," was a bad choice. For poor Mackintosh, no matter how courageous and gallant he was, and no matter how much he tried, even to the point of giving up his life, was not a natural leader. He was too impetuous and lacked a balance of judgment.

Ernest Joyce was now leader of the two-sledge team. On the morning of October 13 he called the other five men around him to tell them how he planned to reduce their loads. "Our two sledges have a combined weight of almost 1,400 pounds, and that has to come down. We will, for a start, depot two weeks' rations for each team and dump every bit of spare gear we can manage. I reckon in that way we'll divest some 400 pounds, and each of us will be pulling around 170 pounds. That means we'll have to relay and walk three times the distance, but that will be easier on us than this mad slog we've been enduring. We'll also cut down the agony a bit by cutting off a few miles. We shall go closer in toward White Island and try and avoid the crevasses the ice movement causes there against the solid rock."

He found a new eagerness in his teams that day and saw them pulling steadily, "not the heart-breaking strain as hitherto." Every half-hour they stopped to erect snow cairns as markers for their return journeys, keeping them in line with a peak on "dear old Erebus." They ran into thick drift in the afternoon, but the men were ready to push on until evening. Joyce's diary noted, "All my party are keen and cheerful." In the same entry, he described how their "finneskoes are wearing through and the sleeping bags are full of ice which one's body melts before going to sleep; there is little comfort in our bags." The inconsistency of the climate was such that the following day they were able to turn their bags fur-side out and partly dry them in the bright sun and cold breeze.

Dick Richards recorded the varied nature of the elements they met during their journeys to stack the major depot at Minna Bluff, where the long arm of rock stretched into the shelf ice. The main food depot was in line with a small peak at the rock's tip and with the crest of Mount Discovery in the far distant west. To the south the mountains diverged from the sledging route, and the men could see only the endless ice plain.

"The ice shelf," Richards wrote, "presents a bewildering variety of surfaces. Sometimes we encountered very soft snow, sometimes a smooth, almost marble-like surface on which the sledge-runners left no impression. Yet it is usually soft enough to dig into with a shovel which reveals a frozen crystalline structure. . . . Then, again, there is the so-called 'pie-crust' surface which just took our weight momentarily before our feet sank suddenly by several inches, making walking a tiring experience, indeed. Sometimes entire large areas will drop several inches with a deep booming sound, while in other places large, hard furrows—*sastrugi* (Norwegian name for large ripples and ridges in the ice)—running parallel south-east to northwest are sculptured by the constant blizzards."

When a blizzard hit it was the sledgers' practice to erect the tents and lie in their bags, eating only half rations. "During the bad blizzards it was risky to leave the tent for any reason at all," Richards observed, not knowing how closely his statement resembled the vivid record of the Scott expedition historian, Apsley Cherry-Garrard, in *Worst Journey in the World*: ". . . Outside there is raging chaos. Fight your way a few steps from the tent and it will be gone. Lose your sense of direction and there is nothing to guide you back."

It wasn't only the mad blizzards that confounded the men's sense of direction. The half-hourly halts to build cairns were vital to their safety, especially when they marched in "white-outs"—those times when the "carpet sweeper" wind rolled the whirling drift over them and shut them into a closed white sphere with their burdensome sledges. The scraps of old black cloth tied to the bamboo poles on the cairns prevented them from straying into nowhere, onto that "featureless ice shelf stretching away, apparently endlessly."

Dick Richards also recorded days of utter silence, stillness, and loneliness. "Trudging along, hour after hour, day after day, with a canvas harness over the shoulders and round the waist is a fantastic experience. . . . There was no conversation on the trail. Each step forward was a little advance on the last. . . . All our energies were needed for the job in hand. The silence was profound; the soft crunch of feet in the snow, the faint swish of the sledgerunners serving merely to emphasize that silence. . . . The hours of a day's march seemed endless. I do not know what went on in the minds of my companions while on the march over these months . . . in my case I'd perform long useless computations of one sort or another in my head . . . an automatic reaction to the monotony that was forced upon us, an anodyne to the weariness of the body. We seldom thought about the outside world. We had heard nothing of it since December 1914. We had left all that behind. The outside seemed unreal; the only reality we had was what we saw about us . . ."

Amid the toil—the terrifying blizzards, the tent fabric ripping as a result of the constant banging against the five bamboo poles, and the frantic stitching to save worse disaster—the travelers also found joys and delights "as satisfying as those in civilization," wrote Richards. "The shelter of the cloth tent at the end of a day's march, the easing in the blizzard, a smooth-running snow surface, the sighting of a food depot, and food itself after being on short rations." These were the peaks of existence above the dreary routine of slogging toil and cold, and they produced "a feeling of profound well-being."

Joyce's party arrived at Minna Bluff on October 21. The men had struggled with thrusting head winds, blizzards and drift, and were reduced at times to feeling their way forward while the guiding islands and mountains were veiled behind flying snow and white haze.

The first indication they were approaching the Bluff depot came by way of a mirage. They broke camp that morning by 8, and 90 minutes later Dick Richards sighted a flag to the southeast. They veered their course to meet it, but ran into a "pie-crust" surface. On and on they fought in the direction of the flag, but it wasn't until late evening that they reached the depot. By then Richards knew that he had seen the flag from almost 10 miles away in a mirage that had led them to their destination. He suffered snow blindness for his keen sight, and was treated that night with slivers of cocaine beneath the lids to ease the pain.

There was a note at the depot from Mackintosh, who had departed two days before, leaving behind 178 pounds of provisions. Joyce recorded his attack of frostbite that night: "my nose is one black blister."

With lightened sledges they hurried back north the next day, their first haul of the season to the Bluff completed. They came on October 26 to the stores they had left on the outward journey, including precious food to satisfy their appetites. They sighted an upturned sledge; with it Richards found a small Kodak film tin sealed with a note inside, which they read while standing in silence in the snow.

In March 1912, Apsley Cherry-Garrard had left the upended sledge there as a marker. He was about to return to Hut Point after spending almost a week at One Ton Depot, waiting in vain to sight the returning polar party. The date on the note was pathetic, Joyce thought—for on that day, less than a hundred miles to the south, "Titus" Oates had left Scott, Wilson, and Bowers in their tent and had walked out on his frostbitten legs into the blizzard to die, hoping his death would give the others a better chance of survival. Scott's entry in his diary for that day was prophetic: "He has borne intense suffering without complaint. He was a brave soul. This was the end."

Cherry-Garrard had known nothing of the tragedy taking place when he penned the note to Scott; nevertheless, the six men were astonished by the formality of the wording. It read:

> Dear Sir,
> *We leave this morning with the dogs for Hut Point. We have*

made no depots, being off course all the way, and so have not been able to leave you a note before.

Yours sincerely,
Apsley Cherry-Garrard.

Joyce took charge of the slip of paper. It was forgotten for almost half a century, until a party from New Zealand found it in 1960 beneath the pillow in the bunk Joyce had occupied at the Cape Evans hut.

There was other treasure in the vicinity of the upturned sledge, far more valuable to the men at the time. They uncovered a cache that Cherry-Garrard had deposited at the site: six boxes of dog biscuits impregnated with cod liver oil. Joyce wrote that night, "At last, we have struck gold in the Antarctic." Scott's dog biscuits would be priceless in the coming weeks.

Meanwhile, Joyce's thoughts had been turning toward methods of speeding their depot-laying journeys to the Bluff. The first journey had been slow, and they had labored long. Now he was worried that it would be late in the season before they could finally strike south with the critical depots for the lower latitudes, and put down the final Mount Hope supply of food and oil.

The six-man party's return from the first trek to the Bluff depot nearly ended with a serious mishap. At Corner Camp they dumped the traveling gear—tents, poles, snow sheets and tools, along with the cookers and stoves—and hurried to reach the bay ice for the six-mile tramp to the hut. The wind began to blow and the drift whirled about round their heads, clogging their snow goggles so they couldn't be worn. Suddenly Joyce, leading ahead on a 20-foot rope, stopped with one foot in the air, poised above a sheer drop in the ice. He was almost over the edge of the Barrier, with tumbled, sharp-ridged ice rocks more than 40 feet below. "By good fortune," he wrote, "I escaped from going over the edge." Then Stevens crashed into a crevasse to the full length of his sledge harness and was jammed between the faces of the ice walls. With care and a struggle they got him free and back to the surface.

The men made the bay ice safely, and then hurried in the teeth of a rising blizzard to reach the hut in late evening. They arrived to find Mackintosh and his party already there with a blubber fire burning. Within minutes there were seal steaks sizzling in the big black pan, along with special delicacies (for the travelers returning from the ice shelf): seal liver and kidneys.

In the combined space of the hut, with the air smelling of burning fat, the nine men discussed ways of speeding the depot-laying. One single journey to the Bluff had been achieved, Mackintosh said, but the whole month of October was virtually gone. If four journeys were needed to build the stock of supplies so the men could then proceed down to Mount Hope, they might be facing a return from the Beardmore far too late in the season.

Richards and Joyce voiced the opinion they had reached on the struggle back to Corner Camp. The only way to reduce both time and strain on the teams, they said, was to use the remaining dogs. With memories of his unhappy experience with dogs the previous season, Mackintosh looked doubtful. But Dick Richards argued: "If they are not used now, when will they be used? Joyce has got them into condition during the winter, and it's common sense to put them to work."

Joyce supported the younger man. Any help in pulling would help conserve human muscle for the drive to the Beardmore, he suggested. "Even if we expend them on the Bluff trips, it will be worth it to save time. They will get short rests in between, and maybe that will give them extra condition for the long run to the south." Four dogs would adjust more easily to the slower speed of the men than six animals in a team following a leader, Joyce argued.

There was no further hesitation from Mackintosh. He accepted the suggestion, and agreed that a three-man party would go to Cape Evans to bring the dogs and to sledge back their food. The decision, reached without argument, clearly marked the point on the expedition when the combined opinions of Joyce and Richards began to prevail over

Hunting seals

those of Mackintosh. From then on there were separate parties working on the ice shelf, to one end but with no single leadership. Joyce's
diary began to show increased assumption of command and direction.
"I had a talk with Skipper, told him I had decided to take five dogs,"
read one entry. Others stated: "I have decided to start south on 3
November, am expecting party back from Cape Evans today," and "I
have sent Richards, Hayward, and Gaze to pick up 12 seals." When
the second trek started, after being delayed by bad weather until
November 5, Joyce noted, "On the way out, the surface soft; the dogs
pulling splendidly, and quite justify my taking them."

Dick Richards confined himself to commenting, "The decision to
take the dogs was most providential. Without them we would never
have got back."

The animals were a welcome sight to the men when they were at last in
harness for the second run to the Bluff. They numbered five in all, four
males and a female, Bitchie, who was in the early stages of a litter.
Frisky, tails wagging, eyes bright, ready for work—and ready to fight—
they made their presence felt from the first time the sledges moved out
of Hut Point on November 5. There had been days of delay, the result
of bad weather and the endless preparations: hunting, killing and hauling in the seals, frying up many pounds of meat for the men and dogs,
fashioning harnesses for a team of five, patching and sewing clothes,
overhauling the sledges. Now, after a "shocking night of weather," the
sky had cleared enough to start the dogs across the ice hills to Safety
Camp on the Barrier's edge.

They were headed by Oscar, the undeniable leader, bearer of the
name that would become legendary in Antarctic exploration. He was
a big dog with a massive head and a baleful eye, a favorite of Dick
Richards, who knew him as "an old reprobate, a dirty dog if you like;
a quick-tempered brute, but he was always there when the chips were
down, pulling his heart in front of the others." With him were two
other Canadian huskies, big Gunner and Towser, that showed not the
faintest inclination to hunt, and were lazy and quarrelsome but were

tough workers. And then there was Con, Richards wrote, "a good-looking, good-living dog, a lively fellow who liked to hunt seals. He was different, the odd dog out, more like a Samoyed type, and the other three hated his guts."

Con had a history; he was given to the expedition by Sir Douglas Mawson, who had received him as a gift from Roald Amundsen. It was said that Con was bred from one of the dogs that went with the legendary Norwegian to the South Pole and back, but that cut no ice with the huskies. The strain of wolf breed in them urged them constantly to get at this intruder. In the end, they did. During a winter blizzard they tore his throat open and killed him. The fifth animal, Bitchie, loved company, both of man and beast, and was intelligent and a good worker in the harness.

Even with the dogs still learning to pull in unison, the second sortie to the Bluff took only eight days—this despite the usual drag of soft surfaces and laborious "pie-crust" snow cover. There was bad weather, too, with one blizzard bringing temperatures so low that the drift was frozen hard and struck the tent fabric "like hailstones." Joyce could not restrain his self-congratulation: "The dogs pulled well. . . . I am more than pleased I had the sense to know the value of them; they are as good as four men—at least, four men in the condition we are in. . . . Gave them extra feed and will increase their diet."

The party had one puzzling encounter. The tracks of an emperor penguin were found more than 40 miles from where the creatures usually gathered. Joyce found it "strange that the bird should be all this distance from the rookery and food."

The men came to the Bluff depot after a heavy blizzard, which required them to spend hours digging out the dogs and the sledges. They found that Mackintosh had been there two days earlier and had deposited 188 pounds of stores. From their two sledges they unloaded 624 pounds, almost double what had been accomplished in the previous haul, without the dogs. "What a difference the dogs make," Joyce exulted. "Now we shall try and get back to the hut in only five days."

To do this he had to take the party closer to the point of White Island, known to be a turmoil of ice close to land. There they came on an extraordinary sight, known as a *bergschrund*, a huge crevasse carved by the wall of a glacier into the shelf ice, made up of deep blue ice some 70 feet from the level of the Barrier and decorated with hanging curtains of frozen snow. It was a natural birthday card for Dick Richards—he was 22 years old that day.

The team of six men and five dogs covered satisfying mileage despite the difficult terrain. They rushed pell-mell across snow bridges; at times even the dogs went through the holes and were dragged out by the momentum of their rush. The daily records were mounting—12 miles, 17 miles on two days running—and Joyce was already planning how they would lay the southern depots.

The extra miles were not gained without cost, however. Early in the afternoon of November 19 Joyce was forced to call a halt. His feet were badly blistered, and he had to don another pair of his make-do fur sledging shoes. His diary tells the story: "If I were in civilization I would not venture two yards . . . the blisters on my heels are as large as potatoes." This did not dampen his resolution. The team walked 17 miles that day, and that night he wrote: "We still have 24 miles to reach Hut Point. Will try to cover that distance tomorrow." They achieved this goal, despite the crevasses and Joyce's own snow blindness. Again, the brevity of his diary is graphic: "Came on four crevasses; suddenly. Keith Jack fell through. We dragged him out; could not alter course; this would be steering along them. Gave the order to rush them . . . one plays one's chances. You're down! You're up! You're out! Your heart goes pit-a-pat . . . stopped at four-o'clock to put cocaine in my eyes. Snowblindness, agony . . . turned lead over to Richards and staggered blind. . . Was assisted to hut."

He had led the party on their record dash from the Bluff to Hut Point, wearing a leather mask with eyeslits cut in it. "There was no rest for my eyes. The man leading is always facing the white ocean . . . it is like pepper in the eyes, or a bit of dust from a steam engine. I don't think I have experienced worse pain . . . the agony was intense."

They rested all day on November 21, and Joyce revived his eyes with dressings of cocaine slivers. They set out south again on the afternoon of November 25, reaching Safety Camp and camping there that night. After three days of hauling through swirling snowdrift, they came on an apparition: two cairns that were moving! Joyce surmised that they were lost emperor penguins, but when the two shapes were approached they proved to be Captain Mackintosh and Spencer-Smith, who had glimpsed their sledges through a gap in the drift and had come to meet them.

Joyce's notes give the first hint of coming troubles. "They had left their camp and walked four miles to meet us. Skipper came into my tent. Padre—who does not look too well—returned. I then gave skipper a good working plan . . . told him what stores we had on the sledges, gave him the list of the last load we had trekked. . . . He quite agreed to my programme. If possible, he will meet us at the Bluff on December 23." And on the following day, "During breakfast had Wild in to pay me a visit. We had a talk over old times. Before he left he said they were 'having a hard time.'"

The dogs and men "put in a brilliant performance" of nearly 15 miles in the next day under the heavy load of 1,400 pounds. They left Mackintosh and his two companions well behind, man-hauling through the soft surface.

In their lone tent that night, as the reliable Ernie Wild heated their hoosh, Mackintosh and his companion Spencer-Smith wrote notes on the day's events. What the Captain had to record of their progress and their exhaustion will never be known.

Spencer-Smith patiently penciled his notes into one of the small diaries Shackleton had provided, one of only three written on those southern journey's that have survived to this day. Spencer-Smith wrote a tight, constrained script, as though conscious of the pressures of space and time that he faced. He had started this record of his adventure with a Biblical quotation from Isaiah: "Thus saith the Lord, Heaven is my throne, the earth my footstool. Where is the House that ye built unto me? And where is my place of rest?" And on the flyleaf the clergyman had inscribed encouragement to his own spirit. He had written, "It's all in the game. Play on!" He needed that encouragement on the night of November 30, 1915. Once more the men were blizzard bound, lying supine in their sleeping bags, shoulder to shoulder, while the mad wind threatened their shelter by slapping the canvas against the cord binding that held their broken tent poles in place.

Spencer-Smith had first noticed the trouble in his leg two days after leaving Hut Point on October 29. "Very sore," he wrote. "It is a comfort to rest in bed and to read." It was his left Achilles tendon, he thought; probably just a strain. He was able to take his mind off his immediate surroundings and his suffering body by remembering autumn scenes in Edinburgh, the city where he had been ordained, and which he loved. He thought also of his two sisters, who were doing church work in India, and of his two brothers, who were now fighting in Flanders.

Little more than a year after leaving Edinburgh Spencer-Smith was in one of the most solitary places on earth, a gale-whipped tent in the Antarctic with the dedicated Captain Aeneas Mackintosh and the laconic and capable naval petty officer Ernie Wild. Mackintosh, in his serious manner, announced now that they would not turn back from the Bluff, but would go farther south to reinforce the depot that had been laid down the previous season at 80° South.

After all they had achieved, after all the miles they had slogged across the ice shelf, here was greater labor and deeper cold—long, long weeks to be spent in the field yet, before rest and warmth and refreshing, uninterrupted sleep.

They found the Bluff smothered with clouds. They slept long despite the blizzard that came in from the southwest. When the snow cleared, they stacked their sledge with stores they were to take to the 80° depot. "We shall then come back and hopefully meet Joyce and his party late this month," Mackintosh told them.

Looking south from the Bluff, Spencer-Smith found hostile beauty all about him: brilliant, hard hoar frost with "an arch of light of pale rainbow colours which seemed to hover above us and follow our trail."

It was a magic that lasted a single day; the next morning they were back in their harness, Mackintosh on the longer rope, Wild on one side and Spencer-Smith flanking him, pulling into a wind full of hard granular snow, hoods pulled over their goggled faces, able to see only the surface a yard or two in front of them.

At last, on December 15, they sighted the flag above the depot at 80° South. Thankful, they unloaded the cache of stores. Before turning north again, Spencer-Smith produced his camera for Wild to snap a photograph of him against the tall snow cairn with the black cloth flying from the pole. Grinning under shaggy brows, Wild had a title for the snap: "First Parson at Eighty South," he suggested.

Running north now, their sledge was lighter—dangerously light. Within days they complained of hunger; on short rations, they had constant thoughts of food during the silent hours of marching. The wind was at their backs, so they rigged the snow cloth as a sail on the bamboo pole that was stepped behind the cooker box assembly. It almost blew them along; on December 21 they covered 12 miles. Spencer-Smith wrote his impression of traveling with wind power: "Run! Slip! Stumble! With poor visibility ahead the order of the day. . . . Hold her into the wind!" He was ravenous that night, and took a book from his calico bag to read before sleep. It was *Gentleman Of London*, and "almost every page speaks of eating."

They sighted Minna Bluff on Christmas Eve. The weather held a promise of clearing for them, and Spencer-Smith dreamed that night of food, of very hot curry and stewed prunes, waking with the thought, "God willing, we shall not go hungry this Christmas Day." They hurried the last miles to the Bluff depot. There, the dreams of eating to repletion came true: They feasted on hoosh with onions, chocolate and cocoa and biscuits. Then Mackintosh sprang his surprise: cigars salvaged from the box he had found on the visit to Shackleton's old hut on Cape Royds. The fragrant smoke brought Christmas to their camp as they sat in the tent together, three weatherworn companions in a great sullen solitude, and sang "Adeste Fideles" and other carols. Then lusty Ernie Wild gave out with gusto in a solo, the only verse he knew from "Christians Awake!" Spencer-Smith's last thoughts that night were that they had more than 600 miles yet to march before they would be back at the hut again—and his leg was sore.

On that same Christmas Day, the two-sledge team under Ernest Joyce was just a short march to the north from the Bluff depot. Joyce was noting his eighth Christmas in the Antarctic. To him "all days were the same on the Barrier." They had been out of their sleeping bags since 5:30 in the morning and had plugged for nine miles, the soft snow at times up to their knees. When a blizzard sprang up to pin them down for the next two days, Mackintosh and his two companions were a mere five miles away. The last miles that Joyce and his men marched on December 28 marked the worst trek they had made to the Bluff. Bad weather and poor going had dashed their hopes of a speedy trip and an early start to the southern depot-laying of supplies for Shackleton and his men.

Joyce's team had left the hut on December 13, after days of intense preparation for the big haul. The last party coming back there, the men were told, would not arrive until well into March 1916. Precautions had to be taken, "in case *Aurora* fails us, and doesn't come back," Joyce said. The seals had to be hunted and harvested to provide for the emergency of the team becoming isolated in the Discovery Hut with the onset of winter. They fried dozens of pounds of seal steak, "to prevent that dreadful disease of scurvy."

Seal meat was also needed for the ravenous dogs, mixed with the cod-liver oil biscuits that Cherry-Garrard had dumped in 1912. The diet would keep them in good trim for the work they had to perform. This was particularly important because the men had to start south a dog short, this time, since Bitchie was near to delivery and had to remain at the hut. "If I am fortunate enough to return," the team leader noted, "I hope to be able to train her forthcoming family into an excellent sledging team."

Stevens, who had now taken Gaze's place at Cape Evans, was on his way across the bay ice to take charge of the bitch, but when he failed to appear Joyce decided not to wait. He hoped to make the Bluff by

December 19, and the weather that day was promising for travel to the Barrier. He fried a supply of seal meat, left a pile of biscuits within reach and tied Bitchie up with a rope.

The party got away at noon, but had not traveled more than a few hundred yards when they heard yelping. Joyce turned to see Bitchie running toward them, tongue lolling happily, her tail wagging with delight. Around her neck she still wore the loop of rope that she had chewed through. The team halted while Joyce took her back to the hut; this time he used a chain to tie her close to her food supply.

In the late afternoon they loaded their sledges with stores from the dump at Safety Camp, then headed east to skirt the rocky islands before turning south toward the Bluff.

"Thank God this is our last load from here. Altogether we have dragged something like 5,000 pounds of provisions to this depot," Joyce noted. "The dogs have done splendidly. I think I will take them to Mount Hope, if they last that long."

The drudgery of the following days, dragging nearly 1,500 pounds on the two sledges through clinging snow, made havoc of their plan to reach the Bluff depot by December 19. On that day the six men lay in their sleeping bags on half rations while the four dogs huddled outside under heaps of blown snow, with only their breathing holes showing. Richards still held himself responsible for feeding the animals, and when the blizzard abated he gave them a hot hoosh of seal meat and biscuits. He speculated whether the men could have conveyed these cargoes without the help of dog power.

The days slipped by, gaining too few miles under their biggest load no matter how hard they hauled. On Tuesday, December 28, they slogged up to the Bluff depot, with the south winds flinging hard snowflakes and fine drift into their faces and the dogs holding their heads down. They had taken 15 days to make this fourth haul, the most grueling journey so far. They found a note from Mackintosh waiting for them there, thanking them for their valiant efforts and saying that he had decided not to wait; he had left two days earlier to haul stores to the 80° depot.

Disappointed at missing Mackintosh and his party, Joyce blamed the hours they had spent digging out sledges and dogs each day: "I don't know what is wrong with the elements lately. . . . If this weather does not cease, we will have to devise some plan to travel in a blizzard. It is the steering that is so difficult; one is liable to turn completely around in one's tracks. But we must push on. If not, our struggle will be in vain."

* * *

On an ice floe in the waste of the frozen Weddell Sea, Ernest Shackleton dispensed his expedition's last few luxuries as a Christmas treat: as much as the men could eat of anchovies in oil, jugged hare, and baked beans, in one single serving; a final "glorious mixture" before the trials to come. He and his 27 men and 49 dogs had been on the floe since October 27—the night that Joyce and his team returned to Hut Point from the first hauling of supplies to the Bluff. It had been a dramatic and traumatic night for the men of *Endurance*.

In the evening Shackleton had ordered all hands onto the ice. "At last the twisting, grinding floes were working their will on the ship. It was a sickening sensation to feel the decks breaking up beneath one's feet, the great beams bending and then snapping with a noise like heavy gunfire. . . . I cannot describe the impression of relentless destruction . . . floes with the force of millions of tons of moving ice behind them were simply annihilating the ship."

Next morning the Boss went aboard the crippled vessel with Frank Hurley and Ernie Wild's brother Frank to retrieve some cans of petrol in order to boil milk for the chilled men. They found a scene of chaos and wreckage: the rudder post was torn out and the stem post split across, while the starboard side and the whole after section had been crushed like a concertina. There were a few mementos to gather from the mangled cabins, though they disregarded useless trinkets such as gold sovereigns. Shackleton didn't even take along the Bible that had been given to the ship by Queen Alexandra, but he did tear out the flyleaf with her handwritten inscription as well as the page he treasured from the Book of Job, with the verse:

> *Out of whose womb came the ice?*
> *And the hoary frost of Heaven, who hath gendered it?*
> *The waters are hid as with a stone,*
> *And the face of the deep is frozen.*

Joyce and Towser

"The Dogs Are Trojans"

On the third-to-the-last day of 1915, the six men at the Bluff depot crawled from their sleeping bags before 6 in the morning to face their most challenging march. They had now spent three months sledging in the snow since leaving Cape Evans. The men showed the wear and tear of the long miles of hauling in their garb and in their faces and in the drag of their feet. They were unshaven and carried the scars of frostbite on their ears, cheeks, and noses. To a man their eyes were bleary, reddened from the occasional attacks of snow blindness and the subsequent treatment with cocaine slivers. Their clothing was ragged and torn, their sledging boots worn thin and their socks patched with old scraps of cloth. Yet each man was ready that day to march out of the depot camp toward the polar plateau, following the tracks of Captain Mackintosh's laboring party; their trail showed clearly, even though it was two days old and there had been heavy snowfalls since.

They were glad for the track Mackintosh had left. The snow was blowing in sheets, and the light was so bad that if it weren't for the sledge tracks they would have had to strain their eyes for features to steer by. The dogs once again pulled well all that day of tramping, and they covered more than eight miles.

In the evening there was a brief clearing in the weather, and looking south Joyce spotted the hemispherical shape of the umbrella-type tent set against the white plain. It was about three miles distant. "I think they have been having a hard time to have managed only this distance in three days of travel," he told his companions. "We'll catch them in the morning and find ⬛t."

That night the south wind flung fresh bouts of snow over them as they lay shivering in their sleeping bags, with only a tarpaulin between their recumbent bodies and the hard ice. Again they faced hours of work spading the snow from the dogs and their equipment. Drift still swirled in the air, and there were heavy clouds as they set off. The light was bad and there was no longer any sign of the Captain's tent. The sledge tracks had also disappeared.

They cairn hopped, using the prismatic compass which Richards kept slung from the bamboo mast, picking up the snow piles that had been erected on the journey from the Bluff to 80° South the previous autumn. All that day they lunged into deep banks of snow, often sinking in to their knees, the dogs floundering but always struggling through, their breaths steaming white vapor as their mouths opened wide to gulp the chill air.

It was the afternoon of the last day of the year before they again picked up the tracks of Captain Mackintosh's lone sledge. They followed the tracks to the green tent that evening. Joyce guessed Mackintosh and his men had been traveling during the night hours, hoping the colder air would give them easier going. From their appearance and the few miles covered, their strategy seemed to have brought little benefit.

Mackintosh and his two companions sat in their sleeping bags, looking "beaten by the weather." Mackintosh's face was deeply lined, his brows knitted in worry and depression. Spencer-Smith was his "usual cheery self," but he was wan and thin. While Wild made tea, Mackintosh told the newcomers that he and Wild had discussed the situation and had found it discouraging. "We agree that there is not much hope of us getting through to the Beardmore," he said.

Richards and Joyce were disturbed by the Captain's dejection. Joyce argued against the gloomy view that they were fated to come through all this fight and struggle only to give up near the end. In his diary he recorded that he told Mackintosh how they must fight their way through to the Beardmore.

At that same time, the Captain, seemingly troubled at the consequences of the orders he was about to give, decided to commit them to paper. In the morning he handed Joyce his written instructions. Their essence was that all hands would proceed to 81° South to lay a new depot, 60 miles on from the one established in the previous season. From there Joyce, Richards, and Hayward would go on to 82°, and beyond if possible.

Whatever reasons lay behind Mackintosh's written orders, they were subject to the play of other forces and pressures. As it had been with the few dozen other human beings who came on foot to challenge this strange and hostile land, its defences of cold, wind, and distance ate steadily—implacably—at human resolve and physical capacity, and this debilitation eroded the will to survive.

Indeed, on one of the worst days of endless trudging, young Dick Richards, just 22 years of age, found this thought strong in his mind: "It would be so easy to sit down and just die—much easier than this endless fight to survive." Richards was the youngest and among the strongest of the group—and perhaps the most resilient, given his youth—yet the thought of death came to him repeatedly during those toilsome days: bending in the harness and feeling the dragging weight of the sledge through long, punishing hours of drudgery; making and breaking camp; heating and eating the same food day after day; digging the eternal snowblocks to build cairns; ceaselessly struggling with the climate; shivering in an ice-crusted sleeping bag; and carrying cold, wet socks inside his shirt and facing each morning the torture of forcing his feet into finneskoes frozen stiff overnight. Then there was the snow blindness, and the red patches of frostbite on the flesh where the lance of the southern wind got through the tears and rips in his clothing. He later remembered the shock of the thought: "Oh no! I didn't want to die. I kept thinking how easy it would be to give up and pass away. And I suppose that is a thought that comes to people in many survival situations."

The conditions began to affect the dogs, too. They also suffered snow blindness, and found some relief from burying their faces in snow—a trick that Joyce himself tried later, when the cocaine slivers were running very low. Towards 80° South two of the dogs, Towser and the Samoyed, Con, developed shortness of wind. Joyce treated them, Richards fed them double rations of a hot hash of seal meat and biscuits, and they quickly recovered. Nonetheless, the men decided to work them in briefer spells, and the dogs were rested every 15 minutes from then on while the men cut snowblocks and built up the cairns that would guide them on the return journey.

The farther south the parties trudged, the more the frozen continent seemed to resist their penetration. The conditions of which Ernest Joyce had complained at the Bluff grew worse. From the forbidding polar heights toward which they trudged, an icy wind swept unimpeded across the flat plain, flinging frozen fragments in their faces, causing the dogs to hang their heads in order to shield their eyes, and piling up layer upon layer of difficult surface for the sledges to cross. The substance clung to the runners so that each mile became a back-breaking attainment, the men's legs burying deep in the drift. To this was added the bad light, and the difficulty of halting every 15 minutes to rest the dogs, build the guiding cairns and check the line of advance.

The first real threat to their safety came as a shock to Joyce, though it was not unexpected. On the third day of the new year his mind had been filled with concern about how the dogs were coping with the added stress. These thoughts had been sharpened as they passed by the cairns they had built on their way home the previous season. On one of these, the harnesses of two dogs that had died were still hanging, silent reminders tied to a bamboo pole. Richards gave the four dogs extra food that night. As it was being prepared, Joyce was called by Irvine Gaze to the second tent. Gaze told him the problem: "Looks as though the primus stove is giving up the ghost, Joyce! It has started to burn away at the top."

The Australian snipped a band of metal from a tin and fixed it around the burner, but this did no more than direct the flame upward, and gave none of the force necessary to create the concentrated heat needed for cooking. This was more than a problem. This was a dangerous development, more serious than death among the dogs, for it threatened death among the men.

There was no more vital piece of hardware on the sledge journey than the primus stove, for it was the only means of producing quick and reliable heat to cook food and to melt snow into water. When men sledged across this frozen plain, the most urgent need was to satisfy their thirst— which at times could be raging. A man could go without hot food for a time, but not without water to drink. Otherwise he could be driven to suck ice or to try drinking snow—and "that stuff was so terribly cold it would likely burn the tongue and cheeks and scald the throat."

Joyce pondered his problem before going to sleep that night. The question was whether to send three men back now, or to stay together until they reached the 80° South depot and then make a decision. Either way it meant launching men on a risky journey, "playing the chances that the crock of a primus would see them through the 200-mile journey." They were six men now with only one reliable burner, the one he'd brought ashore from *Aurora*. (Was that last year?) That cooker stove had done its own share of work, but nothing like what they'd demanded of the two stoves they had picked up on the dump at Scott's hut at Cape Evans—which had already been heavily used by the Scott parties.

How long could the cooker stove from the *Aurora* last if it had to share half of all their heating and cooking requirements for men and dogs? No man could answer that. He must be sure that the remaining primus burners did not do too much work; that would be potentially fatal. He wrote into his log: "Lives depend on that. And I don't want to risk lives without thinking the problem right out. We are now about two days' march from the 80th latitude and our sledge loads must get there and on to 81° South—somehow. We will go to 80th and see how things progress by then. There never seems to be any happy medium in this beautiful country! One thing or another crops up." He climbed into his bag at 9 that evening, telling himself that providence would somehow pull them through.

When the weather improved, just before noon the next day, it was as though some celestial hand had been wiped across the sky. A brilliant halo with bands of gold and violet formed, and then came the gift of the sun's light, glinting on the endless ice and snows as it shimmered on the circle of horizon. The sunlight was so warm they shed their outer garments for the first time in months and turned their iced fur sleeping bags inside out to dry in the heat of its glow.

The sun lifted their spirits and broadened their grins. Joyce took off his sledging boots and socks and washed his feet in the snow, but he left his calves exposed too long, and sunburn blisters soon appeared. "It was amazing," Richards noted, "how the light of the sun brought new life to the men and the dogs."

That afternoon they covered nearly 12 miles before halting for the evening meal. Joyce again examined the defective stove and found nothing to reassure him. He commented to the men that "they'd obviously seen a lot of service with Scott's various parties."

More than ever now, they would have to depend on those four valiant-hearted huskies. He did not say it then, but Joyce knew it would be unfair to ask these men to travel beyond 80° South. It was bad enough that they would face the march back to the hut with no certainty that their stove would hold out. But whatever happened, they would have to take good care of the dogs. It was comforting to know that Richards was proving a conscientious warden, giving them hot hoosh at least every other night.

All next day as Joyce marched, he wrestled with the reluctance he felt in sending men back after they had come so far, and deciding who would return and who would go on with him. They covered another 11 miles that day. After they had eaten he told his tent mates, Dick Richards and the biologist-doctor John Cope, what he had decided.

"We'll probably reach the 80-degree depot tomorrow, lads. We can't wait any longer; we will have to part company. Doc, you will go back in charge of the other party. You've been a great tent mate, but we've got to have the fittest and strongest men if we're ever going to get these depots laid. I'm sorry, but there is no other choice. Hayward will come over here and join Richie and me from tomorrow."

Hayward was a quiet, brawny man who had experience of cold-weather traveling in northern Canada. His strength would be valuable in the heavy hauling that lay ahead. Joyce made this point to Cope who, though showing his disappointment, accepted the decision without question. Shunning sleep, Joyce sat in his bag until the biologist was slumbering, then talked long and seriously to Richards.

Young Dick Richards understood then that, though Joyce was a veteran Antarctic sledger, he was no natural leader. To him Joyce was almost an old man, nearing 40 years of age. Richards realized that if Joyce had true leadership quality and a clear mind he would have sent the other party back at once, and not risked their lives by dragging them to the 80° South depot. Just one more day on this ice shelf with no heating could mean the difference between life and death for them. Joyce told him before going to sleep, "More'n ever, Richie, I'm sure we're going to have to drive those poor dogs right down to the Beardmore . . . even if it means sacrificing them."

Dick Richards had a different opinion. The expedition was plagued, he reasoned, by their secondhand equipment. The unreliable primus stove and the tent that threatened to rip open in every strong wind meant that Mackintosh would not allow them to go beyond 82° South. There he would exercise his authority and take the dogs on to Mount Hope himself with the better equipment. It would then be Joyce and his companions' turn to suffer the disappointment of being sent back along the tracks without the satisfaction of seeing the task finished.

Richards sighted the black flag of the 80° South depot at midmorning on January 6. By midday they were already hard at work rearranging the parties and packing sledges in a gusty wind and heavy snowfall. Joyce's team and the four dogs now faced a much heavier load, a total weight of 1,240 pounds. At this depot they could take on supplies for Shackleton's men and for themselves—a benefit from the work they had done in placing this depot the previous season. There had also been a loss, however, in that they were now in great need of the dogs that had died on that journey.

From here to the Beardmore there was nothing more to aid them in their objective—no more caches of food or fuel, and no other shelter than their threadbare tents. They would have to transport all their own stores and fuel and gear for the next 500 miles or so (as well as the food and supplies for Shackleton's six men), in enough quantity to last them for several weeks. It was a daunting prospect.

When Cope and his companions turned back north they did so with a lightened load, just enough supplies to last them to the Bluff depot and on to Corner Camp. Just the same, Joyce felt anxious. He took Cope aside and warned him to push on in all possible weathers.

"Some advice, Doc," he said affectionately. "Stick to our outward tracks as long as you can. In this thick weather you'll see no landmarks, so stay with the tracks and the cairns we've set up. I'm sorry I can't give you a compass; we have only the one Richie is using. So follow your nose along those tracks, and good luck."

He gave Cope a note for Mackintosh, telling him that they would go on to 81° South and then to 82°, where they would wait to meet up with him.

Farewell cheers rang out, and the three returning men were at once lost in the swirling drift. Joyce headed his party south. He expected heavy going from the continuous snowfall, but was surprised at how well they moved, the dogs matching the men in the forward traces. He called a halt immediately, and went back to the depot for another case of biscuits. Both men and dogs could eat those if they were needed, even though they did add another 45 pounds to their load.

They sledged another six miles southward that afternoon, aided by a sudden wind from the north blowing into their makeshift sail. Joyce described this as a "brilliant performance. If we can keep this up I have no doubt about the success of the journey. We have sufficient food on our sledge to lay all depots . . . I think I will go off to sleep tonight, my mind more at ease."

The next day they were up and away in foggy conditions through which there was a heavy fall of snow crystals, frozen tiny stars of white that fell on their heads and shoulders and decorated the sledge. Again they covered a satisfactory distance with their heavy load. During one of the breaks in the toil—they were still halting every 15 minutes for what they now referred to as "spellos," during which they erected the snow cairns as markers—Joyce and Richards discussed the cargo they and the dogs were carrying.

Joyce said that on sledge journeys a working load of 180 pounds per man was a big weight, and that one could not expect to do more than eight miles trudging a day with that amount of lading. That meant the work load for the three men was around 540 pounds, leaving the other 745 pounds for the four dogs to haul. He always calculated that between 80 and 100 pounds was a fair average for a dog to haul, so it was cause for wonder that these four animals were hauling nearly twice their own body weight; Oscar and Gunner were well over the 100-pound mark, but Towser and Con would turn the scales at no more than between 70 and 80 pounds.

"It's remarkable! The vim they put into their work, they seem to realize what's required of them. These dogs are Trojans!"

In the next few days even more demands were made on both the dogs and the men. Dozing in their bags an hour before midnight on January 8, the men were surprised to hear the dogs barking excitedly. Fearing that the animals had broken loose and were attacking the Samoyed, Con, Richards and Joyce hastily crawled through the tent tunnel to the open air, only to find that the uproar was caused by Mackintosh's sledge party coming in from the north. Mackintosh, in the lead trace, was bent nearly double in his harness and was limping, Spencer-Smith was almost staggering with weariness, and Wild's shoulders were slumped in exhaustion. Joyce and Richards went to their aid, helping them pull the sledge in and then putting up their tent.

Mackintosh explained that they had "made a forced march." It was plain to the other party that they were a spent force. "They are done men," Richards wrote. The reason for the forced march became apparent the next day when Mackintosh suggested he should join with Joyce's party for the dash to the south. "Told him frankly, he would delay us," Joyce wrote in his diary, "but I offered to take some of his load." Some 50 pounds of stores were taken from Mackintosh, reducing his cargo to around 500 pounds and increasing the other sledge's burden to 1,335 pounds.

Even with this adjustment of weight, Joyce's party and their dog team easily outstripped Mackintosh's party. This caused such concern that Joyce and Richards conferred and decided to wait for the others to come up with them to discover the cause for their slow progress. It was apparent that Mackintosh's party was exhausted, so Joyce rearranged the harness and toggled their sledge behind his own.

Mackintosh revealed for the first time that he was suffering from a painful knee. Mackintosh explained his disability as a "sprain." Pulling behind the captain, Spencer-Smith was also a pitiful sight, leaning steeply into his harness, then collapsing exhausted and panting at every 15-minute break.

On Wednesday, January 12, Joyce was assailed by a severe attack of snow blindness and could not lead. He marched at the rear, his eyes bandaged, and stumbled and fell over the few miles they covered that day. Meanwhile, the lame captain took the lead trace and steered their southward passage.

The next day Joyce insisted on marching, though a blizzard faced them with strong wind gusts and snow. With the help of Richards and Wild he began erecting snow cairns every 200 yards, until they had exhausted the supply of black bunting from which the little flags were cut. Dick Richards then produced an old pair of dark trousers from his calico bag, which they scissored into small pieces to mark the new cairns for the return journey.

Developing films

During these few days of slogging, the wind grew colder and made deeper inroads on the reserves of the weakening members of Captain Mackintosh's team. Richards observed that he, Joyce, and Hayward were in fine condition and the dogs were doing splendidly. But Spencer-Smith inscribed a different tale in his official expedition diary: "Have been marching with my Burberry helmet down, in a dream-like state . . . it has been the longest afternoon of the journey. Have found strength in repeating the words of Isaiah, 'They shall mount up with wings they shall mount up with wings.' " He complained of very sore lips and mouth, and of "stiff muscles and quite painful walking."

They sighted the Western Mountains during these days, and saw the "two Mount Markhams" rising above 14,000 feet, "magnificent and noble," in the view of Dick Richards. The comfort of knowing that they were well on course was lessened by the nagging concern over the condition of their two weakest members: Mackintosh, grimly limping the miles away, and the wan and ailing Padre, Spencer-Smith.

On Wednesday, January 19, just as the air cleared to give them a view of the scene to the south for some 50 miles, the almost fainting chaplain confessed, "I had to tell my companions at lunch how weak I was. They gave me much sympathy—and an extra Bovril meat cube all to myself." He bravely hid entries in his diary that read, "knees uncomfortable, feel very cold"; "feeling seedy, head hot, eyes ache"; and, just before his midday confession of weakness, "my heart is rather ricked, I fear, my knees bad, swollen and like a great bruise above and below." Spencer-Smith would not yet admit that he was a victim of scurvy, the scourge of sledging on the ice shelf, a vitamin-deficiency disease that would rob him of more than mere muscular or physical capacity; it would erode his willpower and make him lethargic and indifferent—and a burden to his companions. He acknowedged, instead, that his heart "was rather ricked," and he found some release in strange dreams and in the conjurings of his imagination: "I dreamed the war was all over, and that all the German rivers were now English rivers."

Before the 82nd latitude was reached it had already become blindingly obvious to Joyce, Richards, and Wild that it was utter folly for

Mackintosh and Spencer-Smith to have come farther than the 80° depot. Richards made a down-to-earth assessment of the situation when Mackintosh doggedly insisted on marching south: "We are determined not to allow them to go on to the Beardmore. That would be nothing less than suicide."

They had only the power of argument and persuasion. The Captain would not yield in his resolve to be there when the final depot was laid, when he would keep his promise to the man he admired so much: the Boss. Each grueling day the two weakening men showed further deterioration as they staggered on. Joyce noted, "The Padre complains his knees are giving out; he had been in agony since 81° South"; and "I am very pessimistic about the Padre and Skipper; it seems we shall be dragging them on the sledge"; and further, "The two men are not well; the Padre totters like an old man; it is pitiful to see the Captain get along."

Amazingly, Mackintosh and Spencer-Smith continued to march. Six men and four dogs yanked the two sledges mile after mile when the brief sun shone, showing the land ahead, and when the wild winds hit them in the face and the snowdrift shut them into a tight sphere with no other world but their own stumbling, tramping feet and the dragging sledge. Still, in spite of all the trials, they made the 82nd latitude, and there Richards, Hayward, and Wild joined Joyce in erecting a big cairn with a bamboo pole dressed with a pennant cut from Richards' trousers.

They left some three weeks of food and fuel for 12 men, and at once set off for the 83rd degree. The sledges were much lighter, and the dogs pulled so well that Joyce was exultant: "Distance for the day, 12 miles! At this rate we will have the Mount Hope depot laid in a week from now. Turned in satisfied."

Despite his excitement about their progress, Joyce felt renewed anxiety over the condition of both Spencer-Smith and Mackintosh and their failing ability to pull and march at the same speed as the other members of the party: "It is a great pity that the Skipper and his party did not turn back from 80° South. . . ."

The issue of whether Mackintosh should have recognized his own waning strength and the poor state of the clergyman earlier on soon became secondary to a more urgent crisis. The second of the primus stoves taken from the Cape Evans dump began to fail in the same manner as the one Cope's party had taken back to Hut Point. The punctured metal ring that gave pressure to the flame started to burn away; it was apparent that they could no longer contemplate separating into two parties. They were inextricably bound into one unit now, their existence dependent on their single reliable heating appliance.

As Mackintosh glumly pondered the situation in his tent during the night blizzard at 82° South, he recalled that because Dick Richards had joined the party in Australia he had not signed the customary agreement with Shackleton, a form of contract that limited what members of the expedition might publish about their adventures and sufferings on their return to civilization. There and then Mackintosh pored over a sheet of paper, writing in pencil the form of the contract as he recalled it. When he was done he called Richards to his tent to sign the document, which was witnessed by Spencer-Smith. In the small tent in the snowy wilderness, young Dick Richards grinned. "This must be the nearest to either the North or the South Pole a fellow has been asked to sign his freedom away."

As they marched on toward the remote 83rd latitude, Ernest Joyce remembered that they were now farther south than Scott, Wilson and Shackleton had reached in 1903. They were approaching the Beardmore Glacier, and he lamented, "I am steering right ahead for the mountain which answers the description of Mount Hope, but Padre and Skipper Mackintosh do not seem well. It will mean dragging them on the sledge before we are finished."

That eventuality was far closer than he knew. The drama he feared was about to burst on them with a tragic suddenness.

The sightings Dick Richards made on January 21 put them at the 83rd parallel at midmorning. The reading was taken at 11 o'clock, when the thick clouds had cleared away from the south and lay low and deeply black behind them. The mountain range was clearly defined against the southern sky, but peak after peak rolled into one another and there was nothing on their rough chart that gave the men true indication of their destination, Mount Hope. Richards calculated then that the foot of the Beardmore Glacier was some 35 miles distant.

They camped early that night to give respite to Spencer-Smith, and did not get under way again until 9 the next day, which was a Saturday. The rest gave them little benefit, however. After two hours on the trail Spencer-Smith fell in his tracks, pitching forward on his hands and knees, his head hanging. He was gasping for breath and his face was lined with pain. His companions rushed to his side and helped him to his feet, but he could not stand without support, and he could not walk. Indeed, he would never walk again. They put up their tents and heated some snow to make tea. With Spencer-Smith lying in his reindeer-skin bag, they held council. The Captain, grim-faced to hide his concern, asked for opinions from the group.

The distance from here to the site for Shackleton's southernmost food cache was little more than 30 miles, within the reach of three solid days of marching. They were very near to attaining the objective they had toiled and suffered to achieve, and here was a helpless companion. What should they do? Joyce was direct in his view. Mackintosh himself needed rest, and he should stay and care for the Padre while Joyce went on with the others, laid the depot, and hurried back. It could all be done within a week, he claimed. Richards lent his voice to the argument: Mackintosh was not fit enough to do much of the pulling anyway.

An unexpected voice then entered the debate. The helpless man, still managing to be cheerful, dismantled the arguments of Joyce and Richards, pulling away the support of their contention by smiling and saying, "Nobody has to stay with me! You can leave me here with enough food and fuel and I'll look after myself. I'll be quite all right. I really will, I assure you."

Not one of the four men still fit enough to pull the sledge could be left with Spencer-Smith. The weight of the stores and the obviously difficult country they were about to enter precluded any notion that someone other than Mackintosh could be left behind. When Richards put forth this view, the Captain brushed it aside and, still contending that his knee was "sprained," asserted that it was his duty to continue the journey. Richards felt sympathy for the man, and some admiration for his courage.

Mackintosh was the commander, working with only one eye, crippled by his troublesome knee, obviously run-down and weakened and finding every step a jarring pain—yet he was sticking to his post. He was the professional navigator, and he had pledged to Shackleton that the southernmost depot would be properly laid in the appointed place. His refusal to abandon that duty now placed him in jeopardy. Young Richards was convinced that the Captain was making a serious error in judgment. Both he and Spencer-Smith should have turned back to the north from 80° South; since they had not, Mackintosh should now remain behind.

Overruled by his commander, Joyce hurried the preparations along, shunning delay. "Come on, lads," he called out. "There's not an hour to lose!" His implication was that there was even greater need for haste, since the limping Captain would be in the company. So it was that less than three hours from the time Spencer-Smith had collapsed they were trekking to find the foot of the Beardmore Glacier and the sentinel to the polar plateau: Mount Hope. They were quickly on their way, five men and four dogs, and the scrap of canvas that sheltered the sick man lying in his sleeping bag was soon lost to them in the vast white emptiness.

The Reverend Arnold Patrick Spencer-Smith, aged 31, was completely alone for the first time since he had left England; he lay still in his reindeer-skin bag, straining to hear the last command to the dogs come on the wind, to catch the last whisper of sound from the only living creatures in the wilderness outside his tattered shelter. Then they were gone. He watched the canvas of the old Scott tent quiver in the wind, and waited, thinking they might return, having changed their minds. Then there was only the swish of the drift on the tent. Later he took out his small expedition diary and pencil and wrote, "They have been gone two and a half hours. I can reckon on getting some rest.

They have left me five weeks' food. I found the Skipper and Wild very sympathetic. They gave me a bottle of lime juice . . . in case it is scurvy, which I doubt altogether . . .'

The five men tramped another 12 miles that day before weariness forced them to camp. Restful sleep, however, was not to be had. They were five in a hemispherical (umbrella-type) tent designed for three. Cooking and sharing out the hoosh equally became more difficult and prolonged.

Spencer-Smith also had trouble sleeping in his conical tent with the canvas spread across five bamboo poles. Instead he persisted in reading one of the few books in his bag. It was quiet this night, and finally he fell asleep and dreamed: Here was Sir Ernest Shackleton, eyes beaming, coming to meet him, and with him Frank Wild, Ernie's brother, resplendent in a gold-laced cap. Sir Ernest was clean-shaven and neat, with one motor sledge and one dog sledge.

When Spencer-Smith woke, the wind was rising. He found his knees were not improved and decided he would have a "day of total inaction." But that day and another and another of "total inaction" led to no improvement. He wrote in his diary that his condition grew "progressively worse." He could manage to write only brief notes now. It was so cold his fingers suffered: ". . . went to the door to get snow, felt very poorly. Concocted a comedy in my head, but could not write it down." Slowly he drifted into a lassitude and lethargy that was "half-sleepy, half-dreamy," with times of clarity when he recalled what he was doing a year ago. The drift and the snowfall piled round his tent. "Drift kept me home. Spent day delivering lecture and a sermon—in execrable French!"

Still refusing to recognize the cause of his swollen black gums and the blue-black bruises round his knees, Spencer-Smith penciled the words, "Seems my heart is racked after all. It is humiliating that they will find me no better."

To the south, still some 20 miles from the foot of the great glacier, Dick Richards was digging out the dogs from a "snorter of a blizzard" that had struck during the night of January 24. Inside the crowded tent

Ernest Joyce was examining Captain Mackintosh's "sprained knee." He massaged the joint with the methylated spirits, which they carried to start the primus, and was puzzled because "it is blue; cannot understand how a sprain should remain so long. Of course, it requires rest. . . . What a pity he did not take advantage and lay up with the Padre!"

They were compelled to lie in their bags for the remainder of that day, eating only half-rations, as was the practice, unable to move in the thick drift and snowfall because of the perilous area of disturbed ice that they expected ahead of them. Trekking was possible the next day, and they made excellent mileage to find themselves facing a chaos of mountainous ice in the late afternoon. It was misty and the surface was deceptive under the refracted light, so they put up the tent and spent another restless night. Each of them felt the cold more intensely than before. Richards noted that "Mackintosh kept going through that day but was very lame at the end. There is a considerable area of blue-black discolouration behind his knee."

They left the tent standing next morning, and Joyce, Mackintosh and Richards set off, roped together, to reconnoiter a passage through the turmoil of crevasses and caves and hills of ice. They were close now to where the colossal frozen river, the Beardmore Glacier, fed its slow burden into the ice shelf along a 25-mile-wide front. From its source, more than 100 miles inland on the awesome polar plateau, it fell some 10,000 feet, exerting enormous pressure against the foothills of the mountains and the mass of the ice shelf itself. Joyce described the upheaval as "beyond realization in life . . . a vortex of ice churned into caves of blue appearance." The pressure had thrown up massive hunks of frozen snow to a height of 400 feet, and caused a chaos of countless crevasses with bottoms lost in a dark abyss, a few of them filled with the shattered debris of ice that had cracked and shattered against the rock.

Richards sighted the detached and rounded mountain, several thousand feet high, that answered the description of Mount Hope, and the three men altered their course to find the gap between the mountain and the mainland beyond. In their path was "the result of the violent crushing by the weight of the stupendous glacier. Huge pinnacles of ice rose up in front, and great chasms confronted us on all sides." With patience, however—and with a few falls into crevasses through broken snow bridges—marking their return passage all the way with scraps of cuttings from the dark trousers, they came to an ascent between the mountain and the range beyond.

Here Dick Richards's sharp eyes caught a glimpse of an object in the scene of rock and ice that was alien to the rounded curves of nature, an object of angles and lines. In the difficult light they steered to investigate and found an upended sledge, its tip projecting about four feet from the surface. This, they decided, was the marker Captain Scott and his polar party had left on their outward journey to guide them on their own descent of the Beardmore. Joyce decided it was actually two sledges lashed end to end, which were mostly snow-covered. "We are on the right track," he declared.

Richards remembered this scene vividly in later years, "It was a beautiful, calm day, the sun shining brightly. . . and everything on a gigantic scale, full of colour and magnificent, simply magnificent. The ice of the great glacier was flanked by sheer, steep rock faces that were splashed with vivid color."

Joyce was terse, but equally as graphic. "We saw the Great Beardmore Glacier stretching up and away to the south . . . a glorious spectacle, a mighty silence, fitting recompense amidst our trials." One of the world's biggest frozen rivers, running down from the sky above the awesome polar country, the Beardmore had been discovered by Shackleton in 1908. Now it was to be his great staircase down to this depot they were laying at Mount Hope, the food and fuel that could carry him on his journey north across the Ross Ice Shelf.

Richards looked with wonder at the glacier and noticed dark patches on the gleaming surface. The belief that the sacrifice and the suffering the men had endured had been worthwhile was still strong in their minds— so strong that Richards would later say, "If we did not believe that Shackleton could come across the continent, why were we pulling our very guts out to lay that depot?" It seemed likely that the Boss and his party were even then somewhere on the 100 miles of ice gradient, climbing down to the saddle behind Mount Hope to seek the warmth and sustenance these men had dragged the length of that terrible ice shelf!

And so he scanned the gleaming expanse with his keen eyes, and there, showing dark and distinctive against the face of the glacier—some five or six miles distant—was a round shape, hemispherical even, like the dome-shaped tent they were using—Shackleton's chosen type of tent! Richards went down flat on the snow-covered saddle, propping his elbows to steady the old binoculars against his eyes, and stared, waiting in hope, watching for movement, for signs of life. For one moment the vision cleared—a movement in the ice haze—and he could see plainly that he had been looking at a big rounded boulder that had been caught up in the glacial flow. There was no sign of Ernest Shackleton's transcontinental party.

*   *   *

A thousand miles beyond the South Pole, which itself was 500 miles from where Dick Richards stared hopefully at the round rock, two men sledged across the frozen Weddell Sea for two small cases of lentils, a treasure trove of food. The castaways of the Imperial Trans-Antarctic Expedition were at their second camp on the sea ice, living on a giant floe that was drifting inexorably northward towards the South Atlantic, away from the coast where the historic crossing was to have started. For two months they had lived this way, ever since the last sighting of the doomed *Endurance*, which Shackleton had described: "her bows overridden and broken by the relentless pack . . . the tangled mass of ropes, rigging and spars that made the scene desolate and depressing."

The men of the Shackleton expedition had existed for a time on the floe they called Ocean Camp, until it began to split and threatened to dump them all into the icy sea. Then they struggled to a more solid floe, which they christened Patience Camp, where they were to live in spirit-crushing circumstances for more than three months. Already Ernest Shackleton had noted how "apathy seemed to fall upon the men at our great disappointment." Food was so short and inadequate that it was a cause of perpetual anxiety to him, and he sent out parties to search for seals and penguins to supplement their depressing diet of half–sledging rations every day.

For their kitchen they built a wall of blocks of ice and topped it with a tarpaulin, and they looked for miracles from a cook who had little but blubber for heating. "Our rations are just sufficient to keep us alive," Shackleton wrote. ". . . We feel we could eat twice as much as we get. Our craving for bread and butter is very real . . . the system feels the need of it."

The few seals and penguins they could find to kill, the extra scraps of food salvaged from the remnants of the shipwreck, even the hope that winter storms would burst open the sea ice and allow them to take to the boats—none of these could save Ernest Shackleton from his most horrifying decision. At the very time when Mackintosh's men and their four valiant huskies were hauling his food and fuel to the Mount Hope saddle, Sir Ernest was near to tears writing in his diary: ". . . we need all the food we could get for ourselves. I have had to order that all the dogs except two teams should be shot." It was the worst action he had had to take so far, and he "felt the loss keenly."

Wild and two dogs

"Death Stalks Us From Behind"

T he glacial ice was a living thing. During the night the five men were frequently jerked awake, startled by a range of explosive sounds reaching their ears, sounds like sharp rifle volleys, rumbling artillery bombardment, the crackle of pistol shots; startled also by the vibration reaching their bodies from the ceaseless, relentless pressure of the Beardmore Glacier thrusting its mass into the prodigious ice shelf. All around them the chaos of frozen upheaval was being shaped and reshaped constantly. Yet as they lay through the night hours in the tent, the men knew a sense of satisfaction, even peace. Mackintosh had expressed his relief, borrowing from the poet, "Something attempted, something done." Young Dick Richards had his own consolation for the past 16 hours of backbreaking toil, "At last, in the face of all the difficulties, we have placed all the depots for Shackleton."

Charting that last dangerous course through the shattered ice to the saddle behind Mount Hope had taken nine hours to achieve. With the drive of urgency powered by the memory of the sick man lying alone in a tent on the ice plain, they had rapidly stacked the sledge with the final stores they would haul for other men, and then had retraced their path into the frozen madness, over crevasses, down frigid gullies, up steep slopes to lay that final depot—food in the calico bags they had cut and sewn and filled with Scott's discarded pemmican back at Cape Evans, and the precious fuel, and a bonus of biscuits—enough to last six men for three weeks. When it was done, the blocks of icy snow they cut and built into a tall cairn were marked with the discarded Scott sledge and bamboo masts that carried three fluttering flags 15 feet above the skyline—an obvious, prominent mark for the overlanders climbing down the mighty glacier.

On that last day of depot-laying they trudged a distance of 22 miles to and from their most southern camp, the Captain hobbling all the way. Their battered sleeping bags of reindeer skin were molting now (the hairs were getting into their evening meals of hot hoosh), but they were beds of welcoming embrace after this day of crushing toil and danger. Four days had passed since they had started their march from the tent in which the Padre lay waiting. Laid on the evening of January 26, 1916, the Mount Hope depot represented a monumental effort of continuous exertion with niggardly resources. The effort had, that season alone, lasted for more than 21 weeks—a total of 148 days of hard labor and suffering that had so far cost the lives of more than a dozen husky dogs, and put at risk the lives of nearly as many men.

Some 400 miles of difficult travel now lay ahead of them in the fight to regain the shelter of Hut Point. It was a depressing prospect of more months of slogging against the surface and the elements. However, Joyce found means to cheer his comrades in the crowded tent. "Every step is a step back along the trail—and maybe when we get there we'll find the ship is waiting for us," he told them. In his diary, always written no matter what the circumstances, he was more realistic: "Now for the long haul back to Hut Point. The dogs are our only hope. Our lives depend on them."

The howling, snow-filled wind blocked any thoughts of travel the next day. They stayed in their bags for warmth and ate breakfast at mid-day, saving a meal. Later, when the blast eased enough for them to break camp, the wickedly reflecting light turned their pathway through Joyce's "vortex of ice" into an agonizing stint. Soon the veteran sledger had to give way, as the pain of snow blindness drove him out of the lead trace and back alongside the sledge with his eyes bandaged, stumbling and falling on the uneven surface. All day long Joyce marched in pain; there were no more soothing cocaine slivers now; his only relief was to copy the dogs and slap handfuls of deeply cold snow on his eyes. "I feel a useless wreck," he complained. "My eyes are a complete blank. Cannot see anything."

It was like that for two whole days, and not until the morning of Saturday, January 29, could he again go to the lead, with hopes of reaching Spencer-Smith by noon. That morning a northerly wind hit them full on. This caused three hours' delay, adding to their anxiety for the brave man lying alone in the old tent somewhere ahead amid the whirl of snow and fine drift. Dick Richards thought of that ever-cheerful clergyman, "a small speck on the vast ice shelf with the only other nearest human beings some 400 miles away to the north. . . . When our small party had disappeared into the south a week ago and the great silence settled down, he must have been lonely indeed."

In the afternoon Spencer-Smith wrote joyfully, "They have come back! How wonderful to hear the dogs and the voices again." They found him totally helpless now, and with his sleeping bag frozen into a fixed shape, since he was too weak to force it to alter to his changing position. Richards saw that although the Padre was cheerful and joyous to see them back, "his condition had sadly deteriorated and it was obvious he could not walk."

Joyce examined the sick man and found his lower limbs black and dark blue, "extending from hip to ankle." This was the same condition that he saw in Mackintosh when massaging the Captain's legs against the so-called sprain. Next he looked in the Padre's mouth and saw that the gums were black and swollen. Richards then looked into a little round mirror and saw that his own gums were black and swollen as well.

Joyce wrote, "We have the curse of scurvy with us . . . every indication of the dread disease! Well, we must get along and make the best of circumstances with longer hours of marching and greater distances—one of the trials of polar regions we must expect. Somehow, I felt after leaving 80° South something like this would occur. If it had not been for their primus giving out I should have sent them back. Our only hope is our four-footed friends."

They broke camp almost at once and stacked the first sledge so that Spencer-Smith could be laid full length, to give him the best possible comfort for the hundreds of miles of hauling that he would have to endure. There was nothing more they could do, other than to get him and the Captain back as soon as possible to some fresh food.

The lightened sledge was now heavy again with the body of the helpless passenger. And the fear grew, as they marched, that Mackintosh too would soon be unable to walk. He could no longer pull any weight, but simply trudged on and on in this grim struggle to cover the frozen miles. As the bitter days went by the other men marvelled at his courage, at the brave way he bore the pain of seemingly endless hours of stumping forward, holding on to the sledge or to one of the ropes, with his condition steadily deteriorating.

The weather also deteriorated, the drift becoming finer as the air grew colder, turning into a state that was almost a powder, which the south winds blew into their clothing and all that they possessed. So the sweat of their labor garnered more and more ice. They covered the Padre in his sleeping bag on the sledge with a snow cloth, which they used on the floor of the tent, but this did not save him from a wet bag that froze about him each night. Concerned about this and the increasingly heavy going they were encountering as they crawled northward, Mackintosh talked with Joyce as he performed the nightly chore of massaging the Captain's swollen legs with methylated spirits.

"Don't you think, Joyce," he suggested, "that we might find the going better if we marched at night and not in the day, when the snow and drift is softer?"

Joyce did not agree. They had to stick to a routine, he argued, or they would never get through. "If we sidetracked it would not be easy to step into line again, and the dogs must be studied. I feel it my duty to nurse them in every sense of the word." Recording this conversation, he added, "I told him he should have realized the state of the Padre's health, having traveled with him for so long a period."

Each day the care of the dogs and the sick men was a ritual. Joyce's diary jottings tell of his resolute and rigid adherence to the routine, to "keeping on line." He claimed that his long training in the Royal Navy had installed an alarm clock in his brain that woke him early each morning. When he was cook for the week he would reckon to be up and about before 6 in the morning, first stirring the men, then stirring the steaming pot on the cooker from which the pint mugs were filled with breakfast—fatty, meaty pemmican hoosh, which warmed and nourished them for the day's slogging labor. After this came a pint of hot tea in the same mugs, and a hardtack biscuit, all rapidly consumed.

Stockinged feet were then thrust—painfully—into the work-worn and frozen finneskoes, and personal effects were stacked into calico holders. Sleeping bags were rolled and tied, sledging garments donned, and the tent knocked down and furled, while at the same time Richards or Joyce or both furiously dug out the dogs from their heaps of snow and cleared the sledges for loading. Then the separated dogs— always tied to the 20-foot lead rope to prevent them from fighting— were harnessed and attached to the sledge front. The sledge itself was about 12 feet long, weighed 60 pounds, and had flexibility for travel on the uneven surface with its joints bound together with greenhide thongs. The sleeping bags were rolled and stored behind the plywood front box in which the cooking gear and fuel were carried, and behind which was stepped the bamboo mast on which they could sling the snowcloth as a sail when the wind was favorable. Preparation for travel usually took upwards of two hours, and much longer than that when the weather was bad.

Once started they would heave in the harness, pulling with the dogs through piecrust surfaces, in deep, cloying snow, or over marble-hard ice, halting every 15 minutes to rest—for three minutes only, though, to prevent themselves and the dogs from getting too cold.

It was customary, when supplies allowed, to halt around midday for "lunch." The tent would be quickly erected and the primus lit, ignited first by burning methylated spirits to heat the burner ring, then the snow would be melted to boiling water for a mug of hot tea, a single biscuit, and a slim stick of plain chocolate. The afternoons always seemed like entire days of endless bondage, plugging forward in the sledge harness for hour after hour, with thoughts of the evening hoosh coming upon them like a dream of home and comfort somewhere ahead in the cold monotony of their progress. Around 6 in the evening, unless the going was good enough to encourage one more hour of pulling to make an extra mile, they would halt and stake out the dogs on the long rope. The tent would go up quickly and the snow-cloth would be passed in through the canvas tunnel, whose round opening was tied like a long sock from the inside in an attempt to keep out wind and drift. The stove would soon be roaring its blue flame of warmth and life for the exhausted men and dogs. The animals would be fed first, a hot mess of seal meat, while it lasted, with pemmican and mashed biscuits. The sleeping bags and other gear would be passed in through the tunnel and the evening meal prepared, the menu exactly the same as breakfast. A slab of snowy ice would be cut in the floor for a latrine and when the call of nature came one man would call, "Heads under!" and the others would pull the cowl of their sleeping bags over their faces while the hole was used and the icy block replaced. It was primitive and uncomfortable, but it was a sensible routine. It was Ernest Joyce's "ton line" pattern of sledging. Now, with a recumbent passenger, a limp body in pain, as well as a walking invalid who hobbled like an aged man on a ski pole, the routine was extended and more complicated. For the hundreds of miles northward that remained to be covered, the pattern of camping had to change.

They traveled the northward trail from 83° South with two tents and two sledges toggled together. The motivation of the four dogs and four men, no longer fit and strong, and now suffering from the first influx of scurvy, was further handicapped by the advancing season and the worsening of the going underfoot. Each midday at the lunch break and every evening Spencer-Smith was lifted from his couch on the sleeping bags aboard the sledge directly to the snow cloth, and the tent was erected above his head. His two tent mates were Mackintosh and Ernie Wild, so the main burden of caring for the sick man fell upon the kindly but somewhat taciturn Yorkshireman—duties he performed with utter unselfishness and unfailing kindness. Although Mackintosh, near collapse after each day of trudging behind the sledges, gave some help with the tent chores, they had to be carried out primarily by Wild, in a display of endurance matching that of his more famous brother. Each morning, each midday stop and each evening, Wild heated the food and gave aid and comfort to the two sick men. He washed and cleaned the helpless parson and disposed of his excrement, without hesitation. So faithfully and unobtrusively did he give these services that he was fervently blessed by Spencer-Smith, and openly admired by the other members of the struggling party.

"I could never ever speak too highly of Ernie Wild's devotion to the two sick men," Dick Richards would say, many years later. "He tended the Padre with a devotion that could not be surpassed, for more than 40 days, on a journey of more than 300 miles and in circumstances that became increasingly difficult."

In the agony of the journey, often fainting from pain when he was being lifted to and from the sledge, Spencer-Smith gave his own example of forbearance and courage. Richards wrote of him, "Spencer-Smith never once complained. He was always ready with a cheery word and a smile and tried to make our task easier by his manner." But the Padre was declining; at times the malaise clouded his mind and his thoughts wandered for relief, as Richards saw it, "into more kindly climes." Some were memories of the world he had known, and when he was well enough and lying in the tent he would prop on one elbow and slowly pencil a note or two into his official diary. Nowhere does this writing show any fear of the chasm of death that yawned before him. His legs were burdens of pain—the action of the scurvy tightened the rear tendons of his knees, and as his thigh muscles weakened from inaction his legs were bent nearer and nearer to right angles.

Spencer-Smith had the kindly Ernie Wild to tend him and the tough veteran Joyce to reassure him. There was the chance, however small, that they would get him back to the hut, to the fresh meat of the seals. As the bucking sledge rode over the uneven ice known as *sastrugi*, jerking and swaying, throwing weight onto his crippled legs and pain into his head, he would write of excursions in his mind: "There I was on a warm sunny day, walking with pals in Edinburgh" or "strolling in Gray's Inn." He was comforted by images of the London where he had been born and raised. Then the wilderness would be with him again, and he would write, to the sound of the tent canvas rattling the poles, "Oh, the wind carries a note of personal animus!"

The elements—the blizzard winds and horizontal sheets of blown snow, the lack of living things and fresh nutriment—and the long, long days of slow crawling across the frozen surface were enemies to his resolve, to his faith that all would be well after trial. Little comfort came from the monotonous diet, made up of a mug of pemmican hoosh, a biscuit and weak milkless tea, but it was always accepted with smiling gratitude and good manners from the patient Ernie Wild, and with thanks to God for blessings received. The mind could always look elsewhere for comfort: "I keep thinking of new milk, cheese, salads, brown bread and butter and jam, sometimes pickles and new laid eggs."

The depot at 82° South came into view after five days of arduous travel. Hauling two sledges, one laden with the weight of the sick man, for 60 miles had been such a drain on their energies that Joyce insisted on a rearrangement. Mackintosh did not want to agree, Joyce wrote in his diary, but the second sledge had to be abandoned and everything—cargo, gear and food, and the invalid—had to be borne on one sledge. This made fresh demands on the time taken for packing and camping, but the delay could be countered by sledging more hours if they were to cover the critical distance of about 14 miles a day.

By the second day of the new month of February they were tramping more than 16 miles a day, but this encouraging development was weakened by the continuing incursion of scurvy. For the first time Joyce noted that the Canadian, Hayward, had become a victim, for his "gums are black and protruding, his knees are of the same colour . . . scurvy has caught us in its net." There was bad news of the Padre: "His lips are bloodless, and his breathing far from normal. I feel dubious about his heart." At the same time, Mackintosh was giving an incredible display of courage. His ankles were "swollen out of all proportion, and it is beyond my powers to understand how he moves along. In these vast wastes, what an asset is pluck!"

But high courage gave no relief to Captain Aeneas Mackintosh. Each painful step forward was followed by the misery of another, of another hundred, of another thousand, a lasting distress that continued across the hostile wastes. The depot in the blank of white drift at the 81st latitude was still 60 miles away, which meant there would be yet another 60 miles of suffering to attain sight of a pile of frozen snow-blocks, a remnant of a tattered flag on a bending bamboo pole, whipping and shredding its substance away in the wild wind; a few calico bags of pemmican and a can of fuel; and then the desolate ice-crusted arm of Minna Bluff would be the next staging-post to be dreamed of, as of some marvellous landfall.

The farther north the men struggled, the more the alien continent appeared loath to allow their escape. Every aspect of its harsh climate was being flung at them in their desperate floundering. But courage and the driving spirit of survival were so strong in the travelers that, invalid passenger and crippled captain notwithstanding, they slogged the trail from 83° South to the 80th parallel in two weeks, a distance of some 180 miles. That depot being reached, however, there awaited them the "treacherous country" leading to desolate Minna Bluff. The nearest shelter and fresh seal meat, at Hut Point, were still 200 miles to the north. Most certainly the coming stretch to the Bluff depot and their worsening condition would cause delay, so they took on an extra four days' rations at the 80° depot. Joyce recorded, "We are leaving four weeks supply for Shackleton—which should see him through."

They stayed there only long enough to erect tents and heat mugs of weak tea, and to allow time for Joyce and Richards to massage the legs of the Captain and Hayward. Then they were back into the bondage of the harness, heaving with the dogs in conditions that Joyce bemoaned. "This terrible 60 miles to the Bluff is worse than Hell! The temperature is falling, our clothing is dilapidated, our finneskoes worn through—and Mack is growing weaker. . . . If we have to pull two men in I don't know what will happen."

At times it seemed to them that the snow had the consistency of glue. Then they would be jarring their joints on iron-hard ice or wallowing again in deep drifts of snow up to their waists, with the greathearted dogs always threshing and flailing to get them through.

Each long morning and each endless afternoon carried torment of the spirit and torture to the body. In one of his nightly entries Joyce wrote, "I have never known such shocking conditions. This is one of the hardest pulls since we have trekked. The Padre has taken a turn for the worse. It is incredible how a human frame can endure these trials. We are absolutely powerless to aid him further—all we can do is to slog on with the greatest possible speed."

Their very location prompted further reflection on the peril in their plight; for here at 79° 30′ South, on this section of the southern passage across the Ross Ice Shelf, at about this same time of the season some four years earlier, Captain Scott and the last two companions of his five-man polar party had been dying. Crippled with frostbite, helpless and weak from starvation and cold, Scott had written his famous "Last entry . . . the end cannot be far. It seems a pity but I do not think I can write more."

In November 1912, some 30 miles north of where Joyce had taken on four days' extra rations and left four weeks' supply for Shackleton, a search party had found the Scott tent covered with the rime of winter. They had paid their respects by erecting a huge snow cairn over the icy grave of the three men who had died only 11 miles from food and fuel at One Ton Depot, when they had been trapped by a great Antarctic blizzard. Just such a blizzard was about to fall on Ernest Joyce and his hungry companions.

In these few days of titanic struggle to advance toward the stores at Minna Bluff, the last vestige of leadership slipped away from the failing Captain Aeneas Mackintosh. Decision was now arrived at by consensus, with Ernest Joyce and young Dick Richards, the two strongest men in the party, joining to form the most influential force. There was something paradoxical in this situation. In relinquishing control of the mission the Captain grew in stature in the minds of his men. Richards wrote, "Our hearts bleed for the captain in his agony." When they urged Mackintosh to ease his painwracked stumbling by riding on the sledge, his one eye glared with defiance, and he declared that he would not "jeopardize the Padre's chances for his own." He even refused to be tied to the sledge and went on plunging forward on his crippled, bent legs. Joyce wrote, "He is true blue and we all admire him for it."

So they came to the night camp of February 17, 1916. They were about 11 miles from the big Bluff depot to which they had hauled their thousands of pounds of stores. Fatigue now marked every movement in men and dogs. It took much longer than usual to go through the ritual of setting up camp for the night, getting the four animals fed and tethered on the long rope and the two tents pitched within a few yards of each other. The nights were drawing in now, and to avoid cooking in the dark they ate their hoosh and biscuit earlier than usual and then stretched in their reindeer-skin bags to rest. They were hardly asleep when the first assault of the blizzard swept over them: Furious and powerful, the tornadic wind flung frozen drift like pellets being fired at their threadbare tents, as the quaking canvas slapped and the bamboo poles rattled. The gale sounded like the soul of vengeance; it screamed and howled and moaned around the men and animals, all night through and all through the next day. Dick Richards testified that "the blizzard surpassed in length and fury anything I experienced during my stay in the Antarctic. It was impossible to travel—even impossible to see or communicate with the other tent in the howling of the wind. Soon the drift banked high against the frail walls of the tent and gradually restricted our space inside. The sleeping-bags were crowded together side by side, and hour after monotonous hour was spent in them as the days went by. By this time plenty of ice adhered firmly to the hairs of the skin making real rest impossible."

They dared not venture far from the tent for "any personal reasons, and all nature's needs were met inside the quivering canvas shelter. Richards, or sometimes Joyce, would push the bank of snow from the tent tunnel and go outside into the whirling chaos to free the tethered dogs from too great an overlay of drift. This would take an hour or two of stressful toil, shoveling with the face, nostrils, eyes, and ears filled with flying flakes, with weakness from short rations slowing the work down. This labor was necessary, for they recognized the animals as essential to their hope of survival in this terrible country. Hayward was already in an advanced stage of depression from scurvy and, like the Captain would soon be of little use. Joyce's fear that he would soon have not two but three men to drag to the distant edge of the Barrier grew hourly, so every care was taken with Oscar, Gunner, Con and Towser. Without them there was little chance of hauling the sledge to Safety Camp.

On their first full day of being storm-bound they reckoned their resources at three days' rations for men and dogs. The daily allotment immediately had to be halved, and the lack of food and its warming preparation made the creeping hours seem even longer, adding to their misery. To break the long boredom of lying, tossing, and shivering in their sleeping bags, they took to mending their tattered garments, patching everything with discarded calico food bags. Even the badly holed fur sledging boots were bound with these, and when the tent fabric itself split near the tunnel entrance, allowing drift to blow in and threatening to rip the full length of their shelter, Richards and Joyce shared the discomfort of sewing a calico bag over the hole, one man inside feeding the needle and thread to the suffering man crouched outside in the blast of the blizzard.

The portents of disaster were with them day and night. The incessant slapping of the tent canvas, the beat of the angry gale on the slender poles, the whack of frozen fragments into the exposed area of the fabric, all were manifestations of a wild enemy at their door. And time was slipping away, the hours of idleness without sustaining food eating at their resolution and their will to pull through. In the second tent, where the durable Ernie Wild was caring for two ailing comrades, time dragged by even more slowly. Hours of exhausted sleeping were often broken by the Padre's moans of pain or by the poor Captain's restless seeking of a comfortable position. When they were awake, however, Wild the taciturn endeavored to be Wild the garrulous. He would talk of his life in the navy, of his family and his plans for the future, and whether the war would be over when they got back. At those times when Spencer-Smith appeared to sink into gloomy contemplation of the hopelessness of their plight, he would provoke an argument on religion, saying that there could not be a God who would allow men and creatures to suffer without cause. The Padre recognized Wild was baiting him, and in a brief note in pencil confessed to being "cranky" as a result. He attested that the Yorkshireman had rigged arguments with him, and that "I have told him that an absolute belief in absolute good must mean recognition of God . . . but he has not realized this yet."

In the other tent they could not hear Wild's voice unless he led the other two in a burst of song during a rare lull in the wind. There was no lull that Sunday night, however, when they guessed the force of the gale reached at least 80 miles an hour and the tent was almost blown away over their heads. That day saw a major loss in their cold imprisonment. Joyce wrote, ". . . still blizzarding, our position serious. Stores running out, sick men not improving in their sleeping bags, dogs weakening from being laid up. . . . We are up against the biggest calamity of all—no kerosene for the primus."

The men were 10 miles from the Bluff depot, but in these conditions the stores deposited there might as well have been on another planet. To be without means of heat meant dying of thirst in a sea of frozen water. They still had a source of fuel, however. This was the small supply of methylated spirits which they carried to ignite the primus stove, and which they had used liberally to massage the tortured legs of the scurvy sufferers. Now the adept Dick Richards found a means to burn it in a crude spirit stove, which he adapted from the tin mug they had employed to share out the hoosh from the cooker. This proved to be an excruciatingly slow method of melting snow to water and heating the water enough to make weak tea, but it was a salve to their state of mind, as well as their bodies, and it eased a further reduction of rations. Still, even Joyce was despondent: "We are having a hell of a time . . . lying in the same spot for five days so that our bodies have melted a hollow in the ice. Our rations are down to one biscuit a day with a quarter-pint of pemmican—two biscuits for the dogs—to sustain what little strength we have left. We are frozen by night and starved by day."

By Tuesday, February 22, there was still no letup in the blizzard and Joyce held a solemn conference with Richards and the ailing Hayward. "We are on our last legs for food—but we have kept one final feed of pemmican for our dash to the Bluff, and that is some 10 or 11 miles away. If you agree, I think we should make up our minds to go in the morning, come what may! We shall have to trek or to submit to the same fate as Captain Scott and his comrades."

The dogs too were given the last of their food that night, an act that made the decision to march in the morning irrevocable.

When the next morning, Wednesday, brought no lessening of wind and whirling snow, Joyce tried shouting to the other tent the news of their decision to march on through the blizzard. The gale blew his words back into his teeth, so he crouched and went out into the storm and crossed to the other tent. He appeared before Wild and the two sick men coated in white, his beard flecked with snow, his eyes gleaming, and his manner solemn.

"We are warming our last meal of pemmican—and you must do the same. We are going to try and make the depot. Have your last meal and then we will help you take the tent down."

Captain Mackintosh appeared unwilling to stir. He said that he was "feeling somewhat off."

The veteran sledger grew grimmer, looking down his nose at the men in their reindeer bags and the Captain loath to face the lash of the weather. Sonorously he told them, "There is no choice! It is imperative we leave this camp, or we will all go under. We are on our last legs and weakening rapidly. Whatever the cost—we are going."

And then, just before he left the tent, he warned them, "Our food lies ahead and death stalks us from behind."

Football penguins

Coffin in the Ice

T hey formed a pathetic procession. In a closed sphere of wildly whirling snow the famished dogs were white moles floundering through the drift, while the men were shadowy figures, their heads bowed in weariness as they leaned in their harness. Ernest Joyce on the lead rope was merely a blur in the distance. On the sledge the figure of the Padre was a bundle lashed in a snow cloth against the flying flakes. At the rear, the Captain tottered piteously on crooked legs. Every man and every dog gulped great lungfuls of chill air, either in exhaustion or in pain. All movement, all effort was a striving of will against weakness of body and the buffeting blizzard wind.

It had been like that from the moment they decided not to lie and wait for death in the tents. When Joyce told Mackintosh they had decided to march rather than submit, Richards had noted Mackintosh seemed to have lost "all initiative and was quite content to remain. However, he agreed to make the effort and we set about digging out our equipment." So great were the layers of snow, 10 to 12 feet deep in places, that they found this work to be a "prodigious effort." It was then, Richards recorded, that they realized the extent to which hunger and inactivity had weakened them, how their strength had been sapped by the blizzard's assault. It took them all morning before they could drag the sledge to the Captain's tent, knock that down, wrap the recumbent Spencer-Smith in the snow sheet and lift him to the sledge. The sick man lost consciousness during the pain of movement.

They were not able to "set sail" until midafternoon, rigging the snow cloth against the bamboo spar to gain some impetus from the wind hammering at their backs. The wind force was as violent as ever, and the air was full of flying drift. Joyce felt apprehensive; they were marching in conditions they never would have faced if they had had adequate supplies of food, knowing that a slight error in direction could turn them from their course, to be lost for ever in the white wasteland. Richards checked the prismatic compass and watched the angle of the lead rope carefully, and he and Joyce tried to shout directions to each other against the howl of the wind.

They had little chance of going far in the afternoon. After a mere half-hour of trudging, Mackintosh collapsed, his head lolling back and the snow falling on his face and clogging his goggles. Richards caught him as he fell. His final shreds of resolution had been eroded by the increasing effect of scurvy and the lack of food, and his voice was so pitiable that Richards thought him delirious. With the agony of helplessness their commander was crying to them, "I'm done, I'm done for!" over and over. And then, "Oh, my hands! My hands are gone."

Richards felt deeply moved. He was to write in his diary, "I have never been so profoundly impressed with the change in a man's condition." Now he tried rough comfort, knowing every hour lost on the trail increased their peril. "Don't be a bloody fool, Mack. We'll get you a hot drink and then we'll go on again."

Mackintosh did not respond. He repeated that he was finished, that he had lost his hands to frostbite and could not go on any longer. Then he told them, "I don't care what happens. I don't care. Wrap me in a snow cloth and leave me here! I'm done for."

Richards comforted him again, still holding his body from falling into the snow. "We'll take care of you, Mack," he said. "We'll see you through."

The anguish of that time was still vivid in the mind of Dick Richards more than 60 years later, and recalling the harrowing situation still brought tears to his eyes. He remembered lifting the wasted body of the Captain and comforting him while the others threw up the tent against the force of the snow-filled wind: "No argument, Mack. We'll put you in the tent and make you comfortable, and then we'll go on to the depot and bring back food and fuel. You'll be right."

Joyce had his own memories of the crisis. He noted how he tried to jolly the Captain into a brighter frame of mind. "I felt I should cheer him at any cost. Some added strength came to my assistance and I remembered the wager we had made on our race to the Bluff a year before. I exclaimed, 'You Scotsman! What about my magnum of champagne?' This remark changed his thought waves. Even the Padre had to smile."

Grim facts had to prevail against brief humor, however. There were two invalids to be left in the tent, incapable of fending for themselves. Joyce and Richards, now in total command, quickly decided what should be done. It was essential, they agreed, to leave a fit man to care for the two scurvy victims. Hayward was now so far along that trail that he, too, might soon be helpless. The strongest men, Joyce and Richards, should make the attempt to reach the depot. That meant Ernie Wild would have to stay and care for the sick men. When they told the Yorkshireman of their plan he accepted reluctantly, acknowledging the wisdom of the decision. He had, after all, been tent mate to the Captain and had also cared for the Padre since his collapse at 83° South.

Richards recorded that the decision to leave Wild with Mackintosh and Spencer-Smith appeared to be the right one at the time. "He had been caring for the Padre all along with the utmost unselfishness, so it seemed the right course to follow. As things turned out it would perhaps have been better to have taken him with us."

The march to the depot and back would take four days at the very least, Joyce calculated. He, Richards and Hayward placed almost all their remaining food in the Captain's tent. This amounted to 16 biscuits, some four ounces of meat cubes, and a little chocolate. Optimistically, he told Ernie Wild to expect them back with rations and fuel by the following Sunday, February 27. "We shall bring you supplies by then if we find the depot," Joyce said. "If not? What then?" asked Wild. Joyce cheerfully replied, "We live in hopes of a fine day. We'll try to be back in four days." That would entail covering seven miles a day for three days, allowing for one day at the depot to stock up on food, feed themselves and the famished animals, and rest. "The situation looks far from promising," he wrote.

The parting was made as cheerful as their doubts would permit. Joyce took the lead rope, and with Richards and Hayward on each side of the dogs—big Oscar straining in the front—they tramped to the north. Within moments the small dome of the tent with the three men inside was lost to their vision, vanished in the swirl of blown drift and snowflakes. "So we left them there," Dick Richards told this writer. "When we left I had no idea whether we would ever see them again. In the blizzard we were not sure we could find that depot; and if we did, whether we would ever find the tent again in that wilderness."

Joyce wrote his version of that parting and of their brief march for the rest of the day, Wednesday, February 23: "We wished them goodbye and gave them a cheery parting. As we left, the blizzard came on us again with unabating fury. Even with an empty sledge, four dogs, sail set, we found we could not do more than half-a-mile an hour. The surface was so bad that sometimes we sank in up to the waist. After the tent was pitched I found my left foot badly frostbitten and blistered. We sat down to our banquet: one cup of tea, half a biscuit. The dogs did not give their cheerful bark that they always do when we camp for the night. Poor fellows—no food for them."

The blizzard was unceasing. All night it blew and blustered around them, the patched tent quaking under its impact. They could not rest too long; hungry and shivering in their thinning skin bags they were up and about soon after 4 in the morning. Richards melted some snow, cursing the nature of the last of the methylated spirits. "In normal times," he would recall, "you could put a match to the spirit and it would burst into flame. Down there it was so cold it had to be coaxed with match after match to start burning." When the water was warm enough, they made a weak infusion of tea and drank it thankfully while munching another half biscuit. They wasted no time in forcing on their frigid finneskoes and breaking camp.

The snow and wind were worse than on the previous day. They had great difficulty laying their course and were so weak now that every 15 minutes or so they would drop gasping for breath, their backs resting against the sledge for brief shelter. They came on banks of soft snow that stopped them in their tracks as though hidden brakes had been applied to their load. Then, with men and dogs heaving and straining, the sledge would be inched forward in a heartbreaking slow advance, each stint measured by only tens of yards. At best, with utmost exertion, they could not cover more than three miles in a good day. All dreams of trudging seven miles per diem were blown away by blasts of wind with a force they reckoned to be between 60 and 80 miles an hour, and were buried in the layers of fresh soft snow laid in their path.

Ernest Joyce remembered how a month previously this same team—three men and four dogs—had hauled a sledge with a lading of 1,380 pounds, covering at least 10 miles in a day. "As a comparison," he noted, "the weight of this sledge is about 200 pounds all told and, with the same team, making only two or three miles in a whole day."

They camped at noon that second day, exhausted from their efforts, and spent more than an hour in the torment of igniting the dribble of methylated spirits in the converted mug-stove in order to melt snow to hot water. They drank their weak tea and were compelled to halve their biscuit ration. Richards and Hayward went out to the sledge to prepare the dogs for another haul, but the battering gale almost blew them off their feet. They dragged the skin sleeping bags back into the tent, admitting it was impossible to march, and they lay there in the shaking tent with the cold and the hunger growing in them as the hours went by.

It was little more than 24 hours since they had left the other tent, and they had covered a miserable distance. Now they were so cold they felt they had to use more spirits to make a warm drink, but they would not make more inroads into their few biscuits. Joyce brought in the canvas tank they had used to haul the dog food, and in utter desperation they scraped the inside and the corners with their metal spoons for any shreds of seal meat and pemmican left adhering to the fabric. Joyce's diary relates that "it is a very scanty meal. I don't think I ever tasted anything worse, but it had to go down. This is the third day the dogs have been without food." Now it dawned on their minds that reaching the depot was critical not so much for themselves as for the starving animals. "Our idea is to push on to the depot to save the lives of the dogs," wrote Dick Richards, sitting in the tent that day. "The reason for this is a selfish one, since we know we cannot get back to safety if they give up."

The starving animals were already losing their spirit, all except the doughty Oscar. When they were bogged down in the deep drift, it had been beyond their strength to budge the stranded sledge. At those times of crisis some new surge of power was dredged from the lead dog, and Richards noted how "massive Oscar would lower his great head and pull as he never did when things were going well." His superb pulling power sometimes managed to add a little run to the sledge movement, and then the big dog would snap at the heels of the others to make them try harder.

"Perhaps that sounds rather fantastic, but it was true," Richards attested. "These dogs were as individual as humans and we had become very close to them indeed. We could recognize their moods. Like us, they had been on very short commons for many days, and it seemed that Oscar was aware that we were looking for something that would give him a full meal once more."

They were bound to slave in order to try and save the dogs, because that meant saving the three men they had left behind in the tent. All their energy, all their strength of being were now bent towards reaching the citadel, the depot near Minna Bluff. So consuming was this fight for distance that they gave little thought to the problem of finding the tent again—it was somewhere back along the trail, but exactly where they did not know.

When the blizzard had first blotted out the world for them, somewhere near Captain Scott's grave, they had lost their guiding cairns. When Mackintosh collapsed they had not known whether they were to the east or the west of that line of snow blocks they had laid on the outward journey. And there was a further uncertainty: In the frenetic drive to cover the distance to 80° South they had discarded any equipment they considered not vital. Among the items dumped was their sledge meter, an apparatus with a wheel attached to the rear of the sledge, which measured the distance they covered. Thus they had no sure knowledge of how far they had gone, or whether they were on one side or the other of the cairns that would guide them to the depot. "We were weak and the gusting wind would make us stagger; we marched into a white void and could see nothing," Richards recalled.

They sat fearful in their fragile tent that night of Thursday, February 24. Joyce, "The wind came on worse than ever at 8:30. I am afraid the tent will be the next thing to go, and then it will be all up with us. . . . Trusting in Providence for a fine day tomorrow." Their very breaths and the faint steam from melting the snow to drink were a menace, for the vapor caked into stiff ice on the tent fabric, making it brittle and ready to split from the severe buffeting. Richards was concerned with the problem of direction and navigation. His diary read, "It is hard to know what course to pursue when a wrong decision means wasting the working efficiency of our meagre food. A false start means a meal wasted. . . . It is very cold." And there was more to it than the danger of wasting a meal. Unsure of how much ground they were covering, they could easily overshoot the depot—and "never find the succour that awaits us in that featureless wilderness."

The blizzard fell away for a few hours that night, but Joyce's fine day did not come. Instead it snowed heavily, blocking all hope of seeing anything beyond a yard or two. Without wind on their backs to give them a sense of direction, they could not march. They could even have gone back on their tracks without being aware of it. When the wind came again, at 4 in the morning, they started to prepare for the trail. It took three hours to make the weak tea, knock down the tent, carefully furl it against the brittle ice splitting the fabric, and set off north again.

They made a faltering cavalcade, forced to stop every five or 10 minutes to catch their breath and check their direction, always with nagging uncertainty in their minds. Setting the scene and their predicament, Richards wrote, "Sun shining somewhere through the murk— we cannot see where it is—heavy wind and snowfall. We do not know how we stand in relation to the depot or whether in thick weather we have strayed from our course. We are very weak. The huskies work pluckily but they are obviously weak—no food for two nights; Con very groggy. The method of heating takes a great deal of time; a meal of a mug of tea doesn't stay with us very long."

The wind and the flight of the blown snow was their guide. Richards recorded, "It was my job, being nearest the sledge, to lay the course. This could only be done when we halted. . . . In the cold, with bare fingers, it was possible only to struggle with the metal of the prismatic compass for a few seconds before it had to be put away and the hands returned to the mittens." He laid the course along the angle of the rope that stretched ahead of the sledge, moving Joyce in the lead trace to right or left each time they halted. "There was nothing to guide him to keep a straight course, and the best we could do was to note how the rope lay in relation to the direction of the wind on our backs, or over our shoulders—to go on for 15 minutes in this way then stop, and check again."

At midday on Friday, February 25, the heaviest snowfall of the long-lasting blizzard fell and the wind rose again to its former savagery. They were now completely out of food of any kind—other than the crumbs from the biscuits they and the dogs had eaten. The young man's diary told a dismal tale: "Impossible to travel. Have to wait until storm abates. We do not know how we stand in regards to the depot or whether we have strayed off course."

Crouched down under the brittle covering of the tent they had scavenged from the dump at Cape Evans, their minds turned to the famous tragedy that had happened hereabouts on this terrible ice plain. Joyce wrote, "We speak often of my late chief, of Captain Scott and his party. . . . If we had prolonged our stay in the tent another day I feel sure we would have remained powerless to get under way again. We would have shared a similar fate. . . . If the worst comes we have made up our minds to carry on and die in harness on the track."

Their danger increased that night. Joyce feared they had already passed the depot. There was no food and no spirits left to heat their drink. Then the tent split again down the front, near the tunnel entrance. Vic Hayward was nearing a breakdown. Formerly a beefy man with a taciturn manner, he was changed. Toil, hunger, and scurvy had eaten away the substance of his resistance. Joyce noted, "I am doubtful if Hayward can stand the strain another day. He is down in the dumps and strange." Chosen by Shackleton for his experience in the cold north of Canada, Hayward was now near to babbling in distraction and distress, and played no part in the torment of repairing the tent. Richards and Joyce took turns squatting in the 60-mile wind, with the temperature down to 20 degrees below freezing, passing the needle back and forth while the calico food bags were stitched over the rent in the fabric.

There was no comfort of a hot drink to be had when the task was finished, and so they curled up in their skin bags to try and restore some warmth in their frozen limbs, and were then shocked to hear Hayward ranting about the food outside the tent, in the snow. "We can have meat," he was saying. "We can kill one of the dogs and eat its flesh. That would keep us alive."

Richards was horrified. Joyce sat upright in his bag and stared at the man. "Don't you know," he asked, "that it will put us all in jeopardy to lose a single one of those dogs? Not just us, Vic, but our comrades back there in the other tent! We depend on them to trek us in. If we lose one then it will mean goodbye for all of us."

Richards tried to cheer the depressed man by saying the blizzard had to let up soon, and that tomorrow could be a clear day in which they would find the cairns and reach the depot. Suddenly Joyce remembered lines from his favorite poet, whom he introduced, much to the delight of Richards, as the Kipling of Canada—Robert Service. He quoted,

> It's the plugging away that will win you the day
> So don't be a piker, old pard!
> Just draw on your grit; it's so easy to quit:
> It's the keeping-your-chin-up that's hard.

The words gave all three of them encouragement. Joyce scribbled in his diary that "after this poor Hayward took in another couple of holes in his belt to stay the gnawings of hunger and was more his old self."

Through the last hours of Friday, February 25, the vicious winds tore at the tattered tent. The three men lay in the skin bags, which were now little more than frosted shrouds; their bodies were ice-cold without food or fuel, and hope was dwindling along with the diminishing warmth of life. Feeble and famished, they no longer had even the luxury of shivering. The fight of internal vital organs to maintain a flow of blood tortured their bodies into violent heaving, a convulsive jerking to force a flow from the slowing blood circulation. Sleep was totally impossible; they were allowed only short periods of exhaustion between the onsets of spasmodic jumping. Their plight was at its most desperate; they were at their lowest ebb, moving inevitably towards surrender into cold death. They fell into apathetic silence; and then, an hour after midnight, the silence extended about them. For the first time in endless days of howling wind and chaotic snowstorms, there was quiet. The tent fabric was limp above their heads, and there was no swish of the frozen flakes on the fabric. There was a stillness that Ernest Joyce found "uncanny."

Suspicious that this was only a momentary lull, they crawled from the tent to stare southward. Without the gale flinging drift into their faces, they could see a break in the southeast, among the lowering snow clouds. It was a hope of the finer weather that Richards had wished for a few hours earlier. Yet he cautioned against being too ready to press onward to the north. They might already have overshot the depot, and so would never find the cairns leading to its location. On reflection, however, they saw they had no alternative to marching, other than to turn into the sleeping bags and stay in this camp until death overtook them or the gales ripped their shelter to shreds.

Breaking camp was a simple operation. There was no fuel to melt snow, no food to be eaten, only the tent to be knocked down and stowed on the sledge with their bags, and the dogs to be readied and harnessed. So great was their weakness, though, that every movement was an effort of will. The start to the north was faltering, with both men and dogs reeling and tottering. Richards recorded, "We could move no more than a few yards at a time, so short was our wind."

This painful process of feeling their way forward was made in a difficult light and no wind, with only the angle of the rope against the sledge to guide them. Then, after nearly an hour, the younger man lifted his eyes to look despairingly at the wasteland ahead and saw a blur, a smudge of dark color against the pervading whiteness. The flag above their depot appeared in the distorting diffraction of light to be only a few yards in front of them. In reality, it was three-quarters of a mile distant. The sighting brought joy and sudden release. The effect on the dogs, said Joyce, "was electric. They gave a joyful howl, the first we had had from them in six days." For the shambling Vic Hayward, however, the sighting relaxed the coil of tension in his mind and he fell against the sledge, yielding to the pain of his swollen legs, his resolution dissolved, his will to go on banished.

This collapse put a new strain on Richards and Joyce. The dogs wanted to race with their last energies to the depot, but Hayward, lolling helplessly, had to be helped onto the sledge and covered with a sleeping bag. Then they had to cross that great gulf of snow and ice that lay between them and the food and fuel that was life for them all. It was the longest three-quarters of a mile they had ever known. The trek took them two hours to accomplish, and then another hour was spent erecting the tent. "My God," Richards entered in his diary, "but we were terribly weak." Ernest Joyce, describing their simple tasks, remarked how feeble they had become from starvation and toil, for in ordinary circumstances a tent could be spread in five minutes. Joyce reflected: "If this depot had not been sighted today we could never have pitched that tent again. I do not think there has ever been a weaker party to arrive at a depot—Arctic or Antarctic."

There was further cause for depression of their spirits. They had been so many long weeks fighting their way across the ice to the foot of the polar plateau and back that they longed for some contact, some link with other men, with the outside world. There had been an arrangement that if the ship came back to Cape Evans, a party would push down to the Bluff to leave word. Now they found a tin with a note tied to a bamboo pole, but it was from Cope saying how he, Gaze, and Jack had won through to here with their faulty primus. But there was no word other than that reassuring news. No soul had been here with tidings of *Aurora*, and that blank cut deep into their emotions. The ship was their symbol of a link with the world, a symbol that had not materialized. They could only take the most pessimistic view. Dick Richards was gloomy and apprehensive: "I think she must have gone down with all hands." Thus their relief at reaching food and shelter was overshadowed by fears for the future.

The first demand on their strength was now to be the rescue of the three men waiting in the tent back along the southern trail, but before they set out the faithful dogs had to be given food and rest. Hayward was ensconced in the tent, and the other two men began the laborious job of digging through the snow layers for the cases of stores that had been somewhat scattered by the blizzard. First they found dog pemmican and biscuits and fed the animals. The men expected that the dogs would fall on the food with wolfish appetite. Yet some caution inherent in their nature prevailed, and the animals ate slowly and carefully, setting an example to the starving men. The need for restraint became apparent after Richards uncovered the supply of oil and methylated spirits, which had been stored separately to prevent it permeating the food supplies. For the comfort it would bring, they lit the primus and reveled in its roar and blue glow. They melted snow and mixed a dried milk preparation, but when they drank this mixture they could not keep it down. They tried again, this time mixing the drink with oatmeal for substance, and this proved successful. They spent the next few hours repairing their footwear and the new tears in the tent fabric, then they had a weak dish of hoosh and biscuit. "We can feel strength returning to our bodies," Joyce noted, "then we must get our legs in trim for the walk back to our comrades." The food restored Hayward to effective duty. He and Richards worked on arranging the stores in the depot, and selecting and packing those they would haul back to the Captain's tent. The depot was "untidy," Richards found, and it took some effort to put it in order. This done, they determined that they would start back along the trail at 5 the next morning. They retired to their bags fed and warm.

At 8 in the morning the weather defeated their plans. The wind came in at hurricane force and they sat fearful in the shaking tent, waiting for a chance to march south again. "Impossible to see anything," Richards wrote. "We are sitting on our bags, waiting. Dogs and men could not face this, even if a course could be steered. This is awful—held up here knowing that three men are starving—and worse, deathly cold, 10 or 12 miles back."

The blizzard had now raged for more than 10 days, and still great gouts of snow blew over their shelter, smothering their equipment and dogs under toilsome layers, which would demand more strenuous work to remove before their journey of relief could begin. The comforting roar of the primus was little competition against the howl of the angry polar wind. Joyce made an entry in his diary: "Weather continues with fury. Expecting any minute to have the tent blown from over us. This is the longest blizzard I have ever experienced in this country. We have not had one real travelling day in eleven days. The amount of snow that has fallen is incredible, and it is essential that we track south. The Skipper and his party have been without food now for at least five days. We must reach our companions soon." And this was Sunday—

February 27, the day he had assured Ernie Wild they would be back with supplies—and here they sat in the shaking tent waiting for conditions to abate just enough so that they could sight the angle of the rope against the alignment of the sledge.

The delay was not without its benefit, however. They had time to eat another mug of hoosh and drink tea, enabling them to recuperate further after their ordeal of traveling while starved. They had time to inspect one another's condition as well, all three aware that their hope of life depended to different degrees on the others. Each man bore the unmistakable stamp of advancing scurvy. All three had swollen gums falling down over their teeth and turning jet black. Vic Hayward claimed to be feeling much better, but he found it painful to move and obviously could not walk properly. Richards examined the man's legs and saw he had great areas of blue-black bruising from ankle to hip, the same signs they had seen on Padre and Mackintosh. The young Australian spent an hour using his strong hands to massage doses of methylated spirits into the affected legs, and afterward Hayward claimed the treatment had improved his condition.

By noon they had finished the hours of slow preparation. Joyce decided to hitch on an empty sledge that had been left at the bluff depot, fully expecting that they would have two invalids to drag across the 100-odd miles to Safety Camp. The main sledge was no longer the featherweight it had been when they arrived; they now had more than 200 pounds weight of food and fuel aboard, and with their equipment and extra sledge were dragging a total weight of 500 pounds. Not suprisingly, they found they could not shift their load. "We were unaware till then of the full extent the march to Beardmore had weakened us and robbed us of condition," Dick Richards recorded. "The lay-up and the march to the Bluff searched out our weakness." And he recalled, "We had joked at times about how we had taken the Captain's party with us to the Beardmore to see the southernmost depot. We had been confident then in our strength. We wished we had more of it now."

They fought for 20 minutes and covered only 10 yards; then they upended the sledges and scraped and cleaned the runners to start again. The dogs were angry, ready to fight each other, snarling at the men, and unwilling to pull. They would not start south again. Richards declared, "The beggars know the way to Hut Point. Turn them to the north, Joyce! Then we can make a circle and track back." The tactic worked, and Joyce wrote later, "They are cute. They had seen enough of the glories of the southern trail and knew the northward was homeward bound. I turned them northward and at once I was on my back with my legs in the air!"

Although the dogs were fooled into breaking a homeward trail, the blizzard had laid a barrier of snow that restricted their progress to less than half a mile for each hour of slaving toil. The scurvied legs of the men sank into the soft surface, and each yard made the sledge load seem heavier. Joyce grew increasingly irritable and uncomfortable. "His finneskoes are more hole than foot," Richards noted, "and all day he had frozen snow coming in on his feet. It was impossible to mend them at night because the light has gone from the evening. This has been one of the hardest days I have put in."

All the long afternoon they butted southwards with the relentless blizzard flinging the sheets of snow at them. Then the sky began to darken, and they had no means of lighting. They were forced to camp at last in the late evening, while they could still see well enough to pitch the tent, tether and feed the four dogs, and cook their own meal. Hayward was "painfully stiff," and Richards spent the last of the daylight rubbing methylated spirits into his legs. They crawled into the iced sleeping bags to gain some rest during the dark hours, the gale slapping the tent against the bamboo poles.

They were up again at six on the morning of February 28, but their chores took them three hours to accomplish: Joyce sewing food bags over his footwear, Richards rubbing more spirits into Hayward's legs, then feeding dogs and men and digging out their equipment. Joyce ached to make a forced march to reach the stranded men, and so they struggled against the bad surface for the remaining hours until noon, then a torrent of snow clogged their faces, the wind rose again and they could not see to steer. Laboriously they put up the tent, weary and dispirited that they had not reached their goal, though they believed they were in the vicinity. Hoping against hope, they stood outside the tent and yelled into the south wind, but heard nothing in answer except the howl of the blizzard.

The enmity of the hostile ice shelf turned more menacing that night. Hour after hour they had been watching the snowstorm in the wind from the south, waiting and hoping for a break in which they could search for the other tent. Richards kept watch while Hayward and Joyce tried to sleep. To occupy his mind, Richards made one of the lengthier entries in his diary: "Heavy snow . . . Have shouted with no response. A last hope. We knew we could not go farther as we might overshoot their tent. . . . I know I cannot sleep with the thought of those men starving and cold, perhaps within a short distance of help. One keeps wondering how it will all end." And then he recaptured all the travail and disasters that had struck them since they went on from 83° South to lay the Mount Hope depot with food and fuel they now so badly needed. "And now here we are, waiting for this [word undecipherable] to cease. And this seems the end of Mackintosh's folly in going South when done himself and in the company of another done man . . . And now it is too cold on the fingers and I'll stop."

Concern deepened again when he massaged Hayward's legs and then examined his own. The youngest and strongest man left in the party, he had to write, "I'm sorry—I have the dreaded black appearance on the back of my legs, although up to the present it has given me no trouble." In his mind's eye he could see Spencer-Smith starting to falter and the way the condition had slowly defeated the Captain and crushed his will to persist. The young Australian wrote in his diary again, "Hayward is in the same condition, as I fear I will be shortly." And then, "It is distressing to reach here and be prevented by the thick weather from rendering them aid. We can only wait here and look out at 10-minute intervals. I fear what we will find on arriving. . ."

The dark thought was with him as he stared across the space of flying, whirling snow. Death was almost certain to have come to that tent by now. In retrospect Richards would say, "Spencer-Smith was already very weak when we left them there six days previously and they had very little food. I thought he was probably dead. It didn't take much imagination to think that he had slipped his cable."

The days had been without end in the lonely tent. The battering of the blizzard wind had been ceaseless for nearly 11 days, except for one brief let up when Wild was able to peer from the tunnel and discern the hazy shape of Minna Bluff, the point of rescue for which Joyce, Richards and Hayward had set off more than a week before. The stricken Padre had not moved in all that time, and all his needs had been attended by Ernie Wild. Defiantly, with great restraint, they had eked their scrap of food out across the days of the week while they were storm-bound.

It was Monday, February 28, and Mackintosh had recovered enough to get to his feet without help. He now calculated that the other party had been gone a full four days, to cross a distance he reckoned was about nine miles. With that thought, and in his illness, a sense of impending doom settled on his mind. He sat in his sleeping bag and— not too many miles from where Captain Scott, four years earlier, had done this same thing—took from his canvas holder a writing pad, the same lined pad on which he had written the agreement with Richards regarding the southern journey, and on which he had inscribed the formal instructions to Ernest Joyce to proceed south.

In pencil, Mackintosh wrote his letter of farewell to the world. "I leave this record in the event of anything happening to the party. Today we have finished the last of our food. A blizzard has been blowing for 11 days with the exception of one day when the wind fell light, when the horizon could be discerned as well as land round the Bluff. We were left here four days previously in order that Joyce, Hayward, and Richards could travel with dogs and a light sledge to Bluff Depot more easily, returning to us with food of which there is a plentiful supply at the Bluff."

When a week had elapsed on a round-trip journey of less than 20 miles, he still clung to the notion that each hour brought relief nearer, "We now expect succour to reach us any time from today, in which case we shall be saved from starvation and these lines will be unnecessary. Yet, I take precaution to leave this should I become too weak and the cold make it harder to write. Smith and myself are stricken with scurvy, the former being helpless and weak. I am able to stand, yet becoming more feeble daily. Wild has signs of scurvy, but is still able to move his hands and feet, and with a meal could travel, and this I am afraid cannot be the same with Smith and myself."

His hands were cold, his fingers stiffening, and the writing straggled as he continued: "We have not yet given up hope, for we trust our comrades. Time passes, in spite of empty stomachs, and we argue, sing and talk during the day and anyone coming along would imagine us to be a picnic party."

Ernie Wild was the unsung hero of this effort to maintain morale in the tent, leading them into songs, prompting discussion on what had happened in the war, avoiding the worrisome question of what had happened to the ship, and regaling them with tales of his boyhood in Yorkshire. He told them how his eldest brother, Frank, had run away to sea at the age of 16 and had been to Australia in the wooden sailing ship *Sobraon*, before joining the Royal Navy and winning a place on Antarctic expeditions, and how he had marched with Shackleton to within 97 miles of the South Pole. If anyone gave their perilous position the character of a picnic party, it was most certainly Ernie Wild. Mackintosh paid his own tribute to Wild's service as he continued his farewell letter, explaining how they'd reached the edge of disaster.

"Briefly, and I feel glad to say that it has not been due to any lack of organization. We have done the work we came down here to do, the laying of a depot at Mount Hope for Sir Ernest Shackleton. We made splendid progress travelling homeward, as much as 18 miles a day (geographical) and this with Smith on the sledge. We filled up with a fortnight's provisions at 80° South as our previous experience had warned us against this region Moore Bay. Instead of doing the trip in a week we have been 11 days getting to within nine miles of the big depot on 18 February, since which date we have been camped."

Now he had to record the painful fact of his own collapse. He wrote, "With the exception of Smith we were able to travel until the blizzard came upon us, when we were laid up six days. After that period when we made a fresh start, I had to admit defeat owing to my inability to stand the strain, our lay-up making me weaker—legs black and blue, gums black and swollen." And that was it—there was no more about his condition, and nothing on the loss of the ship, nor of the loss of the main dog teams in the previous season and its contribution to the danger they all now faced.

"The above roughly explains how we were left here," he continued. "Wild, who could have gone on, preferred to stay here and help us, good unselfish fellow that he is. It must be explained that with the exception of the first trip from the Bluff we have had no fresh food since 9 October. Hence the disease has taken a stronger hold on us than the other party who had the opportunity of reaching Hut Point.

"Yet I leave it on record that all have done their duty, nobly and well. The rest of our simple adventures can be explained by this note, also by other members of the party. This is all that I can say—and if it is God's will that we should have given up our lives then we do so in the British manner as our tradition holds us in honour bound to do. Goodbye, friends. I feel sure my dear wife and children will not be neglected. Signed Aeneas Mackintosh: Commander, I.T.A.E."

This tragic letter was not the last thing that Shackleton's southern commander would write. It was, however, his last message to survive.

Soon after striking camp on the morning of the last day of February in that leap year of 1916, the keen eyes of Dick Richards saw the blur in the white rolling drift to the south—less than half a mile distant from where they had spent the past anxious night. At once the dogs had an objective and started to yelp with excitement. In the tent, Ernie Wild heard their barking above the sound of the wind and clambered through the tunnel entrance to stand staring at the hazy figures of the men and dogs hauling the sledge towards him.

After living on starvation rations for a week, haggard from the strain of caring for two invalids, he at once reached for his sledge harness and tottered towards the three men to help pull the sledge across the remaining distance. Richards and Joyce were touched by this gesture. Richards noted in his brief diary, "Thank the fates all are alive. Wild is a great chap. What broke us up on meeting was the fact that when he heard the dogs he unemotionally reached for his harness to come and help us in. We had had three days' food by then but he had had little or nothing for six days. Some of us broke down and cried."

The noise brought Captain Mackintosh from the tent and Joyce recorded the reunion. "Poor Mack, he crawled from the tent very weak, could just stagger and started to thank us profusely for our journey. He told me they owed their lives to us. I told Wild to cook them some food . . . but not to eat too much in case of reaction."

Joyce had fully expected to find at least one death in the tent. Instead, he wrote, "The Padre, poor fellow, has had to stay in his wet sleeping-bag and is very weak." The urge was to leave the sick man undisturbed for as long as possible, but they could not risk delay; every hour was now crucial in the fight to reach Hut Point some 100 miles to the north. They had no choice but to start as soon as possible. With three sick men—two almost helpless and one totally incapable—they would have to push on and travel in all weathers. Although these men had been without a hot meal for nine days and had lived on scraps for a week, Joyce decided they would try to move at once. It took them an hour to dig the Captain's dome-shaped tent free from the wall of snow, and then they prepared the two sledges toggled together, each one to be a couch for a sick man.

Mackintosh again decided to try and walk, and with the aid of ski-poles he went hobbling ahead in a half-squatting stance. By the time he had covered about 50 yards and had fallen into the snow, they were lifting the figure of the long-suffering Padre onto the sledge. In pain from all movement, the brave man reminded Joyce that they had made a tryst to meet in London to take some cheer to the homeless men who slept on London's Embankment.

Richards and Joyce carefully strapped him into his sleeping bag on the sledge, so that the jolting would not dump him in the snow; then they lifted the tent floor cloth to put over him as protection against the blown drift. Beneath the cloth they saw a deep recess which the Padre's unmoving body had melted away during the 12 days he had lain there. It had the shape of a human form; and they knew that if they had missed finding the Bluff depot, and failed to return with food, that recess would have formed a coffin in the ice for the uncomplaining clergyman.

* * *

On February 29, 1916, the day of the six men's reunion on the Great Ross Ice Shelf, Ernest Shackleton and his castaways were holding a celebration on the drifting ice floe in the Weddell Sea they had named "Ocean Camp." "More to cheer the men than for any other reason," Shackleton recalled, "we used the last of our cocoa." From then on their only beverage—other than a very occasional drink of a weak mixture of dried milk—would be water. Their midday meal was merely a biscuit, but then a special treat came lumbering from the water onto the ice platform: a huge sea-leopard. Ernie Wild's brother Frank immediately snatched up a rifle and shot the great beast. When the carcass was flensed of its blubber and butchered, they found several undigested fish in the stomach. Frank Hurley scaled these and they were fried in the blubber fat over the crude stove. Shackleton wrote, "So we had our only fresh fish meal during the whole of our drift on the ice."

Spencer-Smith

Chapter 8

The Bamboo Cross

The blizzard gave them little respite. From the moment they left their camp of reunion the polar gale seemed to grow stronger and colder. Raking down from the frigid plateau and sweeping over the vast open ice plain, its frozen fingers probed their tattered clothing and touched their skin with red blotches of frostbite. Yet this ill wind also blew some good for the straggling caravan of sick and faltering men. It came from behind, filling their snow-cloth sail with wind and making progress possible. They were so weak now that without its force they could not have begun to move the sledges forward. Furthermore, it meant that the four dogs were not hampered by the drift stinging their eyes.

Those four incredible animals had earned undying admiration from the men. Rangy now from months of incessant work, cold conditions, and poor food, tough Oscar held the leadership without flagging, his big bony head thrust forward, shoulders straining into his harness, and growling with anger when the wind fell away and the heavy sledge dragged them to a halt. Con, Towser and Gunner also knew they were traveling north—towards shelter, warmth and fresh food. As long as the strength of these animals lasted, Earnest Joyce knew the men had a chance to survive.

Even with the help of wind and dogs, the men covered a bare three miles in the final hours of leap year day, 1916. When the light was dimming about them, they made their awkward camp, with its time-consuming routine. They unpacked the invalids, spread the first cloth, erected Mackintosh's tent, lifted and carried the fainting Spencer-Smith inside, then carried Mackintosh in. After that they repeated the ordeal with their own tent—an effort demanding extra care so as not to split the brittle canvas or rip apart the rough patching with the calico food bags. Next there were the dogs to tether and feed, a task that fell on Richards, while Joyce and Wild unpacked the sledges and carried cookers, stoves, sleeping bags, and rations into the two tents. Then came the curses as frozen fingers fumbled with matches to ignite the spirits that had been poured into the metal tray around the primus burner, to start the heat that would melt the snow packed in the cooker can and warm the solid pemmican into a hot mash.

Joyce was dejected that night, as he faced in his mind the responsibility of leading this party of sick and sickening men across the toughest hundred miles of their long journey. He viewed the prospect as "tragic." A man lay on each sledge, helpless and immobile; another was very seriously incapacitated, hanging on the sledge as they hauled. The men doing the work were all sickening as well, everyone hit by the dread scurvy. "The sun has not been out for weeks and our sleeping-bags are wet through and worn out. Our clothes are in tatters, our finneskoes in a dilapidated condition, tied up with spare food-bags. My feet badly frostbitten. Hope to reach the depot tomorrow. Poor Padre . . . he has a wonderful spirit and is very cheerful."

But a brave face and a cheerful smile concealing pain could neither mask grim facts nor prevent the setbacks and shocks they would suffer in this fight for life. "What a prospect," Joyce exclaimed. "A hundred miles to go, with Richie, Wild and I already pretty weak. I dare not set a course to cut corners as I did on the way out. I cannot risk it with three sick men." There could be no dashing over the snow bridges, across hidden crevasses near the long arm of Minna Bluff or close to the rocky islands. They would have to veer out into the ice shelf and tramp north, in hope, to Safety Camp. The distress into which they had now come weighed heavily on the veteran's mind that night, costing him needed sleep. On his shoulders rested the responsibility of guiding this handful of relics into the shelter of Discovery Hut—with the helpless men, himself, Wild, Richards and the four worn-down dogs all ill for want of fresh meat that they could not hope to reach until they were off the cursed Barrier and near the tide cracks.

A hundred miles to go! If they were lucky with the wind and made five miles a day, and suffered only brief lay-ups from blizzards, then they would still be another three long weeks on the trail, growing steadily weaker and weaker. What would be the outcome? Would the price of their folly in working those first dog teams to death last season and in not putting equipment and stores ashore from *Aurora* be that they would die in their tracks, perishing on the ice of the shelf?

The memory of Captain Scott remained with Joyce when the men climbed out of their icy sleeping bags at dawn the next morning to face the haul to the depot at Minna Bluff. Even after three hours of toilsome preparation, spent breaking camp and stacking gear and invalids on the sledges, the fate of Scott and his last two companions Wilson and Bowers hovered on the edge of Joyce's mind—so much so that when he observed a dark smudge to one side soon after starting he told himself this was the flag over the cairn that had been erected over their three bodies. In the fearful conditions under which his party plodded north-ward, Joyce could be forgiven for forgetting that Scott's grave was actually well south of their present position. The men had been out now for six months, fighting the hostility of this terrible ice plain and its lethal climate. In this season alone they had come close to slogging across 1,500 miles of snow and ice to lay the Shackleton depots, with no other support but their own muscle and sinew and the four dogs— Trojans that they were. This matchless journey had come after the hard season of 1915 and the disasters of the winter. Death was most certainly at their backs now, for they were frail wraiths compared with the sturdy men who set out south to the Beardmore.

Petty Officer Ernest Mills Joyce felt the weight of his responsibility very heavily indeed, and on this first day of March he decided it was critical that they reach the big depot at the Bluff as soon as possible. Once there, the nagging worry of being caught again in a long blizzard without enough food and fuel would be lifted from his mind. From then on they would be able to eat, and to burn the primus just to keep warm in the tent—luxury indeed! That was something they could strive for!

It was a long, hard slog to the depot. They began in a whirl of drift soon after 8 in the morning with the godsend of a gusting wind at their backs. The temperature was now well below freezing as they fought through drift that clung like rough sand on the sledge runners, and over uneven outcrops of ice that sent the sledges bouncing and bucking so that Captain Mackintosh, who was not as limp as the Padre, was twice thrown off the rear sledge into the snow. In the trance-like state in which the men were hauling on their traces, his fall went unnoticed the second time until Wild happened to see that the sledge was empty of its passenger. Richards and Joyce trudged back to find Mackintosh lying in the snow.

As the two men helped him back to the sledge, Joyce admonished him with a warning: "You must shout if you fall off, Mack! Shout loud so we'll hear you, otherwise we will have to leave you here. We won't be able to come back."

Pitifully, Mackintosh replied, "And a good job, too."

During a brief clearing of the air that long day, the men had a sight to cheer their hearts and give them added hope. For the first time since they had marched south from the Bluff to lay the distant depot at the foot of the Beardmore, they saw Mount Erebus standing against the northern sky, belching its continual column of smoke and steam. It was a massive signpost to safety, for they knew that a few miles nearer than the mountain were the shelter and the tide cracks where the easygoing seals would be lolling and flopping on the ice. "Oh yes," Dick Richards enthused, "that lovely mountain—Erebus is a fine mountain—was beautiful to see, just like seeing home in front of you." Also in view was Minna Bluff, with its food aplenty, and the magnificent Mount Discovery and Mount Lister rising from the western Victoria Land, all symbols of a familiar landscape after the months on the dreary monotony of the ice shelf.

When, at the end of that long day of laborious hauling, they came at last to the depot, it was evening with the light already fading. Richards saw the poor dogs, their eyes pathetic with questioning, sagging from the same weariness that burdened his own young frame. It had been one of the hardest days they had known together, and they all deserved their expected meal of hot mash. However, there was to be no immediate hot food for dogs or men. Instead, the team was faced with a sudden crisis—the shock of critical loss. The poles to the conical tent were missing. Without them it was useless—without them life-saving shelter was gone.

Richards wrote in retrospect of that moment: "For too many weeks our condition had been getting lower and lower. We had been losing the power of concentration and this had bred carelessness in which we took risks. We were not so meticulous in packing and lashing the gear on our sledges as we needed to be. Now this loss put us in a perilous situation. Without those tent poles I would say that our goose had been cooked."

Despairingly he clambered onto the higher of the two sledges and held the cold rims of the old binoculars against his eyes to peer back through the drift-filled air and the dying light. He was trembling with relief as he told his worried companions, "There's something dark back there. Keep your fingers crossed it's our bloody tent poles."

Dick Richards did not hesitate to face the extra mile or two to collect the lost poles. There was no question in his mind as to who should make the extra journey. His readiness to walk for another hour was consistent with the traits that Joyce had come to admire in his tent mate and would later cause the veteran to say, "Every quality one needed to find in a companion on the ice shelf was in Richie's heart."

Richards shrugged off the matter. "Of course I was the mug who had to go back! I was the youngest and then probably the strongest of the party. Joyce could have gone, but then I always tried to ease things for him by doing the heavy chores about the camp. I thought of him then as an old man, nearing 40 he was, in the way young men in the early 20s think of a man that age. It seemed right I should go, and I went." He found the poles near where Mackintosh had fallen into the snow, some three-quarters of a mile back along the track. When he got back to the depot and they put up the tent, he fell into his sleeping bag, noting, "I am more exhausted than at any time on this long journey."

The men were all so toil-worn and ill that night that the other disappointment on reaching the depot did not seem to register in their minds. Not until just before they started their trek the following morning did Joyce note the fact in his diary: "There is no word here about the ship." He had held to the quiet hope that *Aurora* had been carried away with the bay ice and would have broken free by now, and that when they came to the edge of the Barrier she would be there in open water near Hut Point, waiting for them. Dick Richards, with some rest and hot food in him, looked back to when they tottered into this depot at the height of the long blizzard, seeking only food and heat for themselves and the three men back along the trail. "I think our senses were dulled by our poor physical condition, and though there was no news for us at Minna Bluff—as Joyce had arranged—it made only passing impact on our minds. We had food now and could turn some of our thoughts to other matters. We knew more certainly that we were condemned to spend a second—and probably much harder—winter in the Antarctic. We doubted whether the ship was afloat at all."

On the morning of March 2 they took their new provisions from the depot. Joyce listed these as four weeks' supply for his party, thereby leaving six weeks' supply for Shackleton and his men. He also sat in the tent before it was collapsed and wrote a note to Shackleton recounting their situation and what had happened. This was sealed in a tin and tied to one of the flag masts. Shortly before 10 the slow progress began again in heavy drift with a southwest wind, the veteran "thanking Providence that the last part of the endless trek had begun."

By noon that day the wind again attacked them, rising in strength to an estimated 60-mile-an-hour blow, and they managed only two hours of travel before putting up the tents for a rest. In the strong wind, and with their weakness, this took more than an hour. They had a brief lunch and then emerged to try and march again. Joyce noted, "The drift had been so thick that when we came out of the tents after our break the only thing showing above the snow was the mast of the front sledge." Nonetheless they tried to march, going once more through the chilling job of digging out their gear and the dogs and getting men and animals into harness and on the move. Determined and desperate to cover the miles, they kept on until after 8 in the evening, when Joyce was stimulated by judging they had marched some 12 miles that day. The south wind had helped them well along their way, but the next day they were trapped by its strength. The Joyce diary reads, "It has been blowing a howling blizzard all night. Found to our utter disgust it is impossible to travel . . . another few long hours in these rotten bags."

For some of these anxious hours they could keep their minds from their increasing plight by repairing what they could of their clothing and their sledging garments, as well as those precious mittens they wore inside their gloves. All this time Joyce watched his sick tent mate. The formerly brawny man, Vic Hayward, was causing deep concern. Richards noticed how the man was losing his mental grasp; his speech was slurring and at times he talked nonsense. Joyce listed more obvious symptoms of scurvy: ". . . gums swollen and turning black; joints of legs also swollen and turning black; feet can hardly bear any pressure on them; elbows stiff and sore, pupils of eyes enlarged. So, no mistake—this is scurvy; and the only possible cure is fresh food. I sincerely hope the ship is in; if not we shall have to climb the hills by Castle Rock, which would delay us another couple of days."

That night, despite the food and their burning of the primus for some hours, the cold seemed to strike up through their tent cloth and stab their vitals more fiercely than ever. In their ice-crusted sleeping bags, now almost molted of hair, their bodies started the agony of spasmodic violent heaving that passed for shivering, making sleep itself a torment. They prayed with fervor for a turn in the weather. Next morning they had a fine wind, suitable for each sledge to carry a sail, and they moved a few more miles. After lunch Hayward and Captain Mackintosh displayed touching bravery. While the sledges were being readied for the trek they took ski poles and tried to hobble ahead for a few yards, to lessen the burden on their comrades. They could not go far, and for the rest of the day the two sick men joined Spencer-Smith on the sledges as the dogs, Joyce, Wild, and Richards hauled them across the snow. It was a time which Dick Richards logged as "one of extreme hardship for us." He wrote later, "We were getting slower and slower making and breaking camp . . . taking longer to get a start in the mornings. 6 March was a typical day. We rose at 5:30 and it was four hours before we set out. We pitched a tent for lunch at 12:30 and did not get under way until 2:30, then marching on until it was nearly dark at 8 p.m."

At times during those long hours of heaving and hauling, either plunging through deep drift or skidding over ice, the wind would take hold and be so strong that the sails would have to be reefed. At other times Richards and Wild rode on the sledges to keep them from overrunning the patient dogs. Dick Richards tramped much of the time near the bow of the sledge bearing the hapless clergyman Spencer-Smith. During lulls in the storming wind Richards would hear his voice, halfsmothered by the flap of the sleeping bag, reciting prayers, sometimes in Latin, sometimes in English. He would ramble, going back in his mind to his days at Cambridge and Edinburgh. When the pain overcame the mind and the voice, Richards knew that by now Spencer-Smith was sinking fast, and that he was bleeding from the bowels, with never a word of complaint and always a smile to reduce the burden he was on the others, most especially the attendant Ernie Wild. Even in his illness and pain this remarkable man had concern for others. When his helpless body had sunk more than a foot into the ice in what he came to call Starvation Camp, as the trek was being made to Bluff depot to bring back food and fuel, the Padre always managed some little entry in his official expedition diary, recording how Wild had stirred him into arguments with the statement that every word in the English language, bar one, had its rhyme. "Took him up on this, literally, and we had quite a good fight." He also recorded how Wild's need for the solace of tobacco became so strong that he had smoked tea leaves in his pipe.

He wrote such snatches as "Very cold, wet and weak—but not dead yet, thank God!" and "The other party must be at the depot by now. God's in his Heaven—we shall last another day or two yet." When help arrived, he scribbled not of his own relief and gratitude for food and warmth, but of the men who had made the heroic journey to bring sustenance to Starvation Camp: "Joyce & Co have had a terrible time; on their last legs when they got to the depot . . . We have had the closest of calls, *Deus det incrementum.*"* He pitied Vic Hayward, describing the "poor man as almost hors *de combat.*" Their primus stove, he observed, was "playing Old Harry. It takes an hour-and-a-half to get into a meal."

On Sunday, March 5, which the Padre noted as *Quinquagesima*, the Sunday before Lent, his pain was the worst it had been so far. He scratched into his diary, still in the same tight writing, that the day had started calm, followed by a "good southerly," and that he had been on the rear sledge this day and felt it to be "a skittish little thing." For the first time his diary reveals him turning to a drug for relief. It reads, "Bad gripe—one gram of opium afternoon and evening." Nowhere did he reveal how he had obtained the vial of 10 opium tablets that had been in the small sledging medicine box.

The following day the Padre noted that they had come on a small depot laid by Dr. John Cope's returning party and "had depleted it," and how they had then bumped forward another nine miles. When he was laid in his bag in the tent that night he confessed to "feeling seedy all day." The wind had fallen away in the afternoon that Monday, and the burden of the laden sledges became so overwhelming that the men

* "May God give the increase."

again went through their gear and dumped every item they thought they could discard without adding to their danger. "After a most exhausting day's work we had covered little more than three miles," said Richards. Joyce noted in his diary, "a great strain, three weak men, four tired dogs, staggering along with three men on the sledges. Sledging under normal circumstances is solid hard graft. In this case it is almost heart-breaking, at times. Richie and Wild are two good pals, in spite of hard gruelling. . . . Our patients are not too cheerful, poor fellows. They have been wet through for weeks, and being trussed on a sledge is a terrible experience."

Another heavy day followed, although the sun shone through the haze. It was the finest day they had enjoyed for months, Joyce claimed, "all land in sight which is very pleasant—and what a rest it is to my eyes having been in the lead since we started in October—nothing but the white ocean to face, and nothing to relieve the eyes." This day Mackintosh and Hayward again managed courageously to hobble a few yards, but soon broke down in pain. The brave gesture was made when the wind fell away and the sunlit ice shelf was stilled. Without the southerly wind they were helpless now. All of their pulling, men and dogs, would shift the sledges only a few yards. The black prospect Joyce had feared so long now stared them in the face. Progress had become impossible, the nights were closing in rapidly, and the cold was growing intense, with their sleeping bags twice the normal weight because of ice. Richards observed that Captain Mackintosh was in a continual daze, Spencer-Smith unconscious for much of the time, and the suffering Hayward "somewhat unbalanced, mentally." He added, "We just could not go ahead and we were still some 40 miles away from Hut Point, so after our meal on the evening of Tuesday, 7 March, we called Ernie Wild over to our tent and held a conference on the situation."

Without discussion it was plain that any delay in making some adjustment to their situation could be fatal for all of them. Richards recalled saying to the other two men, "The Padre is almost at his last gasp and we've got to get him in if we are to save his life. But as it is we

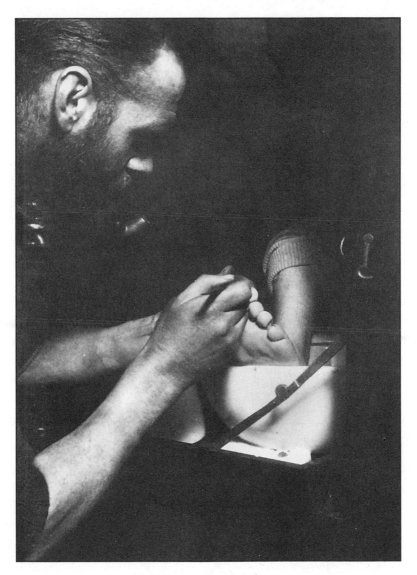

Attending a frozen toe

may none of us get in at all. There seems only one thing to do. We have to lessen the burden on the sledges."

In his diary Joyce recorded presenting both Mackintosh and Hayward with the fact that one man would have to be left behind on the Barrier if the rest were to get to Hut Point. The veteran wrote, "poor fellows, I am sorry for them. I explained I would leave three weeks' provisions and would come out again as soon as possible. The Skipper volunteered [and] we told Mackintosh we proposed to leave him there with provisions while we pushed on to Hut Point and returned as soon as possible." Mackintosh's dulled senses were prepared to accept the decisions made by the three fit men. Although his capacity for clear thought had vanished, he was nonetheless aware of the crisis and the reality that they would all perish unless one man was left behind.

Richards attested, "He acquiesced without complaint or comment. But let me say—not for a moment did this brave man lose his courage or his nerve. He understood that we could not possibly leave Spencer-Smith with him—two helpless men in a tent on the Barrier with the temperatures dropping fast was out of the question. It seems in our judgement at that time that it was right to try and get the Padre and Hayward in to Hut Point. It seemed obvious to us that we had to leave Mackintosh and he was quite willing to take what we said without argument. . ."

On that night of March 7, 1916, the Padre registered the decision in his little notebook, warming his fingers near the blue flame of the primus as he wrote, his thoughts in his sickness reaching out across time and space to his family, to his father and mother and brothers and sisters, as though some omen was in his mind. Something led him to dedicate this entry to ". . . F. M. H. R. O. T. D. Bitterly cold. Bag frozen stiff and in a bad position . . . only three miles as wind dropped. Decided to depot O.M. tomorrow and push on to Hut Point with the invalids. Hayward's legs are very bad now and even Wild has a touch [of scurvy] in the teeth. Hayward and I will be left at H.P. and the others will come back at top speed with seal meat and C. [Dr. John Cope?] and fetch O.M. with whom we leave three weeks' food."

These were the last words he was to write in the little diary that he had started with the quotation from Isaiah, which held the phrase "Where is my resting place?"—and at the back of which he had written, "Ever your loving Tony," with four crosses.

In the other tent Ernie Joyce was making an entry in his own diary, deeply moved at the prospect of leaving a man alone out on the Barrier. It seemed a hard decision to him, and there was also the pressing concern at the deterioration in himself, Richards and Wild. He wrote, "I am afraid that one of us will give in. If so, the whole party will go under. Scurvy has got us, our legs are black and swollen, and if we bend them at night there is a chance they will not straighten out. So to counteract that we lash pieces of bamboo to the back of our knees to keep them straight. There is no possible hope of help from Cape Evans if the sea-ice is broken up. However there is one chance the party from Cape Evans may be at Hut Point. 'Provi' may be good to us tomorrow and send along a southerly. If so, we will not be compelled to leave anyone behind."

The morning brought no realization of his hope, and, after a "rotten, sleepless night," the men set to work installing Captain Mackintosh in the smaller conical tent with his provisions, what books they had left, and a supply of oil for the primus. They were forced to take with them the larger and newer tent, in which five men could be crowded.

The preparations took four hours to complete. Then came one of the more emotional moments of their long fight for survival. Each man shook hands with Mackintosh, a casual parting gesture, that each felt could also be a final farewell. Joyce chatted with his commander for a short while, finding the sick man to be a little vague as Joyce tried to comfort him and give him heart to face the forlorn solitude he would have to endure, the days of gazing north across the empty icescape for sign of rescue.

"Keep watch, Mack. Look for us in about eight or 10 days. We'll bring you some fresh seal meat and that'll make the difference. I'll leave one of the sledges here for you to ride back and we'll travel lighter that way.

Meanwhile, try to move about every day, try a little exercise, till we come for you."

They marched away into the north, leaving the sick man alone in the old ragged tent with its patches of white calico. Joyce reassured himself, "It was the best thing. It was only carried out after careful thought."

The first two hours of the morning were calm, and they could see ahead to smoky Erebus. Joyce as usual was in the lead trace; behind him were staggered tough old Oscar and Gunner and Towser and Con the Samoyed, with Richards on one side of the sledge and Wild on the other, and the nearly helpless Hayward riding on the side with the Padre, now bleeding steadily from his bowels, in his sleeping bag lashed above their load. They still had trouble moving the single sledge, finding that the weight of two bodies caused it to sink deeper into the banks of drift snow. Then the wind came out of the southeast and filled their little sail and they made some headway, marching an estimated eight miles. Richards did not hear much from Spencer-Smith that day other than when he spoke of severe pains in his stomach. There was little they could do for him: His sleeping bag was badly iced, and the only aid they could give was to get him to the hut as quickly as their drained bodies could manage. The urgency was so strong in them that they trudged on until it was dark, then camped and cooked without light. Richards fed the dogs, declaring that they too were suffering from scurvy. Ernie Wild heated the pemmican for their meal and made tea from the water melted from snow. It was very cold. Joyce looked at his thermometer and found the reading down to 30°C below freezing. While the preparations were under way, he tried to enliven the clergyman with tales rummaged from his memories of the days when he and the Captain had worked on sailing ships. It was of little use, and all four men were distracted by Spencer-Smith's obvious suffering.

The Padre had been ill for almost two months now, and they had hauled him from near the polar plateau on a bucking sledge. This night he was in pain and seemed semicomatose, but it was not

Spencer-Smith who kept them awake all night. Richards noted in his diary, "We were all unable to sleep because of the extreme cold and the iced condition of our bags."

Throughout the dark, cold hours the sleepless men could hear the Padre moaning in pain, and they ached for the bitter night to end and for the light to come, when they could make a dash for the edge of the Barrier to save this gentle churchman. In the early hours of the morning he roused Ernie Wild, and there was a febrile quality in his tone as he asked the time. When Wild replied that it was about four o'clock and Spencer-Smith demanded, "Have you lost your bearings?" they knew he was delirious. Half an hour later, when Dick Richards sat up in his bag to end the convulsive leap of his shivering, he found that Spencer-Smith was staring at him across the small tent. With fright in his voice the Padre asked, "Richie, when your heart is behaving funny what's the best thing to do? Sit up or lie down?"

Richards did not know the answer, but said he thought the most sensible thing would be to lie still and try to keep warm in the sleeping bag. The Padre did not speak again, and Richards thought his advice had been accepted. The silence lasted until the first pale light of day was filtering through the green dome tent. When Richards sat up and looked across at the clergyman, he could see that Spencer-Smith was lying with his head back and uncovered. The faint light glimmered on the ice that had formed on his beard, his brows and his eyelids. The Padre was very, very still. The truth came as a stab in the heart, and Dick Richards called, "He's gone! I think he's gone."

Back at the Padre's Starvation Camp, Ernie Joyce had warned that death stalked them from behind. The heroic fight to the Bluff depot and back had been of no avail. Death was with them now, in this crowded little tent. The spirit of this brave man had been extinguished by malignant scurvy. Another victim would be buried in this wan ice-cap at the earth's end. Dick Richards could hear the kind voice begging him to let up when he was desperately hauling the sledges toward the Bluff: "For God's sake, Richie, you'll burst your heart." Now had come this awful defeat in the tent, a moment of death that remained still vivid in his mind more than 60 years later, when he told this writer: "Oh, but we were saddened—so very sad. We were within a day or two of getting him to the fresh meat that would have saved him . . . and we had lost him. Our spirits sank low. We had hauled him for hundreds of miles, and the jolting and jarring of the sledge at times must have been almost unbearable. Yet not one word of complaint did I hear him utter. It was a tragic time—tragic indeed, after all he had endured."

Four men in that tent, all suffering to differing degrees from the intolerable conditions of this lifeless frozen plain, which had taken this companion and could soon take their own lives—four broken-down, tattered wretches, relics of the slavery of hauling sledge loads for some 1,500 miles, their joints turning black, their gums already black and swollen down over their teeth, their faces carved and lined from the vicious blast of the polar winds—they were now at a loss to face this finality of death. Ernie Wild crawled out through the canvas tunnel to stand staring north while the freezing air turned the tears solid on his cheeks. Crippled Victor Hayward, nearer than any of them to succumbing to scurvy, could see himself lying as a corpse in a sleeping bag, and was overcome. Joyce and Richards, both sorrowing, helped the fainting man from the tent and laid him on the sledge, covering his head against the wind. Then they turned to their sad duty. The tent was taken down from above the body. Richards and Wild took turns with the spade to dig a shallow trench in the compacted snow. When the time came to inter the corpse, however, the three men combined did not have the strength to lift the cadaver and lay it in the shallow hole. They could only roll the dead body over and over and, as Joyce wrote, "simply let it fall into the grave."

They built a cairn above the grave with rough-cut snow blocks. Wild took two lengths of the bamboo they had tied behind their knees at night and lashed them into a simple cross, which he thrust into the snow above the Padre's head, vowing he would come back with a more suitable memorial. The eulogy by Joyce was as simple as the burial. "We had carried him for 40 days across the wilderness, and he had been ill for 67 days. He was always cheerful, never complained, although at times on a weakening heart the travel would have been agonizing and require much fortitude to bear."

Standing bareheaded in the cold south wind, the three sorrowing men joined in the Lord's Prayer, with Joyce committing this body to "God's Acre" and his soul to the comfort of the Lord. That was the burial service for the Reverend Arnold Patrick Spencer-Smith—man of God, priest of the Episcopalian Church—on the waste of the Great Ross Ice Shelf, on Thursday, March 9, 1916—a mere eight days shy of his 32nd birthday. Other tributes would come in the years ahead, on the other side of the world. In Edinburgh, his diocesan bishop would speak of him in the church he loved as a "man of gentle equable disposition with a mind naturally and deeply religious." His enduring courage would be remembered for many years by those who had known him.

Now the three men turned to the sledge, burdened still with a helpless man, for Vic Hayward was now so deeply affected that Joyce wrote, "He had fainted. At first I thought that he, too, had given in, he was so still. He came round later." With one last look behind them, the three men turned their backs to the grave and to the polar wind and strained in their harness to try and reach the edge of the Barrier.

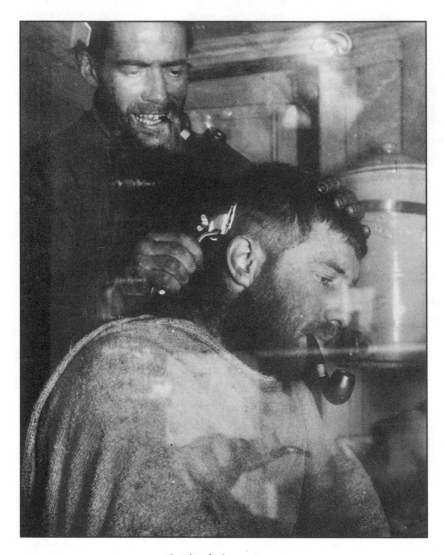

Cutting hair on *Aurora*

Footprints of Folly

Southward from where Ernest Joyce stood on the loaded sledge the great ice plain shimmered and dissolved into nothingness. The distant meeting of far mountains and sky was masked in chill haze and drift stirred by a low wind shearing down from the western slopes. Joyce stared into this lifeless panorama through the old binoculars, as he had done so often in the struggle back from the Beardmore Glacier. From this perch he could not see the small snow cairn they had raised over the body of the Padre, nor could he hope to pick out the little tent, a day's march farther south, where the stricken Captain Mackintosh clung to life, waiting for rescue. Now that they were close to the Barrier's edge, Joyce had felt compelled once more to take a look south, with the hope—almost dead in his mind—that history would repeat itself for him, that his eyes would again be the first to see the dark blur against the white wastes, the alien smudge that would in time resolve into midget figures of men hauling sledges on the last leg of their historic trans-Antarctic crossing. But no! On this March day in 1916, no dark patch in motion met his red-rimmed eyes. The terrible plain was empty of movement and life. There would be no repetition for him of the events of early February 1902.

At that earlier time, peering through a powerful telescope from Observation Hill, behind the hut, he had caught a glimpse of "a black speck, almost indiscernible," which he had claimed to be the first sighting of the returning southern party, consisting of Captain Scott, Dr. Wilson and Ernest Shackleton. Aboard the ice-bound *Discovery* other men had declared this to be a trick of light on the Barrier. But it proved in fact to be an ice mirage, for the following day Stoker Lashly sighted the three men from 10 miles away.

As Joyce stood now near the Barrier edge, with the deserted wooden hut and the empty bay behind him, he recalled vividly the return of the Scott party in 1902, the ship decked with bright bunting, "rainbow fashion," and the cheering men in the rigging greeting the weatherworn, weak men, staggering from toil, exposure and incipient scurvy—three men who had traveled farther south in the world than any human beings before them! Once aboard, the three had told of slogging to 82° 17' South, only to find a great mountain chain blocking the path to the South Pole, and how in the fight back from that southern extremity of the great ice plain they had come close to losing their lives.

That greeting echoed in Joyce's ears, together with the words Captain Scott left of his own feelings, of how the return to life from the ice plain had seemed unreal to their worn and dulled senses. Scott had written: ". . . How can I describe this homecoming? How we clasped the hands of friends . . . How for the first time in three months we shaved our ragged chins and sponged ourselves with steaming hot water; how we sat at a feast which realized the glory of our daydreams. . . . It was a welcome home, indeed . . . it seemed too good to be true that all our anxiety had so completely ended and rest for brain and limb was ours at last. For 93 days we had plodded with ever-varying fortune over a vast snowfield and slept beneath a fluttering canvas."

With no sign of ship's masts poking above the lip of the ice field, and no voices raised in cheers, Ernest Joyce declared, "What a different homecoming for us poor souls!"

Nevertheless, the Ross Sea party of 1915–16 had been out twice as long as Scott's 1902 journey—and it had traveled farther south, heaving and hauling food for six other men, for almost 200 days using discarded equipment and suspect heating gear, and had met with much misfortune. And this party, which had gone without a bath or change of clothing for the last 15 months, and without any fresh food, was not straggling back to any band of welcoming shipmates. "Nothing ahead for us," Joyce commented ruefully, "except a cold cheerless hut—no comforts, no coal, no lighting, no provisions. No happy return for this party! Our whole trek has been one long agony of mental anguish."

Yet, glum as Joyce felt, that cold, cheerless hut—now only a few miles across the bay ice—beckoned as a sanctuary, a refuge for tattered relics from the ice shelf, a shelter to be reached and welcomed if no more lives were to be lost in this attempt to conquer the Antarctic. There was further anguish of uncertainty in his thoughts: Where was Ernest Shackleton now? Was he somewhere back in that haze, doggedly pushing north, stopping at the food depots they had laid for him? Was he following this party's footsteps north from the foot of the Beardmore? Or had he and his companions perished in that awful vastness beyond the South Pole? Had the slogging and the suffering and the Padre's death been in vain? Had the journey been a futile sacrifice? Joyce's own weakness, and that of his feeble and sick companions, added to his despondency. He wrote in his diary, "It is remarkable how weak we are."

This last grueling day had been a grim struggle for distance through all the hours of daylight and well into the night. There was always the oppressive thought that Hayward might collapse completely at any moment. March 10, 1916, was entered in Joyce's log as "the worst day we have spent." Still striving to approach the Barrier edge, they had fought their way up the rocky protuberances near Cape Armitage until an hour before midnight, and there they had met a stunning setback.

"To my utter consternation I saw open water in the bay. And this meant we had to retreat up the slopes for another two miles. It was heartbreaking; just getting our gear and Hayward up those last slopes so we could get to the hut was pitiful. Two miles were like a hundred-mile trek."

It was 2 in the morning before they lay shivering in their sleeping bags, Joyce claiming worries too great to allow sleep. With the first glimmer of polar light he crept quietly from the tent and climbed a prominence, there to gaze into the brightening bay scene with a leaping heart. The ice was in! What he had seen through the drift and gloom of night had been an open lead. Not only was there ice on which to sledge their sick companion, there were also seals aplenty, lolling about in thrilling numbers with promise of the fresh meat the men craved.

Joyce hurried back to the tent to rouse his exhausted comrades. Wild and Richards stared at him with bleary eyes as he told them that the ice was in the bay. "It is a godsend," he said. The frozen sea water had lifted from their flagging bodies the daunting prospect of hauling their gear and the sick Hayward for another two days over rocky slopes to round the Point. Joyce noted, "I'm certain we should never have succeeded in taking Hayward over those hills in our state. I am greatly relieved."

It cost more hours of slow travel to reach the bay ice, and once they arrived there the sight of the seals lolling on the surface brought an extra strain. Joyce enthused, "The bay was full of seals. What a welcome sight, but the dogs, almost maddened with hunger, became very excited—electrified! There is no mistake—they know the seals are their food, that their journey is nearly over. It was a tough job to keep them in, we are so weak."

The last few yards of the long journey brought Dick Richards the most pervasive and primitive urge of his life. They had come ashore, to climb the ice foot of the slope leading to the hut, and nearby at the edge of a tide crack a few fat seals lolled, invitingly vulnerable. He stopped his pulling in the sledge harness to stare at the creatures, and a great desire swept over his whole being. The call for blood—for fresh blood—was nearly irresistible. "I had the strongest desire to rush to one of those animals and cut its throat and drink the blood that I knew would hose from its neck. Extraordinary! I had this instinctive and compelling feeling in me that this is what my scurvy-stricken system needed. It was almost overpowering. I am certain that had the hut been farther away than it was, I would have killed one of those things and I would have drunk the blood for which my body was crying out. And that strong feeling has remained always vivid, in the forefront of my mind."

The hut also called, however, and so they trudged the last few yards—turning away from living food imprinting the moment graphically in Dick Richards's memory. "We were so weak, our clothes in tatters; and we were dependent on our own efforts to rescue our leader still out on the ice shelf—and there was nobody at the hut, of course. Dark and cheerless it may have been, but to us it was security. Snow had seeped in everywhere, the door was solidly iced up and we had to pass Hayward in through the window, which we forced open."

That simple act taxed their waning strength. According to Joyce it presented a last drain on their remaining energy. "He is but a bag of bones, yet we had to struggle to get him through that window—and he can thank his lucky stars that he is here now."

Wild and Richards went back out at once to sate their bodily craving. They stunned and killed two lazing seals, their flensing knives quickly slicing the blubber for the crude stove. Joyce took the role of cook, but he hesitated to sear too much of the meat they brought, fearing the reactions of near-starvation: "Our digestive machines may not be equal to the strain, at first. Our tummies are not in very good order." He discovered a packet of dried vegetables and mixed these with a spare serving of meat in the big black frying pan, then served small portions to both the men and the animals. Those marvelous dogs! "The dogs are jewels," Joyce would say, "those wonderful stout-hearted creatures saved all our lives—especially old Oscar. But for him, and Gunner, Con and Towser, we would have shared the fate of Captain Scott." Like the human beings they served, the animals, though

ravenous for fresh meat, ate sparingly in the first few hours of settlement in the old Discovery Hut. Men and dogs alike were invalids.
There was some concern that Hayward might not recover. The entry
in the Joyce diary that day summarized their situation.

"For 193 days we have toiled under extreme temperatures and suffered untold agony to carry out an objective which we have now accomplished. For 15 months we have been without change of clothing or a
bath. Now, Hayward's legs are deep black, his gums so swollen they pro-
trude from his mouth. He is certainly not himself, his eyes are dilated,
brain is not clear. He is in a state of semi-coma. We will have to wake
him out of that. Wild, Richards, self, have not escaped, legs black and
gums swollen but now we have some fresh meat."

The first night back in the old hut gave the men little comfort or rest.
Their first fresh food for months—though they ate sparsely—was too
rich for their shrunken stomachs, and the digestive reactions disturbed
them through the night. The absence of the tent flapping above their
heads made them restless. Within a day, however, they were claiming
to be feeling the benefit of the fresh meat, though all were still very
weak. That first morning brought the gift of a spell of sunshine, and
before they went seal hunting Richards and Wild helped Joyce carry
Hayward out to sit in the glow. Joyce also took their sleeping bags outside, and turned them fur-side out to free them from some of their
accumulated ice. He weighed the bags while in the hut and found their
normal weight of 10 pounds had increased by around four times, an
increase caused by frozen condensation.

The sunny idyll did not last long. A sharp wind came hurrying off
the ice shelf loaded with drift, and in minutes the bags were coated and
Hayward was sitting like a white snowman. Joyce could not find the
strength to lift the sick man through the window, and so Hayward had
to sit and grow whiter until the seal hunters returned.

The difficulty of adjusting to the richer food affected the dogs later
that day. Greedy Oscar, the biggest eater of the four animals, over-
indulged so much that he spent some hours rolling on the ground

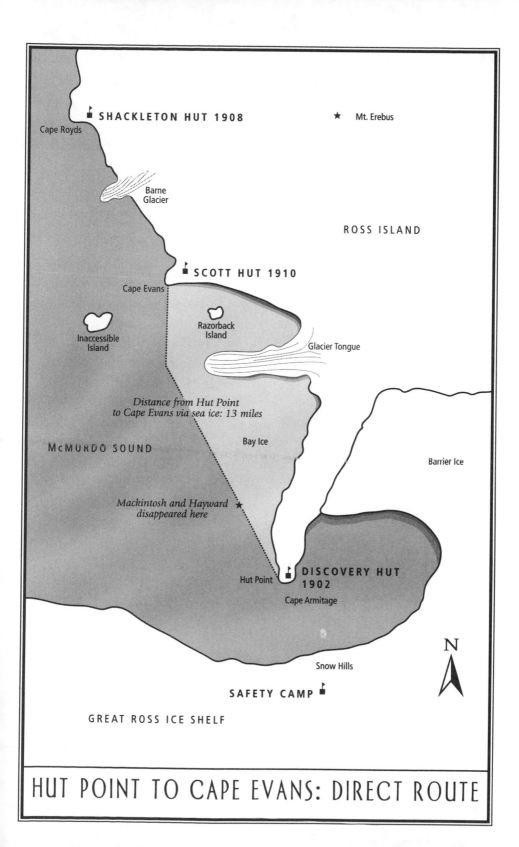

SHACKLETON HUT 1908
Cape Royds
★ Mt. Erebus

Barne
Glacier

ROSS ISLAND

SCOTT HUT 1910
Cape Evans

Inaccessible
Island

Razorback
Island

Glacier Tongue

*Distance from Hut Point
to Cape Evans via sea ice: 13 miles*

McMURDO SOUND

Bay Ice

Barrier Ice

*Mackintosh and Hayward
disappeared here* ★

DISCOVERY HUT
1902

Hut Point
Cape Armitage

N

Snow Hills

SAFETY CAMP

GREAT ROSS ICE SHELF

HUT POINT TO CAPE EVANS: DIRECT ROUTE

groaning with a stomach ache. By evening these afflictions were passing, and Joyce hopefully noted a return of strength and a growing
brightness of manner, which boded well for when he would have to
turn the dogs' faces to the southern trail again.

He could spare them little time to convalesce. The situation of the
lone man left on the ice shelf weighed on his mind. Every seal in sight
had to be slaughtered, he ordered, and as much meat and blubber as
they could collect would have to be sledged to the hut. With the rising
gale winds of winter ripping out the sea ice between Hut Point and the
hut at Cape Evans, they had no immediate prospect of making a crossing for many weeks. Furthermore, they would need fresh meat for the
journey out to liberate Captain Mackintosh from his plight, as well as
enough cooked meat to last the helpless Hayward for at least a week,
and a stock of blocks of blubber to keep the hut fire burning, remembering always that storms and blizzards would reduce the number of
seals coming up onto the ice.

They spent only two full days at the hut. On the evening of March
13 Joyce decided to move again. He wrote, "Our sledge-mate is out
there on the ice shelf, and we shall have to brave the elements tomorrow." He was still concerned, though, as to how the dogs would react
to being driven south again so soon. He was more confident about his
comrades: "I think our strength will carry us through; I will take raw
seal meat for the dogs."

They resisted the desire to sleep and laze in order to ready themselves for the journey on the morrow. They overhauled the sledge,
mended rips in the tent fabric, patched their footwear and clothing,
and cooked seal steaks for stacking in food bags. In his sickness Victor
Hayward became depressed at the thought of being left alone, and so
they tried to cheer him. Wild and Richards cut the blubber for his fire,
and Joyce fried his supply of meat, assuring Hayward they would be
back within six days, that they would make forced marches to get back
off the ice shelf once and for all.

They lay in their bags close to the blubber fire that night, striving for
a few hours sleep. Joyce made a diary entry, "Turned in, feeling better.

Ready for the fray tomorrow to rescue our lonely mate out there in the great white silence."

The valiant dogs gave them no trouble and, with the three men, willingly faced the run south. In the early afternoon of March 14 they tramped again towards Safety Camp, the frozen plain carrying a chiseling wind with a temperature 20 degrees below freezing. They made the sorriest spectacle of any party that ever left the historic old hut. "Looking at us," Joyce noted, "one would think we were the worst crowd of ruffians unhung! Our clothes are patched with food-bags; our finneskoes half-fur and half-calico bags; and our faces bear no resemblance to white men. We are a crowd one would shudder to run up against in the dark."

Nevertheless they marched well and bravely, tackling a journey they reckoned would be nearly 90 miles, with the length of the nights closing down fast on the length of days, and the wind and cold becoming daily more vicious. The frozen plain and its scurvy, however, had not yet done with them. On their first night back on the ice shelf, with the cold so intense that the steam from the primus coated the tent fabric with an ice lining, they again knew the agony and threat of scurvy in their joints. Joyce examined his comrades and himself and pronounced, "We are all nothing but bags of bones. The flesh has gone from our limbs." Since they had had only two days on fresh meat, they thought it wise to bandage their knees with the bamboo sticks to avoid them bending and becoming fixed in the cold night.

There was little time to sleep. They were up again before 5 the next morning, their patched finneskoes frozen stiff and the ice crackling in their sleeping bags, and were back on the trail soon after the first pale daffodil light crept across the frozen plain. They had the blessing of a clear, windless morning, and with their bellies replete with seal meat and hot tea the men strained in their harness and encouraged the dogs to hasten south across the snow, each man filled with the urgency to reach the solitary Captain in the old tent. This was a march of rescue, a march of relief. It did not have the grim aspects of their earlier struggle south from the Bluff depot in the 12-day blizzard to find the three men waiting at the Padre's Starvation Camp, but it did embody a strong element of comradeship and respect. Joyce, Richards, Wild—all three knew a closer bond on this march, each recognizing the faults in the characters of the others and accepting them, and cementing the fellowship that had grown over the long months of their fight to reach and return from the foot of the Beardmore. In this fusion of companionship they reached a union beyond brotherhood that would last for each of them as long as they lived. They had faced death together on this terrible frozen plain, had suffered together and survived. They had experienced the emotion of which the great Douglas Mawson wrote when he was a thousand miles to the west, some three years earlier. "When comrades tramp the road . . . through a lonely, blizzard-ridden land, in hunger, want and weariness, the interests, ties, and fates of each other are interwoven in a wondrous fabric of friendship and affection."

On this march south the three men—these "bags of bones"—knew that same bond of wondrous friendship. On their third day they met with a sad reminder of how closely they were linked with each other's fates, for at midmorning they came upon a forlorn mound of roughcut snowblocks, the cairn under which Spencer-Smith was now part of the ice shelf.

After lunch that day, standing atop the snow mound that had marked a small depot, Joyce looked south through the binoculars. Suddenly he exclaimed, "I can see him! He's all right. What a relief for us all!"

A mile or two to the south, visible through the cold haze, Joyce had seen the fragile tent, still standing after the southern blasts, and outside, leaning on a ski-pole, gazing hopefully to the north was their commander, Captain Aeneas Mackintosh. It was a greater relief to their minds than anyone admitted. Dick Richards would dismiss that last march south as "all in a day's work," but in all three of the comrades there had been an underlying anxiety about the exile waiting out on that white wilderness. To leave any man alone out there was a prospect to contemplate with concern. When they left Mackintosh he had already pushed his reserves to the limit in the fight from Mount Hope, marching when normal men would have dropped, and he might well have been in the same final, lethal stages of scurvy that had taken the life of Spencer-Smith. Now he had been out there alone for nine days and eight nights.

The Captain was alive—but he was not well. The combination of illness and debility in the isolation of the ice plain had laid a mark on him, so that when they came to his tent in the early evening he did not seem to comprehend when they told him that Spencer-Smith had perished, and that Hayward was ill in the hut, and that the ship had not returned. Richards noted how the captain seemed "dazed by his long vigil on the ice shelf." Joyce recorded that Mackintosh called this day of rescue "the greatest day of all my life which I shall always commemorate." He also talked of the long, lonely hours, and how in a semiconscious state he would rest in his sleeping bag and have conversations with imaginary people visiting his tent. The men soon saw he was quite ill, and learned that he was bleeding from the bowels. They gave him a meal of minced seal meat and pemmican and then quickly collapsed the tent and loaded him onto the sledge.

They drove themselves and the dogs hard in that last journey to the north, making a record 20 miles on their first full day. Joyce sat in the tent in the evenings with the Captain talking over their affairs—and found Mackintosh "peculiar." This was understandable, however. As Joyce wrote, "What an experience! Left alone on the Barrier, wondering if the party had made it to Hut Point, whether anybody would be coming to help him. Poor chap, he is in a bad way, but I hope to have him in safety in another three days. My mind is easier for the first time since we left him on the Barrier."

On the evening of March 18, delighted to find the sea ice firm enough for sledging, they carried the sick Captain up the ice foot to the old wooden hut. They found Hayward dejected and still ill, but they cheered him with their arrival and soon had food cooking on the steel plate above a blubber fire. Richards fed the faithful dogs, and soon the five men sat on the boxes near the stove to eat, all in better spirits than they'd known for a long time. Ernest Joyce was optimistic: "This will be our home for some months, I should think, and now we have arrived safely it rests with us to get the patients well as quickly as possible—with fresh meat and judicious exercise. I am more than thankful that this long journey is finished. We have struggled hard since last September and suffered hardships I did not think the human machine could stand." In his diary that night he remembered their loss. "The irony of fate is that poor Spencer-Smith should have gone under only a couple of days before we arrived back."

They looked at Captain Mackintosh's legs that night and found them "a heavy blue from the hip bone down to the knees and with blue stripes to the ankles, very hard and swollen . . . cannot walk, his knees fixed at 45 degree angle." Hayward had made little advance; he too was bent "like a very old man with his knees still black and gums swollen out of his mouth." Joyce, Richards and Wild still had the swellings and black marks of scurvy as well. This parade of affliction seemed to stir a realization in Mackintosh's dulled senses. One by one he solemnly shook each man by the hand, saying he owed his life to them, and then thanked them collectively for the work they had done in laying the depots. It was an emotional moment; they were all touched by his simple expression of gratitude.

Joyce expressed his feelings in his diary before sleeping: "During the sledging season of seven months Richards has been my constant companion and tent-mate. A whiter man never existed. The comradeship of Richards and Wild—especially after the collapse of members of the party through scurvy—was worthy of the highest traditions of polar service. Regardless of themselves, they carried out to the uttermost all that was required of them." He linked them with his special "brotherhood of the south," and calculated they had marched together for almost 200 days, covering more than 1,600 miles in that single season.

Through 14 Antarctic winters the wooden structure Captain Scott had ordered erected for emergencies in 1902 had been assailed by blizzards and gales. Countless storms had flung torrents of frozen granular snow at the external planking, abrading the timbers down below the grain so that the heads of the fastening nails stood clear of the wood. Now, in 1916, the structure rocked and creaked under buffeting winds. There were chinks in the walls that let in fine drifts and chilling drafts, and the place was half-full of snow and solidified ice. In the northern corner was the ramshackle stove—a sheet of steel stretched over a crude arrangement of bricks, with an old flue above to allow some escape of smoke when the direction of the wind was favorable.

This cramped area formed the center of life for the five frigid hermits who had barely escaped the penalty of long travel on the ice shelf. Here they faced the prospect of living under primitive conditions for at least one third of a year, barred from any other human contact by 13 miles of dangerous bay ice. They could reach the four men encamped in the Scott hut at Cape Evans only by a perilous precipitous overland route that involved crossing glaciers and ice-clad mountains, which would have been suicidal in the wintry conditions. Joyce decided they would have to accept at least a four months' stay in a hut "almost falling to pieces," which after the sledging journey was a "sanctuary" in which to recover on a copious diet of seal meat.

The two invalids, Mackintosh and Hayward, were equipped with makeshift crutches so they could totter a few yards at a time as their strength returned on frequent meals of meat and the few dehydrated vegetables and the little porridge other parties had left behind. A cache of old biscuits from the 1902 Scott expedition added to their provisions, with both men and dogs sharing the cod-liver-oil-impregnated biscuits, to which Joyce attributed the resistance of the four dogs to the serious onset of scurvy. That fact had been all-important, he noted, for if just one of the four dogs had gone under, then without question all their lives would have been lost. Beyond this there was a grim—at times gruesome—sameness to their food supply.

With typical understatement, Sir Ernest Shackleton later commented on the rapid recovery of Mackintosh and Hayward from severe scurvy. In a necessarily limited reference to the life led by the exiles at Hut

Point in his book about his own adventures, *South*, he wrote that there was "plenty of fresh food and dried vegetables available."

Dick Richards recorded a totally different account of the "appalling situation" suffered during their four months at Hut Point, "I have positive recollection that there were virtually no provisions at the hut. The little left by previous parties were very soon consumed—and we had none of our impromptu sledging rations left. The old Scott biscuits were musty, some fifteen years old, and these went mainly to the dogs. There was absolutely nothing in the way of general provisions no flour, no sugar, no bread. The sole food we had from the middle of March until the middle of July—four whole months—was seal meat. That is all we had— morning, noon, and night."

In that cheerless, confined corner of the old hut with its constantly smoky atmosphere there was little to give comfort or lift the spirit. The men rammed hard snow into the cracks between the wall boards to try and shut out drafts. To keep their beds above the fat-strewn floor they laid old doors or planks on kerosene tins and spread their thread-bare reindeer-skin bags on these. Most hours in the hut were spent in these bags; for as the long winter night closed over them and storms came with greater frequency and increasing violence, keeping the killing cold out of their bodies became a vital factor in survival. Night and day the blubber fire was kept burning, so that their lives depended on a supply of seals. Dick Richards described this existence as "living the life of primitive troglodytes." Fresh meat for recovery from scurvy became almost a by-product of the vital need to provide fuel for their rickety hut.

Richards wrote, "We would throw those cut blocks of frozen seal fat—about six inches by two—into the fire and they would melt and flare and some of the fat would run down through the cracks between the bricks and across the floor. When this was thick enough, we would scrape it into a tin of some kind and use it for lighting. A piece of string or a strip of cloth would float in the melting fat and burn and give us a crude kind of candle. It was then coming on to 24 hours of darkness every day and these burning wicks were all we had to see by. On days when the wind veered and the blubber smoke filled the space we could see almost nothing."

This situation was especially hard on Ernest Joyce. More than six months on the ice, usually in the lead trace, staring day after day at the white wastes, with frequent bouts of snow blindness, had affected his vision. He could not see well enough to read the few books they had carried with them—books that were read over and over again in the months of seclusion. Among these, notably, was *For the Term of his Natural Life*, and with Wild or Richards reading passages to him, Joyce solved one of their shortages. He heard how a character—a convict in Australia—had made salt from sea water. They had run out of salt at the hut, and without it the seal meat "was very unpalatable." They filled a cooker with sea ice and kept it boiling on the blubber stove. Joyce recorded the result: ". . . extracted a pound and a half of salt."

As the long dark weeks followed one another into April and then May, the basic needs of the hermits at Hut Point evolved into an even more demanding troglodyte existence, that of the remorseless hunter-gatherer. Blizzard after blizzard roared up from the polar regions—lasting at times for more than a week, such as one that did not relent from April 19 to May 3. The five smoke-grimed scarecrows would crouch day after day by the stove and watch the stock of blubber dwindle perilously, knowing that without the flare of seal fat they would not survive. Seals had become essential to survival. The drive to scour the ice when the blasting winds fell away was compelling, and this burden fell mainly on the two fittest men—Dick Richards and Ernie Wild. And a burden it was. The two men would take the dogs and a sledge and push into the winter night, travelling up to 20 or 30 miles a day to find the tide crack or the ice holes through which the fat creatures would emerge. Success was neither certain nor easy with the increasingly rare appearance of the seals. When they did come on an animal, the burden turned to trauma and the chore to bloody horror.

The innocent seal would lift its nose in curiosity, as though offering itself up as a victim. Then in the dark the iron-shod club would crash into its skull, and when the creature fell stunned, flat on the ice, the razor-sharp flensing knife would slash across its throat. Dick Richards later recalled the scene: "The arteries spurt the life-blood like a hose. You can't see it in the dark and the blood covers and soaks your boots and your clothes."

The action of harvesting the body of the victim seal was also branded on his memory. "We had to hold the knife in a bare hand. In the dark, with such a sharp implement, and under the greasy conditions, a slip would be dangerous."

The blade would rip the length of the seal's belly, and immediately the bare hand would be thrust into the still-warm entrails to avoid the frostbite that comes suddenly with the air temperature down to 30° below freezing. One by one the flongs of blubber would be ripped away to expose the skeleton and the submerged meat; the quickly freezing blubber flongs would then be thrown like lengths of timber onto the sledge, the meat would be carved away, and the robbed carcases would be left to stain the snow.

There was ample meat for men and dogs, despite their voracious appetites, but the blubber fire was even hungrier, demanding its fuel around the clock—so that between bouts of blizzard weather Wild and Richards would relentlessly comb the shore seeking tide cracks and seal holes, day after day, week after week. The total grew in Joyce's tally: 10 seals, 20 seals, 30 seals—fat hairy seals with skins like pigs, young seals, male and female—and once, in the dark, a saber-toothed sea leopard. With each passing week into winter's depth the growing need to keep warm added to the hunters' burden.

By mid-April, the terrible signs of scurvy had all but vanished in the three fittest men; only Mackintosh and Hayward still showed some blue-black staining in their legs and their slightly swollen gums. Richards, Wild, and Joyce were regaining vigor and some weight. Joyce wrote "I feel like a rubber ball on this diet. We eat so much seal that Richie and Wild can just about cope with our needs."

There was scarce relief from the grinding routine of survival at the hut. For the first time in almost two years, they tried a barbering operation. Joyce found a pair of scissors in one of the sledging medical boxes and a long and painful session of cutting hair ensued—to little purpose:

Their beards were down to their chests, and the hair of their heads fell down to their shoulders and was matted and glued with the fat and smoke of the burning blubber. There were reading sessions, Wild and Richards speaking the lines from a dog-eared copy of *Lorna Doone* or one of the Padre's books, which had been brought in with his effects. They had many discussions, and speculated often on what had happened in the war with Germany, what had happened to the ship, when they might expect some relief from the outside world, and indeed whether anybody in the outside world would know of them or be bothered with a few castaways if there was still a war going on. The topic that became most prevalent as Mackintosh and Hayward recovered from scurvy, though, was how soon the ice would be firm enough for travel to Cape Evans.

About the third week in April, hope had run high that conditions would soon be right for sledging across the bay past Glacier Tongue to the other hut. On April 18 Joyce trudged north across the ice, keeping close to the land, and found the frozen surface quite firm. He told his companions that with another two or three days of low temperatures the journey would be worth trying. The next day a blizzard came rampaging up from the south. It lasted a whole week, and when the air cleared they could see the dark smudge of open water within a half-mile of the hut. All the weight-bearing ice had been swept away up the Sound.

The disappointment and delay struck hardest at Captain Mackintosh, though this did not become truly apparent until they sat at their morning meal of seal meat on May 8. Facing their eighth week of duress, the captain's decision seemed to come out of the blue. His one bleary eye swept over the faces of the three men—Joyce, Richards and Wild—as they sat finishing their food.

"Hayward and I," Mackintosh said, "are going to walk across the ice to Cape Evans today."

It came as a bombshell, even though the three men knew that these two invalids had walked frequently to regain their strength, and that on the previous day, a Sunday, they had strolled a mile or so in the direction Joyce had taken prior to the weeklong blizzard. The others' doubts, implicit in their sudden silence, lay not in the question of their weaker companions' strength lasting throughout the journey of 13 miles. It was born in the strange suddenness of the decision.

In this moment of tension Joyce did not speak. Instead he got to his feet and went out through the door from which they had cleared a passage to the outside and stood staring south. In a minute or two he was back by the stove, his eyes grim in his hairy face, his voice sonorous. Using the naval formality of address he warned, "Now, look here, sir, you can call me cautious, but I wouldn't go to Cape Evans today, not for all the tea in China!"

In the southern sky above the dark smudge of Minna Bluff, he had seen the gloomy portent of impending blizzard. The darkening clouds massing in that direction, he said, were his "weather pilot." They gave him warning of what was about to strike.

"Oh, nonsense, Joyce." Mackintosh brushed the caution aside. "The weather is fine, the ice is firm. We tested it yesterday—and we are going today. Just walking across; no sledge, no equipment. Be there in a few hours, I think."

Richards thought Hayward looked doubtful after the blizzard warning, but felt the Englishman did not want to challenge the Captain's decision, having given his word. An excuse was ready-made for Captain Mackintosh: Four of his men were at Scott's hut at Cape Evans. He had not seen them for months, and he wanted reassurance that all was well with them. For Richards and the others this motive was too trivial, too illogical. The Cape Evans hut was a hotel compared to their abode, and the Captain's concern should be with the men at Hut Point. Richards said later, "I incline to the belief he liked his comfort, that he couldn't stand these bed-rock conditions we suffered. Cape Evans was a palace compared with Hut Point, and that outweighed all else in his mind. Nothing we could say would dissuade him. We could not stop him going, short of physical force, and there was no question of us joining that foolhardy journey. We made him promise to make for the nearest shore at the first sign of bad weather."

It didn't occur to any of them to remind Mackintosh that at this time the previous year *Aurora* had vanished, carried away on the ice sheet blown out by blizzard winds.

There was, however, bitterness as well as concern in the minds of the three remaining men as they prepared a bag of fried seal meat and watched the preparations for the duo's departure. Yes, they remembered how they had strained nerve and sinew to haul these two men— only just now recovered from scurvy—from the certainty of a frozen grave on the ice shelf. The two had been restored to a state of health by the devotion and dedication behind the steady supply of seal meat and blubber fuel, by the crushing burden of seal hunting in the terrible winter conditions. Now here they were, putting all at risk again, despite advice from wiser heads and greater experience.

Joyce expressed his worry in his diary. "I fail to understand why these people are so anxious to risk their lives again. They could walk to Cape Evans in less than four hours perhaps but . . . it would be hell to be caught on thin ice in a blizzard . . ."

The impetuous decision bit even deeper when Joyce recalled how Mackintosh of all members of the party should have known best the treacherous nature of the bay ice. In December 1908, Captain John King Davis had taken command of *Nimrod* and brought her back from New Zealand to McMurdo Sound in order to bring Shackleton home. The vessel had come up against solid ice some 20 miles from the Cape Royds hut, and Mackintosh—recovered from the loss of his right eye—volunteered to take a party over the ice to learn the news. With three crewmen he sledged away from the ship, envied by his companions since he would be the first to learn whether Shackleton had reached the South Pole. The party was hardly out of sight, however, when one of the crewmen strained a leg. Mackintosh sent him, with another man to help him, back to the vessel, and went on with a fireman named McGillan.

The following day strong winds started to break up the sea ice, and in the next 24 hours Davis was able to con the ship to a mooring off the Cape. On going ashore to the hut he found no trace of the second officer or the fireman. Faced with this crisis Davis took *Nimrod* back along the island to look for the two men, but the ship was caught in pack ice and driven across the Sound for a whole week. On January 14, off the remote northern tip of Ross Island, a flutter of green canvas was seen. The tent that Mackintosh had carried, now ripped by the gales, stood on Cape Bird, and bore a message held by a safety pin saying that they had fought ashore on a floe, and when provisions were running out had decided to try and reach the Cape Royds hut overland.

The redoubtable Davis still held some warmth for his junior officer, whom he had viewed as "undaunted by his injury, an eager and adventurous spirit which nothing could quell . . . a man who was ready to take the hundredth chance." He did so on this occasion, attempting to cross 24 miles of terribly crevassed, difficult and unknown mountainous terrain.

It was a "hair-raising journey and they did not know where they were until by chance one of Shackleton's party happened to see them within a few miles of the hut." Joyce recounted these details to Richards and Wild as they stood together watching Mackintosh and Hayward start across the ice. In their final minutes, under pressure, Mackintosh again assured them that in the event of a strong blow coming on they would make for the land. Then he and Hayward marched away, carrying only a few personal possessions and a bag of fried seal meat: no tent, no sleeping-bags, nothing for an emergency.

It was an eerie departure, with only a twilight glimmer to lighten the midday Antarctic scene. Richards, Wild and Joyce climbed a snowclad hill above a sharp drop to see them go across the bay ice. The hill itself was a pointer to depressive thoughts. It was known as Vince's Hill, for it was here in 1902 that Ernie Wild's brother Frank had helped erect a cross to one of the Antarctic's first casualties, George Vince, who trod a slope too steep and too slippery for his fur boots to grip and had crashed to his death on the sea ice hundreds of feet below. Ragged, their eyes red-rimmed and skin blackened with blubber fat, the three men at Hut Point now stood and watched the two figures dwindle to dwarf size. As Richards described it, ". . . They grew fainter in the dim light against the vast expanse of sea ice in the north."

When the two travelers could no longer be seen the three survivors turned back to the hut, silent in their resentment at the needless risk being taken. Richards wrote, "We were still acutely conscious of our recent experience on the ice shelf and the tremendous toil in getting these two men back. . . . We'd worked our guts out to get them into the safety of the hut, so there was some bitterness in seeing them go against advice."

They had not been back in the hut for much more than an hour when the wind began hammering the wooden structure. Quite soon it was a blizzard, blowing with the strength they had come to expect at that time of year. It hammered at their shelter for three days; only when it was safe to go outside did they risk the journey that their concern demanded. They walked onto the ice and followed the footsteps the two foolish men had left in the ice crystals of the frozen surface. They walked for an hour in the dim light, and then, some three miles from the hut, the footsteps ended. The ice from here on was a different color. Dick Richards reached forward and pushed a ski pole into the surface. It went in quite easily, the ice was so thin and so new.

They stood together in the cold gloom peering at the ominous signs at their feet, thoughts of disaster unspoken. Then they turned away, silent in their apprehension but still trying to find hope. There was a finality in the entry Ernest Joyce made in his diary that night; it had the sad ring of an epitaph: "The fate of those foolish people we do not know. Such is life, after dragging them back from death. Mackintosh's previous experience should have proved a warning . . . the Antarctic is a hard mistress."

* * *

The day Captain Aeneas Mackintosh and Victor Hayward trudged to oblivion in the dark waste of McMurdo Sound, a storm-tossed open boat crept through the cold mists of the far south Atlantic Ocean carrying Sir Ernest Shackleton and five shipwrecked comrades to final safety. The six men, suffering from thirst and near total exhaustion and chilled to the marrow, peered thankfully through the murk, soon after midday, at the forbiddingly sheer cliffs of South Georgia.

The little craft had survived huge seas and gales from 400 miles south of Cape Horn, and had ploughed through nearly 1,000 miles of wild sub-Antarctic ocean to try and bring help from the island where 17 months before, *Endurance* had sailed out to meet her doom in the Weddell Sea ice. Here, off South Georgia, on May 8, 1916, they had yet to scale the soaring mountain chain to reach the remote whaling station on the opposite side of the island—but this day marked the landfall of an open boat journey that has been hailed as an epic in the history of sea travel, coming as it did after all that had followed the "mortal wounding" of their ship in the pack ice.

Twenty-eight men in number when they left the tangled remains of *Endurance*, they had survived the winter months on frozen platforms of ice, drifting, drifting endlessly with the changing winds, escaping from one great floe to another as the floes split under their camps until, at the end of the first week in April, the men were able to launch their three rowing boats and pull and sail them to the solid ground of Elephant Island, at the tip of the Antarctic Peninsula. Shackleton had left reliable Frank Wild in charge there and sailed away in this single open boat, hoping to bring aid to the 22 men who were living under two upturned boats—as they were to do for the next five months—facing starvation, frostbite, and the very real prospect that Shackleton's little craft would never reach South Georgia, and the world would never know of their plight or location.

For 14 days, with little sleep, drenched by super-cold spray, yet hanging on to the thread of hope of life, Shackleton and his five companions had executed this classic journey. To complete a thrilling tale of survival that will last as long as there is appeal to the adventurous mind, Shackleton and two companions had to conquer the snow-bitten mountains of South Georgia with little of the normal equipment used for such a task. After days of exhausting strain and heroic effort, they came down to surprise the men of the little whaling station.

Shackleton described how they had brought only an axe and a logbook. "That was all we brought—except our wet clothes—from the Antarctic which a year and a half before we had entered with well-found ship, full equipment, and high hopes. That was all of tangible things.

We had pierced the veneer of outside things. We had seen God in His splendours, we had heard the text Nature renders. We had reached the naked soul of man."

The work was far from done on this day of safety, though. Three men on the other side of South Georgia still awaited succor, and there were to be agonies of delay before Frank Hurley's "castaway Argonauts" were able to be taken off by a ship made available to Shackleton by the friendly government of Chile. Then Shackleton learned that, half a world away, he had other marooned men waiting for rescue from the rigors of the Antarctic.

Sir Ernest Shackleton

Chapter 10

Chapter 10
The Coming of Shackleton

O n the night *Aurora* was taken by the ice at Cape Evano, Scotty Paton, the bosun, felt the captive vessel begin to stir while he was resting in his bunk. Then there was sudden movement; alarmed, he grabbed a hurricane lamp and hurried on deck. Peering over the stern rail he saw the stress-frayed ends of the broken cables dangling and the shore receding out of sight. The ship was caught in a mass of shattered ice; it enclosed the stern and the sides, and was moving. At once the bosun started pounding the deck, hammering on the companionway doors and yelling, "She's away, sor! She's away with it!"

The slumbering ship broke into commotion. Chief officer John Stenhouse began yelling orders into the night air; sleepy men poured from the little companionway, and chains rasped and banged as the anchors were dragged along and the broken cables rattled and tore at the hawsepipes. Relentlessly the tens of thousands of tons of ice, driven by the southern gale into the wind-whipped Sound, carried the little vessel away as it sat transfixed and powerless, like a candle in a massive iced cake. Helpless and frustrated, John Stenhouse stood on the canvas-shielded bridge and looked back to watch the last glimmer of light from the Scott hut fade and die in the whirl of the night drift.

Nothing of this sudden drama, none of the noise that seemed so loud to the ship's crew, was noticed on shore. Not for another five hours would the sharp eyes of young Dick Richards stare unbelievingly above the bank of snowdrift to see the ship's masts had gone. By that time *Aurora* was captive to the ice and wind and had been carried miles away, her boilers cold, the furnaces dead, the steam feed pipes frozen solid. Chief Officer Stenhouse ordered desperate efforts to thaw the frozen pipes, to light fires and raise steam, so that the ship might break out of the massive ice field's frozen grip. He wrote in his log, "We are drifting God knows where! But what of the poor beggars at Cape Evans—and the returning Southern party? It is a dismal prospect for them."

That entry was the opening of a daily record of peril and suffering that the ship and its crew were to endure for the next 11 months, an experience John Stenhouse would describe as "a fearful nightmare."

When the wind fell away next day and the scene cleared, it was at once obvious that *Aurora*'s puny 98-horsepower engine with its single-screw propeller could never break out of this frozen prison. Only the breakup of the ice itself would offer release—if the ship was not crushed like a walnut first.

She was moving north surprisingly fast. In a day or two Stenhouse reckoned they had passed the northern tip of Ross Island, and were moving into the wide reaches of Ross Sea. Soon they would be level with Cape Adare, and each day reduced their chances of reversing course and steaming back into the Sound. The ship was already low on coal and short of fresh water, which meant that even if they were freed, they would face the agonizing choice of either running north for safety to New Zealand or taking a coalless ship back to McMurdo Sound. In the meantime, *Aurora* was under constant threat from increasing compression; the ice around her lifted and rafted and growled. Days and nights were filled with the menacing noises of powerful pressure as the huge floes grated and ground against each other and against the ship's sides. Stenhouse was so concerned that he ordered the preparation of sledges and packaging of rations, in case they had to take to the ice and make for the nearest land. Here, on the opposite side of the Antarctic to where his commander Shackleton's ship was icebound, he faced a similar plight. And again and again Stenhouse wrote in his log of his worry about the predicament of the men on Ross Island. "Through all my waking hours, there is the one long thought for the people at Cape Evans."

Days and weeks passed with no relief in sight. In the midwinter months of June and July the scene around the ship was totally depressing. Stenhouse noted how the upended blocks and thrusting floes made it seem as if the ship lay in a vast frosted graveyard. *Aurora* was defenseless, the men impotent against the massing of the pack ice, and without fires or hot water, cold was an enemy. Nothing could aid them; though Lionel Hooke spent many hours bent over Douglas Mawson's old wireless contraption in the steward's pantry tapping out endless messages to raise the alarm, they went without response. Not until late August could he report hearing transmissions between Macquarie Island and the New Zealand Bluff station. Any hope that *Aurora*'s signals had been picked up was thin indeed.

September brought to the ice-trapped ship a raging blizzard that tore off the mizzen-mast, but also brought some prospect of a break in the ice. Now, having drifted some 700 miles, there was so little coal left that all hope of returning to the men marooned on Ross Island had to be abandoned. All that was left to the men was to make a course for New Zealand as soon as the ship could break free.

After five months of this drifting came some hope of escape. The fleeting summer season was imminent, and there was expectation that the ice mass would disperse as they crossed northwards beyond the Antarctic Circle. Instead, the summer inflicted still more trials and greater peril. Pressure increased so much that the ship's rudder was smashed and the propeller was threatened. As the squeezing of the ship continued, the men came to think of the floes as malignant enemies bent on slowly destroying them. They worked like demons to fend off the disastrous destruction of the rudder, and on the deck saws and nails were used to construct a new, makeshift rudder for when the vessel was freed.

Surprisingly, their breakout came when summer was almost done. In the middle of February there was suddenly open water around the ship's sides, and a long swell picked up the huge chunks of ice, banging and barging them into the rolling vessel. Now a new danger threatened: *Aurora* was leaking, springing water fast, and all hands had to take turns at the pumps while emergency caulking was done to block the leaks in the planking.

In March 1916, 10 months of captivity were over. *Aurora* was in open water again. She was floating due north of King Edward VII Land, southeast of the southern tip of New Zealand, facing 2,000 miles of notoriously stormy waters with little coal and no reliable rudder, and dependent mainly on wind and sails to steer a course. With courage and superb seamanship Stenhouse took the crippled ship north. On March 23 Lionel Hooke made radio contact, and on April 2 the tug *Plucky*, out of Otago, took Aurora in tow and, butting through heavy seas, hauled her into little Port Chalmers the following day—finally ending Stenhouse's 'fearful nightmare,' which had lasted some 48 weeks.

The veteran navigator John King Davis, who had been with Shackleton's first expedition as commander of *Nimrod*, and had also made two voyages in command of *Aurora* with Douglas Mawson, had vowed he would never again go back to the south. In 1914, in London, Shackleton had pressed Davis to take command of *Endurance* for the Weddell Sea journey, and he had declined, Captain Frank Worsley being appointed instead. Two years later, in March 1916, while in southern France, Davis was handed an urgent cable from Shackleton's London lawyers asking him to head a mission to search for the marooned men in McMurdo. When the ship he commanded pulled into New York the following month, he received a wire from the

Admiralty ordering him to "report at once," to take command of *Discovery* and go south to search for Shackleton. Before this journey had begun, however, Sir Ernest had already turned up in South Georgia and was arranging relief for his men on Elephant Island with the aid of the government of Chile. Davis was commanding the *Barunga* in Australian waters several months later when he was called upon once again, this time to command *Aurora* on its voyage to rescue the Ross Sea party.

The arrival of *Aurora* in Port Chalmers, with its news of the 10 men cast away in the Antarctic, had triggered instant action by the Australian, British and New Zealand governments. A total of £20,000 was allocated to repair and refurbish *Aurora* for the journey of rescue, and a supervising committee was sent by the Australian government, headed by Rear-Admiral Sir William Creswell, with four members—among them experienced Antarctic veteran Dr. Griffith Taylor (who had been with Scott), Captain J. B. Stevenson of the Royal Navy, Professor Orme Masson, and Mr J. R. Barter. After this committee decided not to reappoint John Stenhouse to command the refitted *Aurora*, a radio message calling for Captain Davis was sent by Admiral Creswell. Some members of the original crew were retained, but new names were added as well.

Captain John King Davis set out at once for the little New Zealand seaport to take up his old command, the Newfoundland sealing ship he had chosen and purchased for Douglas Mawson in 1910. The love of a mariner for his vessel was strong in Davis, and the prospect of walking the gangplank onto *Aurora* was to his mind "like coming home to an old friend." She held memories of great days of peril and drama; of pitting her little engine against ferocious blizzards in newly discovered Commonwealth Bay, and challenging weeks struggling against the menacing ice pack, going west with Frank Wild's party to find a great sheet of ice they would name for Shackleton; of being forced to leave Mawson to face another winter when he came back from that epic, cruel journey of survival; of Macquarie Island, and battles with great gales in the Southern Ocean. So when Davis saw his "old friend" scarred and battered by ice, he was angered at the folly that had placed her in danger of being crushed, as *Endurance* had been. Captain Davis immediately questioned the wisdom of Stenhouse's choice of Cape Evans as a suitable winter anchorage. It was far too exposed, too vulnerable to blizzard winds and ice movements, he said, while the only proven mooring at that time was farther along the bay off Hut Point, where Scott had anchored *Discovery* in 1902. Davis did not find out until later that the decision not to go south of Glacier Tongue had been made neither by Stenhouse nor by Mackintosh, but by Shackleton himself, because the explorer remembered how Scott's ship had been trapped in the bay ice for two consecutive years.

Captain Davis wasted little time on inquiries or recrimination. His ship was in a parlous condition, and his overriding drive, he said, was to rescue the men marooned on Ross Island. "Those men have to be saved," he declared, and he at once began the months-long task of refitting and refurbishing *Aurora,* an effort that took longer than normal because of wartime conditions. Halfway through his task, however, Davis brought his activities to a halt. Newspaper reports from England told of a concerned Sir Ernest Shackleton hurrying to New Zealand to take command of the expedition to rescue the Ross Sea castaways. Captain Davis found this development deeply disturbing. He had, long before, earned the reputation of a stern disciplinarian and a jealous guardian of a shipmaster's right—under any expedition leader—to decide matters affecting the protection and safety of the vessel he commanded. These firmly held attitudes and principles had involved him in difficult relationships with members of prior expeditions. He had been called, at times, a pessimistic and inflexible man, through one who could also be a warm and genial companion once on land. At the news of Shackleton's coming, he stuck by his master's principles, and foresaw the possibility of a very "distasteful situation emerging."

Davis felt no personal antagonism toward Shackleton. Shackleton had been his leader when Davis commanded *Nimrod,* and he held the explorer in high regard. The present circumstances were quite different, though. This vessel was in debt, and could well be sold to meet the money owed to suppliers and governments. Davis believed that events had revealed bad organization and haphazard planning in earlier days, and that Shackleton had by now expended all his funds. He promptly sent his resignation to Admiral Creswell, feeling that he could not take the mission of rescue if Shackleton was to come on the scene and seek to take charge.

The three governments made a quick joint decision. At the prompting of the Australian committee they rejected Davis's resignation and confirmed his authority. He, not Shackleton, would take *Aurora* to relieve the marooned men, and the work of preparation was to move ahead. Shackleton did eventually come onto the scene, and Davis, hearing that the Boss was in Wellington, went to meet him. They sat looking at each other in the hotel, two men of Irish birth who were unyielding where their principles were at issue and could easily explode into anger.

Davis left behind his impressions of that reunion with his old leader: "I found him changed. His sufferings had left him tired; glorious failure had imposed grave worries—personal and financial. He had re-emerged into a world with little resemblance to the one he had left, and was unable to accept that people's thinking and living was dominated by the war."

Captain Davis found Shackleton resentful, even angry, and not inclined to be cooperative. *Aurora* was his ship, and the men in peril were his men. Davis knew there had to be a judicious approach, and he used the warmth of comradeship for a former shipmate. Disaster, accident and war had created a new situation, he argued, and Shackleton needed to come to terms with new attitudes to, and within, government. Public money was now being sunk into an expedition that was humanitarian—the rescue of men cast away in the Antarctic—and this was being done in the middle of a gruesome and bitterly fought war. If Shackleton insisted on his rights, he would threaten or at best delay the prospect of rescuing the marooned men.

In the greatness of his nature, Shackleton agreed. The vital issue was to save the lives of the men left on the ice, even if he did not go as leader; but he requested that he be allowed to sail aboard *Aurora*. Davis, too, was big enough to yield. However, Sir Ernest Shackleton's name was not to appear in the list of the ship's company in their official report to the Australian government.

Aurora finally left Port Chalmers in late December 1916. Davis recorded that when the tug *Plucky*, which had towed *Aurora* into port, came alongside her, Sir Ernest Shackleton boarded *Aurora* and went south in his own ship, signing on as a supernumerary with his pay fixed at one shilling a month. Captain Davis also recorded complete accord during the voyage. He later wrote of Shackleton: "He was my friend whom I admired. He was a loyal member of the crew and a good shipmate."

In the ramshackle wooden shelter at Hut Point, the three survivors of the epic march to the Beardmore Glacier crouched around the spluttering blubber fire for another eight weeks, waiting to cross the 13 miles of treacherous bay ice to Cape Evans. Each week since Captain Mackintosh and Hayward had vanished into the blizzard-swept bay the air grew steadily colder and the gales that rocked their hut grew more violent, making the capture and slaughter of seals more difficult. While the blizzards continued, day after day, the trio would lie wrapped in their old sleeping bags and watch the pile of seal blubber diminish, longing for a break in the wild rush of Antarctic winter, for a pause long enough to let the intense cold freeze the bay ice solid to a depth that the blasting wind couldn't tear out into the open Sound.

According to Ernest Joyce's plan, in mid-June they should find such conditions for a crossing, with a full moon to light their way past the dangerous snout of Glacier Tongue. When the appointed time came, however, although the ice had thickened to about 10 inches, a week-long blizzard blotted out all light and also opened new water in their path. The next chance of a moonlit crossing would not come until mid-July, and so they settled down to more weeks of squalor and the primitive life of hunting seals, fighting to keep the warmth of life in their bodies and hope alive in their hearts.

They had some trouble with the dogs: Gunner and Towser savaged

Aurora held up by ice

Oscar so badly, he ran away and was missing for several days. The Samoyed, Con, broke from his lead and caused some concern until he came back with blood of a seal coloring his white fur, bringing the cheering news that there were seals somewhere out on the ice, and their blubber stock could be replenished.

In those last long, dark days at Hut Point, the three men found relief from boredom and uncertainty in small things such as trouble with the dogs, and in speculation. Now and again one or another of them would raise the hope that Captain Mackintosh and Hayward were not frozen corpses floating somewhere beneath the ice in the bay, or out in the Sound—that somehow they had escaped and reached the land and made their way across the perilous heights and the difficult glaciers to reach Cape Evans. At other times they talked of the man and his plan for which they had all struggled and suffered—Sir Ernest Shackleton. Joyce was forever asking, Where was the Boss? Why hasn't he arrived?

Long afterward, Dick Richards was to say, "We all thought, of course, that they had probably perished. They should have been across to the ice shelf by early 1916. We reasoned it to be inconceivable that they would come later, since if they were coming at all they would have landed in 1915—if they were going to land at all. I just simply thought they were lost. If they had got as far as the southern depot it would not even then be certain they would get through. Look at us! We were very nearly lost. Men who had come across from the other side would certainly be in a worse state than we were."

All speculation, conjecture, uncertainty and boredom ended abruptly in mid-July. It was the time of the full moon, and it shone high and bright across the dark scene of the bay ice, giving faint mauve shadows—and enough light to travel. Saturday, July 15, saw the wind fall away into calm; it was very cold and the ice sheet iron-hard. It was time to cross to Cape Evans, to that splendid hut they had longed to reach during all their months of primitive existence at Hut Point. They worked with high spirits; they were soon to be reunited with their comrades, back in that palace they had left some 10 long months before to lay the southern depots, the habitation with two stoves and acetylene lighting and a diet that varied from eternal seal meat. All this was in their minds as they harnessed the dogs and loaded their pitiful possessions on the sledge, their boots crunching into the salt crystals freezing on the hard ice. They did not know that nature once again was about to play a dangerous game.

For all that it once had been a sanctuary, that its abraded planks had saved their lives, they left the old hut with no regret, but went eagerly in a direct line across the ice, taking the short route to the tip of Glacier Tongue. They were not halfway across, however, when, without a cloud in the sky, the light began to fade and features of the icescape disappeared into gloom. Startled, Joyce looked up in concern and exclaimed, "By God—look at that!"

They had no nautical almanac to alert them—no means of knowing, no reason to suspect, that they had chosen a day of total lunar eclipse for their crossing. Not until they were close to the headland at Cape Evans did the light return to their world—and it came with unexpected noise: In the brightening scene they could make out a group of dogs on the shore, yelping and barking excitedly. The four dogs in harness began responding in unison. "We had completely forgotten," Dick Richards recalled, "that we had left the bitch with a prospective litter, that these pups who had been born at the base were quite big dogs now. I could see them with their fur silhouetted in faint prismatic colours in the light of the returning moon."

The noise of the excited animals brought men from the hut—four men—and they came together close to the spot on the ice where the *Aurora* had been moored before she was taken away by the frozen sea. There were wide smiles, handshakes, backslapping, and joy in reunion. But almost at once the question was asked, "Did Mackintosh and Hayward arrive?"

The surprise with which the question was received told Joyce, Richards and Wild that their apprehensions were justified and their slight hopes baseless, and they were cast into sadness. Sorrowfully they told the grim tale of Captain Mackintosh's folly, and the sparkle was gone from the reunion. They sat quietly over a meal that Stevens prepared, and told of their long march, the fight back from the Beardmore, the great blizzard that came close to taking all their lives, the death of the gallant Padre, the fight to save Hayward, and then the return trek to bring in the sick Captain—and how those two men had thrown away the lives that just had been given back to them.

The survivors from Hut Point slept that night wrapped in blankets for the first time in 10 months. Joyce, who would not allow comfort to break the ritual of his diary entry, noted, "This ends the Great Depot Journey. To Providence who guided us over the vast Unknown, through our trials and tribulations, we bow our heads in gratitude. One can only say—Thank God."

The months at the Scott hut produced little of the comfortable and easy life the hermits had longed for at Hut Point. True, they could at last shun their smelly, molting sleeping bags and luxuriate in wooden bunks wrapped in wool blankets. There were finally things other than seal flesh to eat, from tins scavenged from the dump heap and the ice tunnels. However, the hunting of the fatty animals still had to be pursued; the blubber had to bum continually in the stove to keep out the killer cold. There were no spare clothes into which they could change, and no heat that could be spared for bathing in hot water; neither was there tobacco to be smoked for consolation. There was only the prospect of living day to day and waiting. All of them felt certain that *Aurora* had gone down with all hands, and that rescue was a long way off. They made an inventory of the dumped food and decided it could last them for nine months or a year, with care, and after that they would "have to live off the land," eating seal meat and using their hides for clothing and boots, since their garments were now in rags and stinking with blubber fat.

Some ease came now for Dick Richards, but it was an unwanted idleness that was sudden and strange. One day in August, for entertainment, they had walked the slope of Erebus behind the hut. Wild had fun sliding down into an extinct crater on a sheet of plywood, until he collided with a rock and broke a bone in his ankle. Richards carried him back to the hut for treatment by the acting doctor, John Cope. For Dick

Richards, the effort of carrying Wild seemed to be the last straw. Joyce marked the sudden event: "All seemed to be going well with us when one day Richie threw up his arms, gave a cry, and fell into a faint."

It had been five months since the terrible strain of sledging had ended, since the time when the Padre had called to Richards to stop straining or he would burst his heart. Now the biologist John Cope— for whom solitude had brought some slight mental aberrations—came to his aid and diagnosed heart strain, though later medical examination showed no sign of this. Still, it was obvious the young man needed quiet and care and a long rest. Joyce, who confessed to "crying like a baby when Richie took ill," noted his distress in his log: "No words can express my sorrow. . . . He had been my constant companion for 10 months and a better pal amidst toil and trouble never existed. Cope held out every hope and with that I have to be comforted. All the same I feel a broken man."

They laid the young man in a cubicle that Captain Scott had occupied prior to going to his death on the ice shelf, and in his long fight for recovery Dick Richards slept in the great explorer's old bunk. From that day, Richards ceased to be an active member of the group at Cape Evans—though in his illness he was of help to the man who looked after him, the biologist John Cope. Isolation and insecurity had caused irrational behavior in Cope, but the responsibility of caring for Richards, who in turn persuaded his nurse to eat more food, returned both men to health. So much so, Richards commented later, that Cope—who had once sat muttering incoherently in a corner—became the life and soul of the group. "Cope's mother was an actress and he was no mean performer himself. He had a fund of stories, and I did not hear him repeat himself. He was a changed man as the result of the responsibility of bringing me back to my health."

Richards remained quite ill for some weeks. He did not see the return of the sun, which, Joyce noted on August 22, "peeped over the horizon, winked and dipped down again." This heralded days of renewed activity. Several searches were made along the shore of the island for traces of the missing Captain and Victor Hayward, without any success. Excursions were also made to the old Shackleton hut at Cape Royds for buried "treasure": soap, sugar, matches, and tinned meats and fish. They found the old hut surprisingly clean after the Scott hut, due, Joyce said, to the fact that there was enough coal left there so that blubber was never burned to coat the walls with black grease.

This visit stirred a renewal of interest in Joyce. He recalled that part of his assignment by Shackleton was to make zoological studies. He took a recovered Wild and Irvine Gaze, and spent a number of weeks at Cape Royds watching the habits of penguins at the nearby rookery.

In December there was one more journey to be made, back onto the ice shelf to fulfil Ernie Wild's pledge to erect a more suitable monument above Spencer-Smith's grave. At the Cape Evans hut the Padre's cousin, Irvine Gaze, and Keith Jack worked on a cross fashioned from hardwood. This was completed by the middle of the month, and then—tattered clothing notwithstanding—Joyce, Wild, and Gaze crossed to Hut Point and onto the Barrier.

Some time later, they came on the poor snow cairn where the Padre was buried. The snow was built up as high as they could reach, and the cross was mounted on this. An inscription, carefully carved, read

Sacred to the memory of Rev. A. P. Spencer-Smith,
who died 9 March 1916. A brave man.

It was a time of deep emotion, grief and memory. In the white silence the three men stood alone with their thoughts: the cousin linked by blood to the dead man; the stoic Yorkshireman who had without stint attended to the most personal needs of his sick tentmate for hundreds of miles across some of the world's most harsh terrain and the man on whose experience and strength had rested the weight of the safety of the entire party in the long, cruel journey that had taken this life. They looked up at the simple cross, muttered their prayers and, with nothing more to be gained from lingering in the sad solitude of this grave, turned north for what was truly their journey's end.

They arrived back at Cape Evans early in January, having searched along the shore over some distance for traces of the two missing men, again without result. The men at the hut were in the same routine of eking out food in expectation of being trapped there for another year at least, before they could hope for liberation to the outside world. The hunt for seals was a daily chore, and Dick Richards, who could now move about somewhat, tried to help by walking to a rise at the foot of Mount Erebus and scanning the ice for the dark shapes of the sea creatures who fed their stoves and kept scurvy at bay.

On the morning of Wednesday, January 10, 1917, this chore was started after breakfast in the usual banal manner. From the rising land the young Australian swept a quick glance across the chilly scene and idly looked north to the ice edge. There was some movement there, but nothing that immediately excited him. Icebergs were known to drift back and forth with the changing tide and wind. He then put the binoculars to his eyes, for a moment he would remember for the rest of his life. "It seemed that at the very time I started to look through the glasses a stoker threw some fresh coal on the furnace, and there was a belch of black smoke, curling into the air. Then I knew there was a ship."

He could not make out the vessel itself; it was still too far away. He could see only the smoke from the funnel smudging the northern sky. He walked back to the hut. The other men were still at the long mess table, and he said, managing a casual tone, "There's a ship out there."

The belief that relief wouldn't come for another year was so deeply ingrained in their minds that one man told Richards not to play the fool. Richards then told Joyce, "See for yourself." Joyce went to the high window, stood on a box, peered through the glass and suddenly yelled, "Ship ho!"

The hut broke into pandemonium. Men were laughing, shouting, shaking hands, and then came the headlong rush to collect the few possessions each would carry away from those two harrowing years in the Antarctic. The dogs were harnessed, the sledge was loaded, and the last journey across the ice started.

The ship was some eight or nine miles away, still coming toward the ice edge, and the men had traveled some four miles before all at once they were whooping with joy. They could make out the lines of *Aurora* and knew that fears of their ship going down with all hands had not been realized. Soon they could see that three small figures on the ice, dark and shuffling, like penguins, were coming to meet them.

"It was a dramatic meeting," Richards was to relate. "When we were still a mile or two apart, we were shouting greetings across the ice."

Joyce soon recognized the walk of one of the men. Shackleton had come out of the north, not from the south by way of the Pole and the ice shelf. When they met the creased, bearded face of the Boss was beaming with delight. "Joyce, old man, I am more than pleased to see you," he said. Shackleton had two other men with him: Captain Morton Moyes, navigator, who had been with Mawson's western party under Frank Wild; and, by coincidence, the doctor from the town of Ballarat where Dick Richards had been teaching, Dr. Fred Middleton.

Shackleton asked Joyce, "How many are you? How many men have we lost?"

After hearing the reply, Shackleton and his two companions walked apart and, to the amazement of the others, lay flat down on the ice. When they came back to the astonished sledgers Shackleton explained this was a signal to the master of *Aurora*, Captain John King Davis, to let him know how many men had perished. Within an hour they met the austere Davis himself.

Captain Davis gave his own account of the relief of the Cape Evans party. He told of the arrival of "the ragged procession" at the ship, and the meal in *Aurora's* small wardroom. "We had expected they would be unkempt. I had not fully anticipated what a profound effect such a long period of isolation could have on their appearance. They were just about the wildest-looking gang of men I had seen in my life. Smoke-bleared eyes looked out from grey, haggard faces; their hair was matted and uncut, their beards impregnated with soot and grease."

He went on, "Their great physical suffering went deeper than their appearance. Their speech was jerky, at times semi-hysterical, almost unintelligible. Their eyes had a strained harassed look—and no wonder! These events had rendered these hapless individuals as unlike ordinary human beings as any I have ever met. The Antarctic had given them the full treatment."

In this dramatic moment, Captain Davis realized his mission of relief had been accomplished. When the men sat down to what he hoped would be "the best meal they had eaten in two years," Davis later wrote, "Anxious as we were to heap hospitality on them, our accustomed natural desire as hosts was modified by the small *Aurora* wardroom which was too poorly ventilated to be bearable for those whose nostrils were accustomed only to the odours of the more civilized world."

For this "wild gang of men" the first hot baths and fresh clothes in two years were followed by free access to tobacco, and many hours of talking and of listening to tales of Shackleton's extraordinary expedition; and of hearing about the horrible slaughter of modern war that, unknown to them, had coincided with their own years of toil and tragedy.

Before the ship left the ice Shackleton led further searches for some vestige of Captain Aeneas Mackintosh and Victor Hayward. This proving fruitless, they erected a cross to the three lost men at the foot of Mount Erebus and left a written account of the visit on the table of Scott's hut. Then, for the last time, they closed the door. It remained shut for another 30 years. Not until 1948, following a second world war, did another man cross that threshold—when the massive American survey expedition under Admiral Byrd paid a visit to the historic hut.

By that time the polar blizzards had shredded the flags and the scraps of black cloth cut from Dick Richards's old trousers to mark the food depots for the six men who would never come. The cairns themselves had been battered back into the snowy surface, and the precious food, for which men toiled and gave their lives, had disappeared into the frozen oblivion of the Great Ross Ice Shelf.

Crew midwinter

Aftermath

Only three men and three dogs returned to the warm world from the fearsome journey that ended the age of manned sledging on the Great Ross Ice Shelf. With Joyce, Richards and Wild came the Canadian huskies, mighty Oscar, Towser and Gunner, bound for a New Zealand zoo, where, it is recorded, Oscar lived an amazingly long canine life, finally dying in 1939. The fourth animal on that last journey, Con, the hunt-loving Samoyed, had been cornered by the jealous huskies during the last winter at Cape Evans. In a wolfish attack he was savaged so badly he died a few hours later. With ceremony and sorrow the men whose lives he helped save buried him at the foot of Mount Erebus.

Two Antarctic survivors became casualties in the Great War. Petty Officer Ernie Wild went into active service with the Royal Navy and died while mine-sweeping in the Mediterranean. The other casualty was *Aurora* itself. The old Newfoundland sealer, which Captain Davis had selected for Mawson back in 1910, was finally sold by Shackleton for £10,000 to meet some of the debts of the expedition. In June 1917, she left the eastern Australian port of Newcastle with a load of coal and was lost with all hands, including the bosun, Scotty Paton. Conjecture surrounds the manner of her disappearance, ranging from German sea mines to an attack by the raider *Wolf*, to sheer lack of seaworthiness after her battering in the Antarctic pack ice. Nothing is known for certain; there are only unconfirmed reports that a life belt and an inscribed bottle were found on a beach in eastern Australia.

Dick Richards bore the scars of the remarkable journey for many years, even at age 90 confessing to "never fully recovering." Yet Richards still retained a lifelong admiration for the expedition leader, Sir Ernest Shackleton. "He was a great man. I think he could have been unscrupulous, but as a leader in difficult situations he was the best of them all, greater than Nansen, or Scott, or Amundsen; and I think he had qualities Mawson lacked. Without doubt he was an amazing man with a personality—just like Churchill's—that was magnetic and most impressive. The journey by open boat from Elephant Island to South Georgia won admiration from Amundsen himself; he said he could not understand how such a wonderful voyage could be made. To my mind it was the most wonderful boat journey ever made."

When Richards met Shackleton and his companions on the ice near Cape Evans in January 1917, it was plain the Boss bore the marks of his terrible experiences. That "wonderful" journey may have, sadly, contributed to the sudden death of the great explorer. In 1918–19 he was handling winter equipment for an expeditionary force in North Russia. In 1921 he answered the call of the south again, and in the little vessel *Quest* set off with his boon companions, Captain Worsley and Frank Wild, among his complement. At Gritvyken, South Georgia Island, he suffered a fatal heart attack at the age of 48. He was buried at the foot of the mountains he had crossed in 1916.

In England, the expedition's other survivor, Ernest Joyce, lived on into his 80s, long enough to learn of the first crossing of Antarctica in 1958 by Sir Vivian Fuchs's party, and of the first overland journey to the South Pole since Scott's, by Sir Edmund Hillary.

Joyce, in a 1929 letter to Sir Charles Royds, told of spending six months in the hospital and of being compelled to wear dark glasses for 18 months, as a result of his time leading the party on the ice shelf. In that letter summarizing the expedition, which Joyce claimed was "almost beyond human endurance," he described how the party had lived "like animals at Hut Point," after a journey that was "without parallel in the annals of polar sledging."

In later years Dick Richards compiled a table of comparison that gave credence to Joyce's claim. His record shows that in 1902 Scott spent 93 days sledging (Shackleton broke down); that in 1912 Scott spent 150 days sledging (the whole party perished); and that in 1908 Shackleton spent a total of 120 days sledging, with the benefit of some pony meat depots as protection against scurvy. The total days of sledging by the Ross Sea party of 1915–16 came to an unheard-of 199, plus the eight-day journey to erect the cross for the Reverend Arnold Patrick Spencer-Smith.

This longest of periods spent by men on the ice shelf was marked by hauling extra loads of food and fuel for other men, and was made without dependable equipment, a secure base or adequate supplies, and with the aid of only four dogs. Richards also concluded that too much food was hauled and deposited at Minna Bluff, and that the loss of the main dog teams in the first season was the result of a "tragic error."

"However," added Richards, "we were the only section of the whole expedition to complete our assignment. We had the satisfaction of knowing that Shackleton and his party would have had sufficient food and fuel over the latter part of their transcontinental journey, and that we had accomplished a notable task and a journey that could rank with what had gone before. That the effort was unnecessary, that the sacrifice was made to no purpose, in the end, was irrelevant. To me no undertaking carried through to conclusion is for nothing. And so I don't think of our struggle as futile. It was something that the human spirit accomplished."

Aurora by moonlight

An Assessment: The Crossing
of the Antarctic Continent

C ould Sir Ernest Shackleton have survived the crossing of the Antarctic continent on foot? Suppose *Endurance* had not been snared by sea ice in January 1915, and the landing had been made at the head of the Weddell Sea. Would the depots laid by the Ross Sea party at such cost then have been worthwhile? It seems almost certain to us, today, that Shackleton and his overlanders would have perished in that terrible terrain. One man in this world who spoke with authority on the prospects of such an awesome journey was Sir Vivian Fuchs (1908-1999), who led the first crossing of Antarctica in 1958 and whose doubts about the success of such a venture grew stronger over the ensuing decades.

Taking into account all the problems met on his own historic crossing, Sir Vivian examined the proposed plans for Shackleton's journey, and became convinced that the explorer never would have made it across the continent.

Sir Vivian received a copy of Shackleton's plan for traversing Antarctica from Shackleton's chief of scientific staff, James Wordie. His detailed analysis of these proposals led him to conclude that the sledgers would not have pulled through even as far as the head of the Beardmore Glacier. The plan shows that had the landing been made in January 1915, Sir Ernest intended the journey to start at once. "I do not believe this was ever a practical idea," Sir Vivian wrote, "because unsupported travelling with dog teams would have required at least three months, averaging 20 miles a day to cover his estimated 1,800 miles to the Ross Sea."

Shackleton's daily average would have been severely reduced by the savage climate; a more likely average would be 15 miles a day, and this would have meant more time in the field. Sir Vivian wrote, "Since he could not have reached his starting point before February 1, the journey could not have been completed before the beginning of May and would more likely have taken until June or July."

After many months on the trail, the conditions would have been appalling for both men and animals. "Midwinter is not the time to be travelling in central Antarctica, for darkness prevails and high-altitude cold prevents movement by man or dogs."

Shackleton would have faced another serious problem, that of food. Sir Vivian claimed the range of a dog-sledge party without previously laid depots is limited to about 45 days. At 15 miles a day, this means traveling a distance of nearly 700 miles.

"Yet, Shackleton had to go more than 1,000 miles before reaching a depot—even if the Ross Sea party had been able to place one at the head of the Beardmore Glacier. I believe therefore that inevitably he would have taken up winter quarters at the head of the Weddell Sea . . . On this assumption it seems to me he would have used the remainder of that first summer to reconnoiter southward and to establish one or more depots for the main journey in the following spring." Sir Vivian held that Shackleton could not have taken more than four men with four sledges and 36 dogs across the continent, and that to achieve even this he would have to have been blessed with constantly good conditions, both in weather and terrain.

"We must also remember that once committed he had very little capability of altering his plan," Sir Vivian wrote. "In those days there was no radio to call forward more supplies in the event of having to turn back. Nor could he convey new instructions to his support party on the other side of the continent if his progress was impeded or the route had to be altered. With some reluctance I concede he could have made 15 miles a day over the distance—if his luck remained."

Had Shackleton used a support party of two loaded sledges for the first 400 miles, it would have been just possible to reach the Beardmore and the depots laid by the men from Ross Island. But Sir Vivian had further qualifications. "I have been compelled to assume travelling conditions would have been good," he said, "that the dogteams would have been efficiently trained and properly fed; and, above all, that the drivers would have been experienced. If one takes into account the terrible story of the support party's experiences, I fear these assumptions are open to considerable doubt . . . the weather even at the height of summer was atrocious on the Ross Ice Shelf.

"If these factors had affected Shackleton's party his chances of success would have been small, indeed. It may therefore be permissible to comment that the loss of *Endurance* may have saved a worse disaster."

photographs

SOUTH ATLANTIC OCEAN

SOUTH GEORGIA ISLAND

Shackleton's Open Boat Voyage

INDIAN OCEAN

FALKLAND ISLANDS

WEDDELL SEA

ELEPHANT ISLAND

Antarctic Peninsula

Ship destroyed

Ice Shelf

Endurance *trapped*

SOUTH POLE

Trans Antarctic Mountains

Beardmore Glacier

ANTARCTIC CIRCLE

Ross Ice Shelf

Western Mountains

Ross Island

ROSS SEA

Cape Adare

66°

SOUTHERN OCEAN

SOUTH PACIFIC OCEAN

TASMANIA

NEW ZEALAND

AUSTRALIA

A N T A R C T I C A